The Cancel Culture Panic

THE
CANCEL
CULTURE
PANIC

*How an
American Obsession
Went Global*

ADRIAN DAUB

Stanford University Press
Stanford, California

Stanford University Press
Stanford, California

The first version of *The Cancel Culture Panic* was originally published in German in 2022 under the title *Cancel Culture Transfer: Wie eine moralische Panik die Welt erfasst* © Suhrkamp Verlag AG Berlin 2022. All rights reserved by and controlled through Suhrkamp Verlag AGBerlin.

Printed in the United States of America on acid-free, archival-quality paper.

Library of Congress Cataloging-in-Publication Data
Names: Daub, Adrian, author.
Title: The cancel culture panic : how an American obsession went global / Adrian Daub.
Other titles: Cancel Culture Transfer. English
Description: Stanford, California : Stanford University Press, 2024. | Translation of: Cancel Culture Transfer : wie eine moralische Panik die Welt erfasst. Berlin : Suhrkamp, 2022.
Identifiers: LCCN 2024007547 (print) | LCCN 2024007548 (ebook) | ISBN 9781503640849 (paperback) | ISBN 9781503641211 (ebook)
Subjects: LCSH: Cancel culture. | Moral panics. | Political correctness. | Social pressure. | Mass media—Political aspects. | Civilization, Modern—American influences.
Classification: LCC HM1176 .D63 2024 (print) | LCC HM1176 (ebook) | DDC 302/.17—dc23/eng/20240223
LC record available at https://lccn.loc.gov/2024007547
LC ebook record available at https://lccn.loc.gov/2024007548

Cover design: David Drummond
Cover art: Shutterstock
Typeset by Newgen in Minion Pro 10/14.25

Contents

Contents

PREFACE

A Global Specter

"When I use a word," Humpty Dumpty said in rather a scornful tone, "it means just what I choose it to mean—neither more nor less."

"The question is," said Alice, "whether you can make words mean so many different things."

"The question is," said Humpty Dumpty, "which is to be master—that's all."

—LEWIS CARROLL, *Through the Looking Glass* (1871)

Fear of cancel culture has gripped the world, an old fear in a new getup. Like many old fears (and many new getups), this one hails originally from the United States. In October 2020, an open letter appeared in *Harper's* in which numerous intellectuals and artists complained: "The free exchange of information and ideas, the lifeblood of a liberal society, is daily becoming more constricted."[1] The venerable *New York Times* fears for freedom of expression in the United States and reports that cancel culture places on a "burden" on it in all walks of life.[2] "No one—of any age, in any profession—is safe," says *The Atlantic*.[3] Several US state governments, as well as governments around the world, have passed, or are passing, laws designed to combat it. Elon Musk, self-proclaimed free speech absolutist, put it more succinctly on the service he now owns: "Cancel Cancel Culture!"[4]

During the presidential election campaign in 2020, Donald Trump discovered the topic for himself. Standing before the postcard motif of Mount Rushmore, he explained that cancel culture "is the very definition of totalitarianism," is "completely alien to our culture and our values," and has "absolutely no place in the United States of America." It is a "political" weapon with the aim of "driving people from their jobs, shaming dissenters, and demanding total submission from anyone who disagrees."[5]

This discourse, which was once as quintessentially American as only a Fourth of July address at Mount Rushmore could be, has long since become an export item. In October 2021, Vladimir Putin, against the backdrop of the preparations for his invasion of Ukraine, gave a speech at the Valdai discussion forum in Sochi. There he attacked the культура отмены as a dangerous Western import intended to gag and enslave Russia—his example was J. K. Rowling. In early 2022, Pope Francis warned against cancel culture as "a form of ideological colonization that leaves no room for freedom of expression."[6] His Holiness did not mention Harry Potter.

But above all, this American idea travels the globe in journalism and books. Articles the world over have cast a gimlet eye on US campuses. An entire class of experts has emerged, even if their expertise mostly consists of having been to a US campus, or knowing someone who has. Long, deeply reported books detail safaris among the "woke" or visits with the victims of cancel culture. Of course, although much of this immense cultural production is preoccupied with the United States, very little of it will ever filter back into the US public consciousness. Fernando Bonete Vizcaíno's *Cultura de la cancelación* (subtitle: *No hables, no preguntes, no pienses*) will not appear in a British or American edition any more than will Nora Bussigny's *Les nouveaux inquisiteurs: L'enquête d'une infiltrée en terres wokes*, Julian Nida-Rümelin's *Cancel Culture: Ende der Aufklärung*, Costanza Rizzacasa d'Orsogna's *Scorrettissimi: La cancel culture nella cultura americana*, Carmen Domingo's *Cancelado: El nuevo macartismo*, or Mai Linh Tran's *Ich bin nicht woke: Eine Widerrede gegen Gendern, Woke, Cancel Culture und anderes Gedöns*. You don't have to speak any of these languages to notice in these titles the clear borrowings from US discourse—the inquisitors, the woke, gender, the new McCarthyism. But there are other aspects that, even if translated, likely feel a little alien to you. Cancel culture has long been a topic of global conversation, but unfortunately one downright Babylonian in its confusions.

This book grew out of my concern that the arguments thus traveling the globe are often selective and biased. Fear of cancel culture fixates on specific trends and data points that, without a doubt, reflect societal shifts requiring answers, but it blithely ignores others. My suspicion is that complaints about cancel culture don't really solve anything, nor are they meant to. They are rather part of a moral panic. This is primarily related to what I will call the *attention economy*: People talk about cancel culture so that they don't have to talk about other things, in order to legitimize certain topics, positions, and authorities and delegitimize others. The problem with the discourse around cancel culture is that it distorts real problems like a carnival mirror—problems of labor and job security, problems of our semi-digital public space, problems of accountability and surveillance. The conversation doesn't offer solutions to the problems it describes in an overly tendentious way, and it keeps us from finding solutions we desperately need.

There's a quote often attributed to Winston Churchill: "A fanatic is one who can't change his mind and won't change the subject." My aim is not to win over those who would like to write the next article or the next book about the thought police, about the young leftist inquisitors or the new McCarthyism from the Left, about the end of the Enlightenment or censorious campus liberals and all the things they are supposedly no longer able to say. No, if these 200-odd pages are an attempt at anything, it is to encourage these people to at least change the subject.

The Cancel Culture Panic

INTRODUCTION

Exporting a Moral Panic

The subject of this book is not—or is not just—the fear of cancel culture that has seized the United States, but also what non-Americans have done with it. Media in western Europe, South America, Russia, and Australia have devoted as much—in some cases more—attention to this supposedly American phenomenon than most US outlets. The German, French, British, Australian, and Russian discourse would not exist without anecdotes and key terms from the United States. But who exactly is afraid of cancel culture, which media are afraid, and of what? All of this differs from country to country. The answers speak volumes about the self-image of national publics, about their perceived or real relationship to the United States, to globalization, to culture, and to questions of identity. Talk of cancel culture has become a *lingua franca* of a self-styled embattled liberalism, but the object itself is fuzzy and what it means is elusive. Which is why it can be made productive in different national contexts.

I will at times refer to the concept of cancel culture as a meme. By that I mean, for one, that the term rarely occurs far from internet culture (although it implicitly demonizes internet culture). More importantly, the term also offers a kind of framework to which different groups and individuals can attach a broad, though far from infinite, number of associated phenomena. This book seeks to understand how a panic that seemed tailor-made for (and almost exclusively made in) the United States caught on in Europe and beyond. I'm concerned with forms of attention and address, with forms of resonance and approval, and with how the internet age interrogates itself—or fails to do so.

After all, while cancel culture always seems to occur within shouting distance of the internet, much of the shouting about it does too—something the purveyors of this discourse don't reflect on much. Of course, many cancel culture anecdotes started with bad reactions to a bad tweet. But, many a book or article about the evils of cancel culture started with bad reactions to bad tweets, meaning the collective freak-out about cancel culture partakes of the exact same media mechanisms it criticizes. The magic of the term "cancel culture" is that you don't have to see these two reactions as the same thing.

Most of those who warn about cancel culture seem to be upset about interactions on Twitter (now X)—from which they deduce things about the broader culture with the same myopia as the people they are mad at. What's more, one of the characteristic aspects of the anti–cancel culture movement on the Right is that it sweeps online personalities—from anti-woke crusader Chris Rufo to anti-LGBT poster Chaya Raichik ("Libs of TikTok")—into actual positions of power in the education systems of individual US states. The authors and consumers of cancel culture stories are exactly as, and perhaps even more, terminally online as the people they complain about.

I make several claims in this book. First, I argue that the longer the discussion on cancel culture lasts, the more it reveals itself as a new iteration of the discourse on political correctness. What started out as a description of specific practices of online debates quickly became a rehash of earlier culture wars. Neither political correctness nor what became of the term "cancel culture" turn out to be particularly well-suited to a sharp diagnosis of our historic moment. But as pieces of discourse that travel, adapt, and resurface, both are extremely interesting. Contemporary characterizations of political correctness, wokeness, and identity politics tend to be vague and inconsistent. What has remained shockingly constant and monolithic is the tone and the characteristic style in which complaints are made about them. The object may be unstable, but the subject position fixated on that object has been surprisingly consistent since at least the mid-1980s.

My second claim is that talk of cancel culture largely governs an economy of attention. It tells us where to direct our attention, what deserves it, and what does not. It relies almost exclusively on anecdotes; it confers automatic relevance on what might at first glance look like minor local imbroglios and thus spares the reader or viewer the hard work of mediating between individual and universal. Any piffle, no matter how miniscule, becomes relevant if we tie it to cancel culture. Talk of cancel culture almost magically dissolves local context, such that events in a recherché Twitter niche, at a small college, or at a publishing house—never previously a big concern to the writer or their readers—are suddenly transformed into major threats to society, freedom, and the West.

This is the aspect of cancel culture discourse that, following Stanley Cohen, I will analyze as a "moral panic."[1] At the same time, cancel culture doesn't just dissolve context. It also creates a new one: It reframes contemporary anecdotes by tethering them to a pool of historical comparisons, which no good cancel culture–essay seems to be able to do without. Whether it is McCarthyism, struggle sessions in Maoist China, the Chinese Cultural Revolution, Stalinist show trials, Robespierre's reign of terror, the GDR, witch hunts, or—most recently—North Korea, a classic anti–cancel culture text constantly builds connections between present and past, anecdote and system, without ever explicitly substantiating any of those links.

My third claim is that the birthplace of the term "cancel culture" is the internet, and the phrase is unthinkable without it. Only in certain online spaces does the term have cogency. There are in fact phenomena in online discourse, particularly in social networks, that tend towards constant emotional escalation, towards scandalization and denunciation, and that can ensnare the rich, famous, and secure as much as the unlucky "normies." Simply put: We *do* live in something of a digital panopticon. Our online personas *do* have a horrible way of making time irrelevant, making us identical with (and accountable for) every opinion we've ever expressed. But while the term describes a real problem, the discourse on cancel culture describes these phenomena inadequately and in some cases deliberately distorts them.

After all, cancel culture associates these broad-based tendencies towards escalation and punitive discourse with specific content: with identity politics, wokeness, moralism. It thus seeks to locate the mechanisms of escalation that it describes as primarily on the Left and among young people and thus to disguise an obvious reality: that in our networked world, impulses towards scandalization are widespread and catch on easily; that great collective energy can develop quickly around emotionally charged topics in social networks; that in the Age of the Influencer, people can rise to prominence who have neither the practice nor the resources by which prominence is traditionally managed; and that Twitter or Facebook in particular can promote a certain universalization of scandal, in which normal users can suddenly be held accountable for their own statements as though they were politicians or celebrities. What is worse, warnings about cancel culture aren't just displaced reactions for these perfectly real pathologies of the digital public sphere but are often also an instance of those very pathologies.

The discourse on cancel culture does not sharpen the analysis of such phenomena, but rather makes their analysis more difficult. Since descriptions of "cancel culture" mostly rehash the threat once supposedly posed by the "politically correct," the diagnosis has a hard time doing justice to the genuinely new communicative situation represented by, say, Twitter. And the term's obvious fixation on *culture* means that the problem is not understood as one of institutions or of political economy. It focuses on "Twitter mobs" that send heterodox thinkers into the "cancel dungeon" or onto the "moral scaffold" via a "shitstorm." And it doesn't ask questions, like "What economic framework is required for angry users on social media (it seems impossible to have social media without angry users) to have so much alleged power?" In this and other matters, the talk of cancel culture often only pretends to name a problem, while in reality it at best reinterprets real (and quite valid) problems according to an old pattern.

My fourth claim is that if the sheer amount of interest generated by stories of left-wing censoriousness, identity politics, and wokeness in the United States seems out of step with their objectively verifiable scale and seriousness, the gap between the two in Europe is far wider. Why a newspaper reader in Esslingen, Valladolid, Szeged, or Palermo should care what students are doing at a mid-tier Seattle-area college is even less clear than why a newspaper reader in Maryland might. There is inherent in the concept of cancel culture a certain delimiting in terms of attention economy. That is to say, it takes something that, at first glance, would seem to only affect the reader marginally, and recasts it as something globally dangerous and threatening. This has made its global reception an important part of the term's political echoes.

Which brings us to my fifth point: Once it has left the US context, it is clear that the global fear of cancel culture always contains a certain degree of anti-Americanism, or at least a leeriness about US global influence. Wherever invoked, cancel culture narratives position that country on the receiving end of deleterious US ideas, as an innocent victim of the ever-looming threat of "American conditions." This ideological import-export model is wrong, both on the export side and on the import one. One reason that stories of political correctness and cancel culture so easily make the leap to publics outside of the United States is that they easily attach to preexisting concerns, questions, and discourses. In other words, as soon as tales of censorship-crazed campus leftists in the United States have made it to other countries, they are no longer just tales about the United States, but are about Germany, France, Spain, Russia.

This hasn't just been the case since the internet and global supply chains transformed our information economy in the twenty-first century. When fear of political correctness spread across the Atlantic in the early 1990s, the ease of cultural transmission had far more to do with the recipient country than with the depth of the problem in the United States. For much of the 1980s, Germany, for instance, had been wracked by debates about the limits of public discourse, often dealing with the Nazi past. Nazi comparisons and mutual accusations abounded, along with worries about what was "no longer" permitted in humor and satire. Then-Chancellor Helmut Kohl was almost scientific in testing out what a German head of state was "once again" allowed to do—visit the graves of fallen SS members with a visiting US president, for instance. As a result, by 1991, Germany was more than ready for a debate on the supposed limits of political discourse, which conveniently centered on faraway America. For German newspapers, PC discourse in the United States allowed a kind of pleasant amnesia about their own earlier debates. The idea that the line between the sayable and the unsayable was dictated by an American or an international (but at any rate, a foreign) discourse promised clarity in the midst of discomfiting complexity.

The United States is the country of origin of the term "cancel culture," and it is also the world champion in exporting anecdotes intended to prove its existence. The more one engages with the imagination that stands behind worries about political correctness and cancel culture, the more one realizes how native it is to the United States. These narratives were developed and sharpened in US universities, their anecdotes thrived on the unique mix of intimacy and volatility that campus environments provide, and they imitate the shape of the campus fictions in which US literature takes particular delight. They were disseminated by an infrastructure largely unknown outside of the US tax system: think tanks and nonprofit foundations set up by wealthy conservative donors, within shouting distance from campus but largely opposed to the established university system. From the various campus watch organizations of the 60s, 70s, and 80s to new establishments like the "anti-woke" University of Austin, the idea took hold that for every position represented on a campus there is a counter-position. And that it is the university's duty to platform this counter-position—yes, this duty is what defines "academic freedom." This idea has taken hold thanks to big money from oil, tobacco, and finance.

In the average PC or cancel culture anecdote, we find certain sacrificial lambs singled out through no (or minimal) fault of their own. This motif seems to work best with an audience schooled in Christian fundamentalist victimization narratives. It is no coincidence that in PC stories, dominant groups turn out to be the ultimate victims. This is a trick that America's fundamentalist Christians have been using since the 1970s. Even in cases in which a victim was simply confronted with contrary opinions, cancel culture–framing lapses almost reflexively into a vocabulary of guilt and punishment—"inquisition," "tribunal," "court," and "incarceration." When I first came to the United States, I occasionally saw the following bumper sticker: "If you were on trial for being a Christian, would there be enough evidence to convict you?" Imagining you're in court, even though you are in no such thing, has been a powerful trick in US public discourse for decades.

But the homegrown character of the panic does not end there: The anecdotes through which talk of political correctness first established itself in the American zeitgeist drew heavily on the fables and stories that made Reaganism plausible to a broad public. Even the idea that the woke exist in a uniquely impervious ideological echo chamber is an old topos of American conservatives, which largely stems from the experience of neoconservative defectors from the American Communist Party. Maybe the big panics happen twice: one time as self-concealing conservatism, the other time as self-deluded liberalism. The cancel culture panic turns out to be both: an artifact of a liberalism that blithely ignores its own reactionary tendencies, or reactionary energy that tactically dons the costume of liberalism.

This deeply local, deeply American narrative, which springs from very specific generational experiences, is radically delimited when discourses on political correctness and cancel culture travel beyond the United States. Appeals abound to the fate of "the" West, "of" liberal democracy, of "the" Enlightenment, of "the" United States. It is easy to assume that such maximalist tendencies within the discourse simply overreact to given triggers. But the opposite seems to be true: Without the maximalist appeal, there is no discourse. Only by way of rhetorical maximization can concerns that would otherwise be clearly recognizable as right wing be parroted in left-wing newspapers, as happens in Germany. Only by maximalist appeals to the Enlightenment can a discourse schooled on Christian fundamentalist special pleading become one about the fate of laïcité, as happened in France. Only by recasting trans people as a dangerous international "lobby" can a media elite in the UK tell itself its merciless hounding of an exceedingly set-upon minority is in truth a courageous defense against bullying and violence.

Perhaps because of the detachment from the original context in the first place, it has been a very easy discourse to export. The more nebulous the knowledge of the phenomenon, the easier and more schematic the judgments about it. But at the same time, there is a specific atmosphere to cancel culture anecdotes that connects with widespread feelings, perhaps globally, but definitely throughout the West. France may not have Title IX, Germany may not have sensitivity readers, Italy may not have monuments to Confederate generals, but certain feelings prevail among sufficiently large segments of the reading public in those countries to give cancel culture stories something to attach to.

What, then, is this mood? It is the sense that certain groups are losing their discursive dominance, that their concerns, which were once thought to be identical with those of "the public" or "the nation," may no longer be identical with them or may even diverge from them. It is the realization that the emotions and opinions of these groups, which once upon a time found almost automatic resonance in party politics and journalism, now may not always translate quite so directly. But above all, of course, it is the sense that the young are no good at being young. Whatever else woke leftists are doing, they are bad at being left, and probably bad at being young as well. They are too political and not political enough, too soft and too hard, too coddled and too pitiless, too paranoid and too superficial, too sensitive and not sensitive enough.

In the spring of 2021, the French press reported that some discussion groups within the largest French student association, the Union Nationale des étudiants de France, were open only to members of certain minorities—certainly a practice one can be of two minds about. But it was a practice that became relevant only because it provoked a veritable discursive deluge. When asked about the groups, Jean-Michel Blanquer, then the French minister of education, warned that the episode indicated that the French were "on a path . . . that leads to things that resemble fascism."[2] Blanquer leapt particularly boldly from tiny incident to a global diagnosis. But the way he framed his warning shows that this isn't just a logical leap: It draws on a specific imagination of transition. It is subjective (as all our imaginations are), but it clearly looks for others who share this sense.

For Blanquer did not say that excluding members of the white French mainstream "was" fascism: He said it led to "a path" to "things" that "resemble" fascism. A lot of things resemble other things, echo other things, or remind the speaker of other things when conservatives or liberals warn of cancel culture: the Cultural Revolution, McCarthyism, the Eastern Bloc, Orwell, the Nazis. In France the talk of fatwas has also proven popular. The fact that in cancel culture discourse absolute trifles lead suddenly and immediately to ridiculously bombastic warnings is not—or not only—the result of intellectual laziness. It invokes a hermeneutic understanding: Either you take this rhetorical leap alongside the speaker, or you don't. A claim like Blanquer's celebrates and instantiates a like-minded community of interpretation: Either his word salad lacks any logic to you and is incomprehensible, or—despite all the nonsense—it reflects a feeling you have harbored yourself and precisely for this reason allows identification. Something that just happens to irritate you—talk of gender identity, debates about dreadlocks, trigger warnings, DEI (diversity, equity, and inclusion) programs—conveniently also turns out to be a threat to Western culture.

At the same time, the discourse appeals to a cultural pessimism that does not have to see itself as conservative and defensive but can present itself (and indeed regard itself) as liberal and cosmopolitan. The illiberals are, after all, the others. On the other hand, the person who freaks out about a change in a children's book, or because of a practice on a campus half a world away, is in fact the guardian of the holy flame of the Enlightenment. The PC panic of the 1990s and the cancel culture panic of our day maintain characteristics of American conservatism, but we need not call it conservatism. The *National Review* famously described its mission in 1955 as standing "athwart history, yelling Stop."[3] This gesture describes quite well the panic surrounding the supposed new limits of free speech. The discourse mourns what once used to be easier to say; it reframes gradual change in the customs of everyday life as mass psychosis, or worse. The cancel culture panic, which reacts in a refracted way to Black Lives Matter and #MeToo in the United States, and to the so-called refugee crisis of 2015 in much of Europe, reinterprets as a conspiracy the experience of a social consensus that the individual does not share.

This cancel culture panic also has a curious position vis-à-vis populist energies in current politics. When it comes to who has brought about cancel culture, the culprit is never "the people"—this too has long been a mainstay of conservative US thinking. Rather, parts of the elite are responsible. "The largest cultural menace in America," the *National Review*'s mission statement claims, "is the conformity of the intellectual cliques which, in education as well as the arts, are out to impose upon the nation their modish fads and fallacies, and have nearly succeeded in doing so."[4] Conformity, intellectual elites, and their sinister and already "nearly" realized project of re-education: These ideas, while they arose from a specific US context, hold international appeal and are highly transferable. They make it possible for writers to combine intellectualism with anti-intellectualism, elitism with critiques of the elite. The "heterodox" thinkers who yell "stop" athwart the freight train of history are more intellectual than the intellectuals, more intelligent than the intelligentsia, but in their heterodox ways they are also advocates for those who have been stunned by the "fads" and "fallacies" of the zeitgeist. They criticize elites without really having to believe their own populism. The problem for them is not elitism per se, but the fact that the wrong elite is in charge.

It is easy, perhaps too easy, to show that this kind of discourse is frequently pure projection. Twitter (X) users delight in pointing out that warnings about PC and cancel culture dwell endlessly on the evils of identity politics but clearly represent a kind of identity politics for members of the white majority; that there is constant carping about "grievance," which would be easier to credit did it not occur in the midst of a near constant stream of whining; that cancel culture critics accuse leftists of the same kind of hysteria and rhetorical escalation that they themselves cheerfully engage in; that Europeans warn in dark tones of cancel culture as a dangerous American import while at the same time cribbing every part of their warnings from US sources; that they babble about "coddling" and "sensitivity" but freak out immediately at he/him pronouns or the expression "people of color." To warn against cancel culture can be deeply revealing—at least, it seems, to some observers. Listening to conservatives and liberals describe the evils of cancel culture is a little bit like the famous duck-rabbit illusion: Either you succeed in seeing the rabbit, or you can't see anything but the duck.

In what follows I will endeavor to avoid cheap punch lines, but one of the basic assumptions of this book is that such superficial contradictions are more relevant to an analysis of the liberal and conservative discourse surrounding wokeness and culture cancel than one might assume. Despite, or perhaps because of, these contradictions, warnings against cancel culture seem to work— at least to some extent—for an extraordinarily large number of well-informed readers in a staggering number of countries and languages. My method in this book is to take the sheer number of anecdotes and articles seriously, to look for patterns, repetitions, and (mis)translation within this proliferation.

The first thing one has to acknowledge in analyzing this discourse is the simple but fundamental fact of how much of it there is. In the midst of endless debates about "language police," "speech codes," or "self-censorship," there flows a never-ending stream of very uniform articles through our daily newspapers. We will see that warnings about cancel culture specifically succeed in non-fiction books, articles in national newspapers, high-brow magazines, and ambitious online essays, where they can appear with shocking frequency. Perhaps Alan Dershowitz is not aware of a certain irony when he complains on various talk shows about what he, as an old white man with Trump-y inclinations, is no longer allowed to say. But in any case, we can know that every time Dershowitz gives these interviews, there must be people consuming them, perhaps multiple times, viewers who believe that people like Dershowitz have been muzzled in society. In order for this discourse to work, these readers and viewers have to either ignore the irony, or at least be able to accentuate it differently.

The cancel culture discourse is characterized less by clear definitions and precise descriptions of social dynamics than by a general feeling of threat. That's why I analyze it in this book as *moral panic*. The discourse consists largely of anecdotes: Even if the average newspaper reader in France, Germany, or Russia cannot give a definition of cancel culture, he or she knows examples of cancel culture and the names of supposed victims of cancellation. Or—and this is also central to my argument—he or she at least knows what stories about being canceled look like.

The type of incident usually deployed in cancel culture texts has a clear shape. If you've read the *New York Times*, the *Wall Street Journal*, *Le Figaro*, the *Times* (London), the *Frankfurter Allgemeine Zeitung*, or the *Australian* recently, you know that structure: A professor is canceled just because he wrote something on Facebook, signed an open letter, said "Indians" in class, gave an interview. Whether the episode happened that way, whether the author researched it at all or repeated it, whether there are important details missing, and whether the author checked them at all—all of that is secondary. As Giordano Bruno would say: "Se non è vero, è molto ben trovato"—even if it's not true, it's well invented.

To be clear, there are indeed such incidents. I will not rehearse them here, as there are many books that quite capably do so—most recently Yascha Mounk's *Identity Trap* (2023) and Greg Lukianoff and Rikki Schlott's *Canceling of the American Mind* (2023). Whether it's David Shor losing his job over a single tweet in 2020; adjunct professor Erika López Prater being fired because she showed a picture of the Prophet Muhammad in class; Justine Sacco sending a tweet when leaving Heathrow and being fired for it by the time she'd touched down in Cape Town; Alison Roman losing her *New York Times* column because she criticized the products of Marie Kondo and Chrissy Teigen; Professor Greg Patton being suspended for using a Chinese term in class that sounds like the n-word; a judge being heckled while speaking at my own university (Stanford): I have the impression that something went seriously wrong when it comes to these individuals, and I can understand why people think they deserve our attention.[5]

The question is how much of our collective attention and what kind of attention. And it is precisely this question that our cancel culture Cassandras usually decline to ask.

A broader public has been talking about cancel culture since 2019. In the following chapters, I will devote myself to various attempts at defining this term and tracing its remarkable evolution over that short period of time. Generally, the term has three interlocking levels of meaning. First, there are new media rituals that can indeed seem deeply scary. They are spread and fueled by social networks. There are people who respond to tweets they have half understood with overblown opprobrium—users who, in principle, turn up the emotional temperature of every online discussion and then misunderstand this escalation as activism. And there are the Twitter cops who expose others to aggression through snide comments or embarrassing recontextualization. The various digital platforms each seem to produce their own forms of these discursive pathologies.

What is worse, employers have clearly had difficulty responding to what Angèle Christin and Rebecca Lewis have called "platform drama."[6] As we shall see in Chapter 2, when the term "cancel culture" first emerged online, it was precisely to critique (but also to establish) etiquette on platforms like Twitter and Tumblr. Most classic cancellation stories are not online stories, but (like Shor's, Prater's, and Sacco's) are about what happens when online opprobrium intersects with corporate, academic, or media employers. The reactions could be panicked, excessive, and overbroad. Of course, those reactions on the part of employers were made possible by a thoroughgoing casualization of labor in those fields—people are easy to terminate or they must work essentially as independent contractors. But this isn't what cancellation stories are usually about. They are about the culture part. Which gets to the second level of signification.

This second level is the claim that rituals on social media are part of a broader cultural shift that has swept up not just the internet but the rest of culture and the public. Although cancel culture started in social networks, this aspect of the phenomenon receded from view the farther the term traveled, or it became auxiliary to other aspects. This is the step where "cancel culture" becomes detached from specific discursive practices and attaches to specific identities. Some people, we learn, are more likely to engage in cancel culture than others. Cancel culture is characteristic of the Left, the young, the terminally online, and emanates from woke bubbles, at universities, in the publishing industry, and DEI-crazed corporate America.

Here the attempt to conceptualize a somewhat unprecedented development in media technology, namely the emergence of social networks, merges with a longstanding and well-established discourse: namely, the warning against political correctness. And it turns out that the type of stories adduced to demonstrate the prevalence of cancel culture very much resemble earlier ones about political correctness. Before Professor Patton got in trouble at USC in 2020 for using a Chinese term that sound like the n-word, Professor Donald Hindley got in trouble at Brandeis for allegedly using the term "wetback" in class—in 2007.[7] Or there was Murray Dolfman, a lecturer in legal studies at the University of Pennsylvania, who in 1985 claimed to have been suspended for calling a student an "ex-slave."[8]

The third level of meaning is the broader assertion that the culture of left-wing censoriousness actively drives social fracture. This thesis seems to me to be particularly widespread in Europe, where the fears about the "division" of society are rampant, in particular because of the rise of right-wing populist parties and the COVID-19 pandemic. The idea is that left-wing censoriousness in particular, including both changes in language and new and insufficiently explained changes in behavioral norms, alienates "normal" people. This level of signification clearly derives from public conversations about #MeToo cases: There the argument that the accused were from a "different generation," who had societal change sprung on them, was quite prevalent. Cancel culture applies this logic to using the n-word.

The moral panic surrounding the supposed threat of cancel culture usually vacillates between the first and the second level of meaning. An active online user's worry that a careless tweet or Facebook post could have negative professional consequences is not panic. In most cases, this fear may be overblown, but it is far from irrational. The panic starts when the undeniable power of social networks and the digital public sphere begin turning the common-sense picture of existing social relationships—who has power and who doesn't, who is vulnerable and who isn't, what can and can't be said—on its head: when transgender students who are rarely interviewed in the media suddenly appear as a dominant group, while members of Congress, presidents, eccentric billionaires, and the entire Russian Federation are seen as their powerless victims; when maximum diagnoses are derived from trifles; when supposedly new threats are tied to decades-old incidents; when media present woodcut-like narratives quite obviously omitting salient context, but recipients nevertheless feel that they have understood a complex situation perfectly.

The concept of moral panic was introduced in 1972 by the sociologist Stanley Cohen. In his book *Folk Devils and Moral Panics*, he examined "mods" and "rockers" as objects of discourse.[9] In the United Kingdom of the 1960s, these subcultures were popular with young people but were also understood—to a surprising degree—as threats to public order. The question "mod or rocker?" was important to certain young people, and governed clothing, lifestyle, and creative expression. But the debate about them ended up being about anything but this: After a few fights involving young people with a mod or rocker aesthetic, the question suddenly became a preoccupation for the older generation, for the authorities, for politics. Mods and rockers were now no longer an issue on Carnaby Street, but in the major daily newspapers, in Parliament, in police headquarters.

MPs went wild with extreme historical comparisons and apocalyptic warnings. One representative spoke of the young people as a "marauding army of Vikings going through Europe massacring and plundering, living by slaughter and rapacity."[10] After any alleged incident involving anyone under the age of thirty, or someone wearing a leather jacket, the press reported on the escalating problem: "A Town in Fear—What Can Be Done To Stop More Fights?"[11] Soon, what Cohen called the "widening of the web" of attention ensued: What had begun with fights in public suddenly came to encompass all sorts of other practices simply because they involved young people. In Brighton, young women camping out on the beach on warm summer nights were arrested by police. Entire styles of music and clothing were suddenly suspect.

This discursive expansion was influenced by individuals Cohen called "moral entrepreneurs." These entrepreneurs interpreted the incidents for the general public, explaining why a fight in Margate and girls on the beach in Brighton ought to matter to a newspaper reader in Leeds. Some of these entrepreneurs were decision-makers—journalists or politicians—but their currency was not so much the law as attention. They demanded that the elites finally recognize the problem, that the state authorities finally do something. They called for control while at the same time selling a wide audience on a pervasive sense of *loss* of control.

Each turn in this dialogue was, as Cohen writes, "rather predictable."[12] Cohen pointed out that predictability with each new turn. If you read his book today, you will be impressed by how precisely his model can be applied to later media hysteria—from the hoopla about heavy metal to rainbow parties, from new fad drugs to drag queens, from gang signs to children allegedly identifying as cats. Cohen described a "moral panic" as follows:

> A condition, episode, person or group of persons emerges to become defined as a threat to societal values and interests; its nature is presented in a stylized and stereotypical fashion by the mass media; the moral barricades are manned by editors, bishops, politicians and other right-thinking people; socially accredited experts pronounce their diagnoses and solutions.[13]

What's more, the press and "moral entrepreneurs" give the panic an amazingly uniform grammar, almost regardless of its ostensible object:

> They are *new* (lying dormant perhaps, but hard to recognize; deceptively ordinary and routine, but invisibly creeping up the moral horizon)—but also *old* (camouflaged versions of traditional and well-known evils). They are damaging *in themselves*—but also merely *warning signs* of the real, much deeper and more prevalent condition. They are *transparent* (anyone can see what's happening)—but also *opaque*: accredited experts must explain the perils hidden behind the superficially harmless (decode a rock song's lyrics to see how they led to a school massacre).[14]

Young people themselves were skeptical about the panic surrounding the mods and the rockers. In the Beatles movie *A Hard Day's Night*, a reporter asks Ringo Starr which of the two subcultures he feels he belongs to. In response, the Beatles drummer deadpans: "I'm a mocker." But as a rule, young people were only asked in the movies, and only if their name was Ringo Starr. The subtitle of Cohen's book is *The Creation of the Mods and Rockers*. Of course, both of these groups were perfectly real. But what became of them in the media was something quite different. The young had lost the authority to interpret their own culture. The moral panic broke away from "particular disapproved forms of behaviour (such as drug-taking or violence)" and instead attached itself to "distinguishable social types."[15] Soon the British public was no longer told to be afraid of specific actions of the mods or rockers, but of mods and rockers themselves.

We see an analogous development in the discourse around canceling: What started out as a description of specific (types of) action increasingly became a way to characterize very specific types of people—young, woke activists, snowflakes, social justice warriors (SJWs), and so on. Cohen was well aware that there was a certain fear behind the fear. After all, the mod and rocker panic shared a moment with the establishment of a youth culture that would itself, by the late 1960s, have a major impact around the world. The mod and rocker panic was a distorted and anticipatory response to the developments leading up to the baby boomer rebellion of the late 60s. In its specifics, it was pure nonsense; there was no civil war between young people with gelled hair and those without. But the social fears that this panic expressed were real. They had a political dimension and, more importantly, they had political effects.

A moral panic is not mere mass hysteria. It has political potency and articulates what is usually an affirmative relationship to existing power and privilege structures. Implicitly, the mod and rocker panic called for very specific heroes and saviors: parents, politicians, judges, and police officers. The villains were young people with messy hair and loud music. The cancel culture panic likewise thrives on the assumption that those in power—from politicians to editors and established writers—deserve their status. The villains are young people with "they/them" pronouns in their Twitter bio.

Cohen's notion of "folk devils" suggests that moral panics are also always folklore: No matter how much they are spread by public authorities, by the press, or even by elected officials, they catch on only because they draw on a reservoir of symbolic fears and meanings in their target audience. This also means that if one analyzes the fear of cancel culture as moral panic, one does so instead of turning to another term as a guide—namely, propaganda. As folklore, moral panics are never as explicit as propaganda and are not as overtly dependent on power structures within politics and the media world. The fear of Saddam Hussein's weapons of mass destruction in the run-up to the second Iraq War was not moral panic, although the media regurgitating the lies used similar mechanisms: deliberate misinformation, concocted by the Department of Defense, presented by the secretary of state to the UN Security Council, and constantly discussed with conviction by supposedly reputable media types. By comparison, a moral panic is more agile, more instinctual, and in the end just more eccentric than that. In retrospect, it can be hard to pin down who, in its grips, argued what. Looking back, it often comes across as bizarre and embarrassing rather than dishonest and manipulative.

That is when there is a look back at all—because moral panics depend on a certain amnesia. "A panic," said Cohen, "by definition, is self-limiting, temporary and spasmodic, a splutter of rage which burns itself out."[16] When the next, similar moral panic sweeps the world— and suddenly it is no longer heavy metal but hip-hop music threatening our children, or trans teachers rather than gay ones—then it is essential that the last cycle of panic is quickly forgotten. "Each appeal," Cohen writes, "is a sleight of hand, magic without the magician."[17] In the 1990s, the sociologists Erich Goode and Nachman Ben-Yehuda pointed out the characteristic development of moral panics: Danger comes quickly and is intensely evoked, but "the degree of fear, hostility, and concern generated during a moral panic tends to be fairly limited temporally."[18]

Cancel culture may be different. Those who foment the fear are effectively describing the same object as the moral panic that made the cover of *New York* magazine in 1991: "Are You Politically Correct?"[19] The assertion that universities "now" increasingly restrict what can be said on campus has been around in this form since at least the late 1980s—always underpinned by the usual selective and frequently misinterpreted anecdotes. What are now "trigger warnings" were "speech codes" in the 80s. What is today's freak-out over DEI was until quite recently the one about (certain kinds of) affirmative action. Why is the temporal extension of this panic so different? After all these decades, why are we still panicking the same way?

That is where this book comes in. It is intended to explain and trace how and why various global publics were so quickly convinced that cancel culture exists, that people knew what it was, and that it posed an existential problem. What did people in these various countries have to forget in order to make the cancel culture debate possible? I want to give the discourse back its history. Certainly, stating that we were warned about the big bad wolf fifteen, twenty, fifty years ago and yet it never came does not mean that it will not come this time. But that's not what this book is about for me. I intend to research the "crying wolf" itself, as well as the public that is receptive to it time and again.

My thesis is that the (re)emergence of this panic just after #MeToo is no coincidence. Its structure and timing closely mimic those of #MeToo and Black Lives Matter. Both #MeToo/BLM and the cancel culture panic identify a relatively transhistorical problem (sexism/racism here, censorship and campus/media illiberalism there) but emphasize a crisis point within that *longue durée*. In both cases, conclusions are drawn about some broader system from anecdotes, and in both cases, there is a reassessment about whose anecdotes and individual cases are worth systematizing at all. #MeToo and Black Lives Matter developed their tremendous social power because they resonated with the everyday experiences of many women and people of color. So, I think, did the cancel culture panic: Before debates about Kantian universalism, before "spirals of silence" and "wokistan," there was—for many of those who are most persuaded by these kinds of terms—probably an awkward interaction on Twitter, a strident student in their seminar, an unkind review of their work. Fear of cancel culture is #MeToo for people who are afraid of #MeToo.

To be clear, this is not to say that these two sides *are* similar. It is to say that purveyors and ready consumers of cancel culture talking points regard them, on some level of awareness, as similar. To them, the fact that the number of anecdotes in both #MeToo and Black Lives Matter is disproportionately greater than in cancel culture is not a shortcoming but probably helpful: Anti–cancel culture discourses ultimately poison the well when it comes to anecdotes, first by not really caring about the anecdotes beyond scoring a few points, and second by not bothering to check or contextualize them. The fear of cancel culture is a kind of malicious parody of the #MeToo narrative: slapdash where the #MeToo story needs to be airtight and interchangeable where the #MeToo story centers the individual woman.

This extends to the very raison d'être of anecdotes in public discourse: The connections between anecdote and system, which Black Lives Matter and #MeToo implicitly make, have been established over decades of theoretical work and empirical research, from intersectionality to feminist theory. Terms such as "microaggression" or "white privilege" (regardless of whether one finds these terms useful or not) exist precisely in order to articulate why it's legitimate to move from a cop pulling over a motorist, or an annoying interaction in the break room, to a more systemic critique. The warnings about cancel culture don't do that work, and don't have to do that work. And most importantly, they tell their audience that *they* don't have to do that work either. Once again, the discourse about wokesters does exactly what it accuses them of. Cancel culture discourse, in order to function at all, presupposes a belief and even demands it. The mantralike connection between the individual case and the system, which is found in PC and cancel culture texts, is pure habit. It simulates relevance and cogency through ritualized repetition.

The threadbare quality of the analogies with which cancel culture doomsdayers operate, the often abysmal quality of their texts, constitute the secret principle of the panic. They are sloppy and careless, and in that haphazard way they transport a powerful message. Power doesn't need to bother to justify itself. In fact, if power made that effort, it would no longer be power.

ONE

What We Talk About When We
Talk About Cancel Culture

> When Harvard University law student Brian Timmons used the expression
> "rule of thumb" in class, he wasn't only guilty of a cliché. He soon found out
> he also was being sexist, patriarchal and insensitive.
>
> —*WASHINGTON TIMES* (APRIL 2, 1991)

In this book, I am not primarily concerned with the question of whether cancel culture exists or whether it is largely a media phenomenon. Rather, I rely on a term used by Erich Goode and Nachman Ben-Yehuda in their book *Moral Panics*: that of "disproportionality." Moral panics are usually based on a possibly significant but limited set of real events: Child abductions do happen; some teenage music fans do commit suicide; gangs do recruit young people and commit crimes. But as the panic goes on, the objective frequency of the phenomenon and its media presence diverge. The panic proceeds by expanding what counts as evidence for its central premise: Through overblown statistics and misreported anecdotes, suddenly anything counts. "Public concern is in excess of what is appropriate if concern were directly proportional to objective harm."[1]

My argument proceeds from the observation that the discourse around cancel culture has exactly this kind of proportionality problem. In this chapter I will argue that attempts to capture cancel culture in data are largely failures. But I also want to show that they are interesting, deeply telling failures, since they reveal certain ambiguities in the discourse, whether strategic or unconscious. These ambiguities, in turn, likely explain the remarkable speed with which concerns about cancel culture have established themselves in our media landscape, and the ease with which they have traveled from US newspapers and magazines to very different media environments globally.

Both in the United States and abroad, cancel culture discourses propose that we are living through a rising tide of (usually left-wing) censoriousness. Those warning of cancel culture point to a tendency in public debate, especially in various online forums, towards dialing up criticism almost from the word go and to an overreliance on ad hominem attacks.[2] Outside of the context of social media, descriptions usually identify a form of criticism that is more punitive than in the past, that is intended to prevent the other person from further expressing their opinions ("deplatforming"), that is well organized (the famous Twitter mob), and that also comes to encompass the defenders of the person attacked in its punitive actions (what is sometimes called a "secondary boycott"[3]).

Secondly, cancel culture is understood as the retrospective erasure of unpopular artists and public figures—especially as a synecdoche of what cancel culture critics describe as a more general project of historical erasure. When the philosopher Omri Boehm wrote in a German-language article about a fight over a statue of the philosopher Immanuel Kant—a surprisingly frequent subject of German-language cancel culture fights—he was at pains to emphasize that the debate was part of something much more ominous. "We are not toppling an 'old white man,'" Boehm wrote, "let alone any particular monument. What is at stake is the fate of universalistic thinking."[4] Canceling thus attacks specific individuals, but behind that attack lurks a broader attack on the premises of the liberal democratic order—it is, as the subtitle of Alan Dershowitz's book on the topic has it, "the latest assault on free speech and due process."[5]

Finally, warnings about cancel culture claim that self-censorship is becoming more pervasive, for example, either in interpersonal matters or—at universities—in the choice of research areas or questions. Even if the cases of outright cancellation were few, these warnings suggest, even if the consequences suffered by canceled individuals were mild, the atmosphere of reticence they generate leads to a discursive narrowing that ultimate hurts—take your pick—the maturation process of our young, the progress of science, productive debate, or a free and democratic society.

Given the supposed scope and multifaceted nature of the problem, the question naturally arises as to how perception relates to reality. Unfortunately, however, the question of reality itself fails to capture reality. It presumes the existence of incidents that either happened or didn't happen and that either unproblematically fit or don't fit a clear category of cancellation. But in fact, cancel culture diagnoses are almost entirely premised on anecdotes, and these stories, like PC stories before them, do not represent innocent data points. They come to us pre-grouped and pre-interpreted, and this is where the problems start. Cancel culture anecdotes are tendentiously composed fables, often based on only one source, which are—at least in the United States—usually purveyed and promoted by politically motivated actors. Treating these stories as straightforward data points means ignoring all that. That doesn't make them false, of course. At the center of the PC panic, Marc Fabian Erdl has written, was an "uncritical reception of sources,"[6] and that captures the process rather well: The cancel culture diagnosis fails to think through how its evidence comes about. We can say that in recent years these anecdotes have increasingly been brought to the attention of a broader public. But that of course says nothing about whether such incidents have in fact become more numerous.

Difficulties with Definitions and Data

A first difficulty that presents itself in treating these stories as unproblematic data points is that the types of incidents taken to exemplify cancel culture are very heterogeneous.[7] There are about half a dozen online databases that are supposed to document different cases of cancel culture. As of July 2022, the list compiled by the website Canceled People contained 173 cases, the database of the National Association of Scholars (NAS) had 228, the Foundation for Individual Rights and Expression (FIRE) had 715, and The College Fix had an impressive 1,566. As alarming as these numbers may appear, closer inspection suggests that the listers use highly varied definitions of who is and who is not canceled. As of mid-2022, only 387 cases appeared in more than one of these lists. Even those who warn of cancel culture do not seem to agree entirely on what it is.

Canceled People for example, lists the French teacher Samuel Paty (who was beheaded by an Islamist in 2020), the Japanese literary scholar Hitoshi Igarashi (who was murdered in 1991), and Donald Trump as victims of cancel culture. The incidents behind their inclusion are so different that it is baffling to think the word "canceling" could do justice to all three. Paty was the victim of a violent political crime. Igarashi was probably murdered for translating Salman Rushdie's *Satanic Verses* into Japanese, but the case remains unsolved to this day, and it is thus difficult to ask the perpetrator(s) about their level of "wokeness." And Donald Trump remains—at least as of this writing—perhaps the most influential figure in the Republican Party, adored by millions and poised to return to the White House in 2025.

Although many celebrities who have been positioned as victims of cancellation in recent years had nothing to do with the university (Dave Chappelle, say, or Woody Allen), the discourse always finds its way back to campus. Cancel culture doesn't exclusively happen at universities, but somehow institutions of higher education are never far when it comes to cancel culture. There is a good reason for this: Conservative institutions have been actively collecting anecdotes of supposed left-wing censorship on campuses for a long time. The relationship with the university structures the understanding of cancel culture (especially in Europe), without most writers considering the obvious question of how representative these US elite universities are for American society in general, to say nothing of German, French, or British society.

On the contrary, reports on cancel culture, whether in the United States or abroad, assume two contradictory things about campus life: First, universities are coddled bubbles; their quirky arguments about privilege, wokeness, and gender theory are hopelessly out of step with normal people and their concerns. Second, the college campus is an incubator for ideas that, if left unchecked, will almost necessarily spread from the leafy quad to a subdivision near you. Campus activities (and activism) are the canary in the coal mine, the kindling for an emerging threat.

But even on university campuses, it is not always clear what exactly "being canceled" means. The website The College Fix, run out of conservative Hillsdale College in Michigan, maintains a comprehensive campus cancel culture database, which gives a good idea of what sort of campus imbroglios count. In addition to various arts categories ("Film," "Music," "Theater"), many of the categories (nine of twenty-one) have to do with the university world: "Building/ Names," "Curriculum," "Honorary Doctorates," "Guest Speakers," "Mascots," "Professor Comments," "Student Comments," "Student Groups," and "Student Event." Others point to controversies over the last five years, particularly within the framework of the Black Lives Matter movement. (By early 2024, the film category had disappeared, replaced with "Israel.")

On the other hand, the individual cases fueling the panic are so spread out in time and context that it is difficult to analyze them with any real seriousness. Among the 228 cases of canceled academics listed in the National Association of Scholars database by the end of July 2022, 35 had lost their job, according to the organization. Between 2015 and 2019 the number of those listed as dismissed was three or four per year. A year later, the number skyrocketed: The list for 2020 includes nine resignations, although several of the people named, as far as I can tell, were "only" placed on a leave of absence. For the year 2021, the database lists seven cases of job loss. Three of these firings (Lora Burnett, Lars Jensen, Daniel Pollack-Pelzner) were preceded by a dispute with the university administration; there was no woke mob or student activism. One (Howard Bauchner) is on the list because he was fired as the editor of an important journal in his field. He remains a professor to this day.

A total of four of the professors listed for 2021 experienced what we would likely see reported in the press as a classic cancel story: They lost their position due to allegations of racism or sexism. They used the n-word, joked about Asians and COVID-19, mocked Black students. Their trespasses found their way onto social media, provoking student or faculty protests, and they finally lost their jobs. In one case—Gary Hypes at Seton Hill University in New Jersey—NAS explains that Hypes was dismissed for being "pro-Trump." This is a bit of an understatement. Hypes wrote on his Facebook page on January 6, 2021, that "War is coming!" and "Finally, just maybe we will have the bloodshed that is needed to fix this country."[8] Hypes denies having written the posts.

My point is not that all of these cases are in fact completely unproblematic, or that certain scholars deserve dismissal and others do not. My point is that the overall picture these cases paint is deeply ambiguous. Most importantly, the increase in the number of cases seems to be primarily a function of increased interest and attention. The curves inevitably flatten out towards the past simply because the people gathering and submitting these stories no longer recall very similar cases from 2001, 2005, or 2009.

But even the figures for our present moment should be approached with caution. The United States is a huge country with 5,000 to 6,000 educational institutions, depending on how you count. Dismissal and sanction mean something very different depending on whether someone is a tenured faculty member or an adjunct instructor whose contract is not renewed; some adjuncts are financially dependent on their teaching activities; others are successful lawyers or entrepreneurs "in real life" and only offer a few courses on the side. Journalist Michael Hobbes, who has been tracing the moral panic surrounding cancel culture for years, has said, "When you go looking for such cases, you will find them."[9] However, what exactly these cases mean becomes less and less clear the more you look at them individually.

As I mentioned earlier, the Foundation for Individual Rights and Expression (FIRE) maintains a database of "Scholars Under Fire." Their database lists 715 cases between 2015 and the end of July 2022. Here, too, the extreme breadth of the cases is striking. We read about decanal appointments thwarted by intrigue, promotions that never materialized, speakers who were uninvited.

Taken together, the incidents collected on the list make a good case that US universities are not always pleasant places to work. But here too, if you scrutinize the cases more closely, you find that, behind the apocalyptic talk of cancel culture laying hold of the university are largely lurid redescriptions of longstanding academic dysfunction. Beyond the bombastic framing about the First Amendment and McCarthyism (which, in fairness, FIRE largely avoids), these stories don't seem to say much more than that on campuses where tenured professors are aging alongside one another, and interacting with a student body that is becoming increasingly alien to them, there are almost inevitably injured vanities and small dustups.

Of the 715 incidents, 20 took place at Stanford. That places the university where I work at the top of the list. A little bit of local knowledge, however, quickly puts this top position into perspective. Most of the Stanford entries trace back to a single contretemps: During the COVID-19 pandemic, numerous professors were bothered by the fact that fellows of the conservative Hoover Institution, which is based at Stanford, spread questionable opinions about the pandemic, especially on Fox News. Mentioning specific colleagues, they put a motion before the faculty senate to clarify and possibly reconsider the university's relationship with the Hoover Institution. The Hoover fellows whom the professors singled out in this motion are on the FIRE list as researchers "under fire." The fellows criticized in the motion turned the tables and demanded that their critics be censored for their attempts to restrict academic freedom. The sum of the first and second group results in thirteen of the twenty entries for Stanford, pushing it to the topmost position on the list. Those who came under fire in this way are all still in their positions; several of them expressed surprise that they had appeared on a list of canceled individuals at all.

Three other colleagues likely would have reacted with less amusement. They are on the list due to a fairly classic cancel case. One professor had read a quote containing the n-word in a team-taught course. Students had objected, eventually extending the complaint to the other teachers on the team. Another colleague was attacked by a group of well-funded conservative activists with ads on Instagram and Facebook over his teaching of critical race theory. None of these are just trifles; not everyone on this list could simply shrug off what happened to them. But these lists are frequently used to paint a very stark picture, and a stark picture emerges only if you look at the data points from very far, probably too far, away.

This is partially a problem of remediation: that is, of how these kinds of lists are used. In April 2023, Steven Pinker and Bertha Madras wrote in the *Boston Globe* about the ebbing "confidence in American higher education," that it "is sinking faster than for any other institution, with barely half of Americans believing it has a positive effect on the country."[10] They didn't mention that this is almost entirely due to truly staggering levels of erosion among Americans who identify as Republicans. But they alluded to the fact that *some* Americans seem to be losing faith in the universities more than others, for they went on to note that "no small part in this disenchantment is the impression that universities are repressing differences of opinion, like the inquisitions and purges of centuries past." For any American reading the *Boston Globe* in 2023, the clues laid in this passage were not subtle: This was a cavil about political correctness, repeating its semantics and metaphors. The article also claimed that the erosion in confidence was "stoked by viral videos of professors being mobbed, cursed, heckled into silence, and sometimes assaulted"—in other words, that it was confirmed by "some alarming numbers":

> According to the Foundation for Individual Rights and Expression, between 2014 and 2022 there were 877 attempts to punish scholars for expression that is, or in public contexts would be, protected by the First Amendment. Sixty percent resulted in actual sanctions, including 114 incidents of censorship and 156 firings (44 of them tenured professors)—more than during the McCarthy era.[11]

The numbers in this passage come from the FIRE database; Pinker and Madras provide the interpretation. The "156 firings" in eight years is indeed likely more than during the McCarthy era. Or perhaps we should say, it's more than were fired during the McCarthy era *as part of anti-communist investigations.* The numbers are contested (as at the time neither universities nor fired professors themselves were keen to come forward about dismissals), but historian Ellen Schrecker puts the number of US college and university professors who lost their jobs for suspected communist ties somewhere north of a hundred.[12] Pinker and Madras clearly invite us to compare that number to another one—that of people who have fallen victim to another more or less circumscribed social phenomenon, likely left-wing cancel culture. What Pinker and Madras *intend* for us to picture is a case like that of two professors at Louisiana State University: They made snarky, racist comments about BLM on Facebook, angry reactions from colleagues and students followed, and they had to resign. And then we are supposed to multiply a case like that by 156.

To be clear, cases like these of course do occur in FIRE's dataset. But the FIRE list doesn't just count those kinds of cases. It tries to collect *all* cases where someone loses their job for speech that could arguably be protected under the First Amendment. In Pinker and Madras's text, we are invited to regard, say, a professor fired for what he claims is left-wing speech as evidence for a left-wing cancel culture.

Finally, we also need to consider the denominator: According to the Department of Education, there were about 1,800 universities and colleges in the United States in 1950. Today there are between 5,000 and 6,000 (depending on how you count them). The number of teachers at these campuses jumped from 190,353 to 987,518 between 1950 and 1990 alone—a fivefold increase. Today, the number of "professors, associate professors, assistant professors, instructors, lecturers, assisting professors, adjunct professors, interim professors" stands at roughly 1.5 million, according to the Department of Education.[13] The phrase "worse than McCarthy" seems calculated to confuse the absolute and relative frequencies of a phenomenon.

But it's a confusion such lists invite. These statistics are not innocent of the way they're being used. If you look at lists like Scholars Under Fire, it is hard to imagine them being used in any other way than Pinker and Madras do. Scholars Under Fire isn't RateMyProfessors.com; it isn't intended for interested individuals clicking their way through. These lists are waiting for a writer—usually in traditional print media—who wants to garnish a broad diagnosis in the mode of Pinker and Madras. In other words, these cases exist in the shape that they come to us mostly in order to be divested of their specificity and combined with a handful of superficially similar ones to make a larger point.

When these lists hit the op-ed pages, the writer relies on the geographic and institutional spread of these anecdote collections to create a feeling of proximity: Cancel culture! Now happening in your hometown! Germany has its own version of the FIRE database—the Netzwerk Wissenschaftsfreiheit (Network Academic Freedom), which collects "Examples from German-speaking countries," even though six of the seventy-four "German" cases on the list as of mid-2023 appear to have happened in France, the United States, and the UK.[14] The original example thus becomes evidence for its own spread.

Cancel culture anecdotes are frequently localized not by providing more detail but by selectively omitting it. "An Oxford-educated professor has been 'cancelled' for the second time in three years as his publisher withdrew his biography of a British imperialist following a petition from a communist philosopher," wrote Mark Bridge in October 2020 in the London *Times*.[15] An opening like this attempts to construct a closeness and immediacy for British readers; and so it invokes Oxford (where the "Oxford-educated professor" turns out to have attended a two-year master's program) because telling a story about "a professor at Portland State University in Portland, Oregon, USA" would sound just as remote and provincial to British readers as it in fact was.

In this case, the "cancellation" consisted in the separation of Bruce Gilley (who remains a professor) from his publisher: Oxford University Press (OUP). The publisher withdrew Gilley's book, at least according to the Heritage Foundation's write-up of the case and The College Fix's database. However, as the publisher pointed out in a rebuttal in the *Wall Street Journal*, Gilley withdrew his book himself and offered it to another publisher. Of course, no one is forcing you to credit OUP's version of events. But it's noticeable that the alarmist texts about the affair omit the publisher's version or the version of the "communist professor"—indeed, basically any perspective other than Gilley's. Gilley's book was published by Regnery Gateway in 2021 (a few months after the planned OUP release). Another publisher, Academica Press, claimed that Gilley had also promised them the book. The upshot here is that a book that would otherwise probably only have been discussed in some small scholarly journals suddenly turned up in the *Times* (London), in the *Wall Street Journal*, and many other newspapers. You can disagree with some, or even most, of the decisions made over the course of the dispute—it doesn't take away from their eminent banality. This is exactly what the concept of cancel culture does: It robs the everyday of its ordinariness, converting the absolutely run-of-the-mill into something uncanny.

From the beginning, some of the most avid recyclers of US campus anecdotes—and indeed the most passionate users of databases like Scholars Under Fire—appear to have been newspaper writers and editors outside of the United States. Here is a description by Jochen Bittner of Germany's *Die Zeit* of the situation at American universities: "In 2001 there were two incidents in which demonstrators tried to remove unpopular speakers from the campus or to disrupt their lectures, but the number increased significantly afterwards: 2015–16 there were thirty-eight such attempts."[16] Bittner's data come from the FIRE list. In half of the cases, we learn, these attempts were considered successful, meaning presumably that either the event was canceled or interrupted. However, these 19 cases on almost 6,000 campuses in another country seem to be such an important phenomenon that *Die Zeit* had to devote repeated attention to them. Column inches are a finite commodity. How they are used, and what similar phenomena do not receive similar attention, sends a message as well. How do you explain such an apparent mismatch between problem and attention? It makes sense only if, like Bittner, one assumes that the thirty-eight cases mentioned represent the tip of a gigantic iceberg—one that cannot be quantified in lists but has to be intuited in each reader's own life. Don't you feel less free to voice your opinion? Don't you remember a time when the climate seemed more conducive to free expression?

Climate Change

Proving the supposed magnitude of the cancel culture problem within institutions is difficult. On the other hand, the claim that the internet, and social networks in particular—with their engagement algorithms, search engine optimization, and context collapse—lead to certain discourse shifts and new discourse strategies seems fairly uncontroversial. What is much harder to establish are the effects of these developments in the real world. Time and again, the spectacle of toxic online behavior is used to frame events that—under a different moniker—would have been discussed as supposed signs of the times forty years ago.

An article that appeared in the *Neue Zürcher Zeitung* kicks off, as almost all of articles of this type do in European media, with a set of anecdotes likely drawn from one or several of the online databases. Here is how it transitions to its broader cancel culture warning: "Admittedly, you can dismiss this as a trifle. However, it's not an isolated case. And it shows a trend that is becoming increasingly evident. Not only in the USA, but also in Europe. And no longer just at universities."[17] The dissolution of boundaries in the relevant anecdotes is based on the assertion that (1) they are not isolated cases, but (2) "a trend that is becoming increasingly evident" and that (3) this tendency seeps out from the United States and from the universities into the everyday life of Europeans. For this, writers rely on a second form of perceptual shift. They invite their readers to reinterpret ordinary experiences in a way that makes them appear dramatic and ultimately pathological. This is especially true when it comes to everyday self-censorship, which is often associated with cancel culture.

Self-censorship is by its very nature a difficult thing to argue about since it is primarily based on a subjective feeling. Whether my inner censor is more sensitive than yours, whether either of them has become more sensitive over time, whether the fears that drive them correspond to reality or not—all this is hard to say with any certainty. Moreover, the feeling that one is unable to say something can of course be effective in silencing a person, even if it is ultimately not based on objective reality. What I feel I cannot say, I may simply not say, even if I could. Statistics on self-reports of self-censorship on American campuses and beyond, are a frequently cited proof for the existence and intensification of cancel culture. In fact, many studies seem to document such an intensification. However, this may well be due to their methodology. One gets the impression that these surveys were created to precisely deliver the kinds of dramatic results that can then be ground up in cancel culture philippics.

In the fall of 2021, a number of well-known scientists and intellectuals announced the founding of a new university. According to the designated president, Pano Kanelos, the University of Austin was intended to counter the "illiberalism" rampant on other campuses, where "faculty are being treated like thought criminals" and "over a third of conservative academics and PhD students say they had been threatened with disciplinary action for their views."[18] The press echo, both in the United States and abroad, was enormous. In Germany, almost all major dailies reported on the event, and several published more than one article. One Italian outlet described it as a university founded by "cancel culture dissidents,"[19] the center-right Spanish daily *El Mundo* described it as "a university against political correctness,"[20] and *Le Figaro* in Paris wrote about the university "with the goal of fighting the woke ideology."[21]

The further the news of the new university traveled, the more directly the articles parroted the university's press release, as well as the description of the alleged cancel culture problem. Most importantly, the data cited to prove the necessity of founding a new university came from the founders themselves. In his statement, Kanelos cited a study by the Heterodox Academy. A typical article in the *Frankfurter Allgemeine Zeitung* quoted historian Niall Ferguson (another founding member of the new university), who pointed to the same study. Heterodox Academy is a think tank led by Jonathan Haidt, another founding member of the University of Austin. According to the study from 2020, 62 percent of college students "agreed the climate on their campus prevents students from saying things they believe."[22] In that study, 1,311 students were asked how "comfortable" or "reluctant" they were to talk about various controversial topics.[23]

Something that this study presupposes as obvious, but that—on a second look—is anything but, is the idea that self-censorship is primarily about sharing an "opinion" about a "topic." Censorship and self-censorship can apply to all sorts of things, but here the subject was the lives of others. The authors of the study wanted to know if a student felt he or she could voice an opinion *about* homosexuality, or *about* the civil rights of certain groups—not whether this student would possibly censor him- or herself with regard to the student's own identity. The authors of the questionnaire seem to have implicitly imagined the students who might be threatened with censorship as white and heterosexual. In other words, there was simply no space in this survey for the answer: "I censor myself—for example, by not making my race, gender, sexuality, identity, or culture an issue."

Of course, this type of censorship occurs at American universities (not least of all at Christian colleges that still expel students for homosexuality), but the framing of the study simply ignores it. Instead, it is clear what sort of censorship the researchers wanted to find: namely, censorship of right-wing ideas emanating from the Left and from people of color. The terms "comfortable" and "reluctant" also suggest the extent of the self-censorship problem the designers of the study were hoping to find. That a student might not be "comfortable," or might even be "reluctant" to exchange ideas about a charged topic like religion, is not necessarily an indication of self-censorship; it simply points to the fact that this topic is controversial.

American campuses pride themselves on the fact that they bring together young people from very different backgrounds. For many of them, college is the first step out of the fairly homogeneous communities in which they have grown up. In that sort of environment, a minimal amount of self-censorship is simply good sense, particularly when there are significant differences to be bridged. In other words, such interactions aren't supposed to be *comfortable*— something these same critics of cancel culture like to emphasize when they worry that students are being coddled by no longer being confronted with ideas with which they disagree.

Talking about "controversial" opinions in such studies is also misleading in its broadness. As a rule, the controversial opinions queried are simply pillars of conservative ideology. This becomes clear in a second study that Kanelos quoted in his press release, but that found less resonance in the articles echoing him. This study, undertaken by political scientist Eric Kaufmann, who until recently taught at Birkbeck College, University of London, showed, as Kanelos put it, that "four out of five American PhD students are willing to discriminate against right-leaning scholars." But Kaufmann's study specifically asked how academics would react to "Trump supporters" and "Leave Supporters" (i.e., Brexit supporters).[24] It was thus deliberately constructed in order to focus on a very specific type of silencing—not a rightward lean so much as very specific policy preferences. When news of the founding of the University of Austin made the rounds in newspapers and magazines, that focus magically disappeared. Instead, the framing suggested that the topics at issue were indicators of freedom of expression in general. Kanelos's framing, and the worldwide acceptance of that framing, thus carried the suggestion that, when it comes to worrying about freedom of expression, certain forms of expression matter more than others.

In the *New York Times* editorial from 2022, the newspaper presented the results of a survey that it conducted together with Siena College. For the *New York Times*, the numbers pointed to a massive problem of self-censorship: "Many Americans are understandably confused, then, about what they can say and where they can say it."[25] The questions found "that some Americans do not speak freely in everyday situations because of fear of retaliation or harsh criticism," largely because the questions already assumed they did.

Among other things, the participants were asked: "How free do you feel you are to express your viewpoint on a daily basis without fear of retaliation, censorship or punishment?"[26] And they were asked to imagine their freedom of expression in the context of specific situations: How free did they feel to volunteer their viewpoint among family, friends, online acquaintances, co-workers, and "medical providers"? In particular, Republican voters (55 percent) said they felt "less free" to talk about political issues than they had ten years ago. At least 35 percent of those questioned stated that they felt "less free" when it came to "race relations."

In its diagnosis of a national "burden" of cancel culture, the *New York Times* pointed out that "only 34 percent of Americans said they believed that all Americans enjoyed freedom of speech completely." The newspaper interpreted this as evidence that people in the United States felt they were losing "a fundamental right as citizens of a free country: the right to speak their minds and voice their opinions in public without fear of being shamed or shunned." This of course discounts another possibility: that the results reflected what Americans have been told about their freedom of expression for decades.

Suppose we accept for the moment that the numbers are an indicator of a change in the social climate. What can we deduce from them? The political scientist Nicholas Grossman has pointed out that the evidence is not as clear as the *New York Times* editorial claims. When asked "to what extent you think all Americans now enjoy" freedom of speech, 34 percent answered "completely," 42 percent answered "somewhat," 15 percent answered "not very," and 8 percent answered "not at all." As Grossman notes, the 42 percent are objectively correct.[27] Nobody in the United States enjoys unrestricted freedom of expression. The "just" 34 percent who celebrated complete freedom of expression likely understood the question pragmatically: These respondents took "complete" to mean what they considered reasonable freedom of expression. More than three quarters of the participants seemed satisfied with freedom of speech in the United States.

While it is, of course, interesting to consider whether, say, Americans feel more free to speak their mind online than offline, it's also quite noticeable that the questions contain a kind of pedagogy. Even if they are meant to reflect a perception of reality, they risk shaping it. As with the question of whether college students feel free to express their opinions, the *New York Times*'s survey questions invited participants to pathologize what is in fact quite mundane. The fact that one is not allowed to say everything is a basic characteristic of social life. The sociologist Erving Goffman devoted his 1956 book *The Presentation of Self in Everyday Life* to the rituals of displaying and hiding aspects of one's self and one's opinions. The fact that you don't just regale your work colleagues with potentially controversial opinions—that you maybe don't discuss abortion when you go shopping or Brexit at the dentist—is not surprising: It seems like common sense. From interactions that are fairly constant over time and utterly quotidian, the *New York Times* sought to construct a crisis. And the neologism "cancellation" allowed it to do just that.

It also managed to suggest a shape of the crisis—not just who was affected, but also which issues merited the label "crisis" in the first place. To wit, it is unlikely that, say, a Black man who is a fervent supporter of Black Lives Matter would go around sharing that position unbidden with, say, his pharmacist or his car dealer. According to the *New York Times*'s definition, this person would be engaged in self-censorship. However, our hypothetical person might see this reluctance as a consequence of societal racism, as a function of living as a member of a minority in a white-dominated society, as a natural aspect of life in a multicultural society. But—and this is the point— he would not see it as a cancellation. It is simply not how we use that term. The *New York Times* picks out very specific forms of self-censorship and uses the neologism "cancel" to elevate them into a supposed threat to a free and open society.

While polls of this sort are questionable indicators of sociopolitical change, their structure and framing do tell us something important about the cancel culture panic. It is probably no accident that they invite those taking the survey (and those writing or reading about it) to take a fairly generalized social experience (in a diverse and large country, one sometimes pays attention to what one says in front of strangers) and reinterpret it into a highly specific and politicized problem (leftist activists suppress the expression of conservative viewpoints in doctor's offices or while shopping). This reframing imagines an individual who once upon a time (before the new crush of self-censorship) was able to blurt out everything that went through their head, without fear of blowback. For this fantastical individual, the mere sense that another person might be bothered by their opinion already impinges on their autonomy.

Furthermore, as we shall see, a certain sense of homogeneity—especially a now-lost homogeneity—in terms of discourse and its participants is typical of cancel culture fears. They respond, in other words, to a somewhat sudden realization that others can hear and have a say—that minorities might respond to (or "clap back" at) things being said about them. Conversely, things that are simply part of everyday life for many Americans who are not white, male, straight, or cisgender are understood as dangerous and as illegitimate restrictions of freedom once they suddenly begin to apply to the majority. After all, non-white Americans have long adopted strategies of self-censorship to avoid attracting attention in white-dominated work environments and schools (code switching). Kenji Yoshino introduced the term "covering" to describe how in the new civil rights paradigm, "outsiders are included, but only if we behave like insiders."[28] Covering includes habits like not bringing up certain aspects of one's own identity. Ask any LGBTQ+ American when, on a cross-country road trip, they would stop calling their same-sex partner "partner." They would likely have an answer ready. These are all forms of self-censorship, but they're not the kind the *New York Times* is interested in.

The term "cancellation" allows the *New York Times* to discover distinctions where there really are none. That is the magic of cancellation: It divides the blooming confusion of microscopic daily interactions into two clearly separated camps; it exaggerates some and normalizes others. It teaches its consumers that the type of discomfort they feel is legitimate and politically significant. Other people's expressions of discomfort are not. More importantly, the distinction explains to them why some discomfort is nobler, more meaningful, more worthy of attention than some other kinds.

This pattern repeats in many countries where opinion surveys have collected data on cancel culture. In Germany, the Allensbach Institute for Public Opinion regularly asks about perceived censorship and social pressure. Here, too, the questions usually convey what kind of censorship matters to the survey: The survey from 2021 inquires about opinions that, as a German saying goes, "can burn your mouth"; among them: Muslims/Islam, patriotism, and emancipation/women. Here, too, it's clear that the study design imagines as its subject an individual who approaches these topics as topics (and not as lived experience).[29]

The framing of opinion surveys gives us one sense of how fears of cancel culture function and how they are reinforced. But what is just as striking is that the fear of censorship, or self-censorship, is characterized by a paradox: It is experienced as new, but in fact has a long history. The themes surrounding cancel culture warnings are in many cases decades old. In the United States, France, and Germany, the vocabulary of this panic has been more or less the same for over four decades.

Consider the famous magazine covers from the first stirrings of the political correctness panic of the early 90s: In 1990, the *New York Times* described the new "politically correct orthodoxy" and warned of a "pressure to conform";[30] the magazine *Newsweek* wondered whether it was "the New Enlightenment— or the New McCarthyism?"[31] *Newsweek* had the words "Thought Police" emblazoned on its cover—and warned that its readers should "watch what you say." Meanwhile, the cover of *New York* magazine pictured a concerned-looking white woman, worrying "Am I Guilty of Racism, Sexism, Classism?" And: "Do I say 'Indian' Instead of 'Native American'?"[32] Their vocabulary is identical in most respects with cancel culture texts of 2019–2021. This is a pattern that recurs wherever warnings about cancel culture have had a perceptible impact on public discourse.

In 1993, *Der Spiegel*, Germany's most influential weekly newsmagazine, wrote that "political correctness" was a "liturgy of inhumane patterns of thought and struggle, left-wing pressure to conform and ultimately of censorship."[33] In 2002 the same magazine warned against the "self-appointed thought police of political correctness."[34] The vocabulary of the cancel culture panic has been present for decades. And when mainstream interest in it flags, more esoteric voices will carry the torch until the journalistic mainstream is ready for a new round. Examples, axioms, guiding metaphors—everything in this discourse is recycled.

The questionable framing of polls, like those of the *New York Times* and Siena, clearly interacts with the odd amnesia about just how long we have been living with this discourse. The Allensbach Institute has presented studies according to which the proportion of Germans who state that one can "speak one's opinion freely" has shrunk from 78 to 45 percent since 1991.[35] At the same time, the proportion of those who say it is "better to be careful" has shot up from 16 to 44 percent. What this data of course cannot reflect, but what might explain it, is the fact that since around 1990, Germans, Americans, and French people have been told continuously that the ambit of what is "sayable"—in whatever vocabulary is currently in vogue—is getting narrower.

Even the studies of the type cited by the founders of the University of Austin can hardly be considered independently of the fact that for forty years university students and faculty have been taught to attach political significance (or any significance, really) to specific types of self-censorship while simply ignoring others. As a college professor, if you write about Chaucer, Nietzsche, Shelley, fruit flies, or inflation for a broader public, you'll have to beg editors to publish you. If you write an essay like "I'm a Liberal Professor, and My Liberal Students Terrify Me" or "My University Sacrificed Ideas for Ideology. So Today I Quit," you too can go viral on X or Substack.[36]

To be clear, this says nothing about the reality of the phenomenon. Just because a population is sensitized to a specific situation does not mean, of course, that the situation itself does not exist. Such effects can show up in relation to real developments. For example, women tend to identify more readily as victims of sexual harassment in situations where a language for such identification is readily available. In this case, sensitization promotes a more accurate representation of reality. But of course things can easily be the other way round. Think of the widespread panic in the United States about the MMR vaccine causing autism. It stems from selective sensitization: Since a single poorly conducted study linked the two in the 1990s, parents take a closer look right after their children get the MMR vaccination and provide anecdotes that reinforce this very connection.

Who Is the Cancel Culture Panic For?

Far more real than an existing cancel culture is cancel culture as an object of discourse. The term almost always works deictically: An author points to an occurrence as an example of cancel culture and then moves on to a general description rather than a definition. The discourse about cancel culture is an invitation to play along at home, encouraging you to apply a neologism to a widening range of events, feelings, and phenomena. But, especially once it has entered the vocabulary in non-English languages, it becomes clear the term "cancel culture" represents at its heart a creative act, even if the anglicism of the term suggests that it is a straightforward import. Whether it's the German *Canceln*, the French *wokisme*, or the Russian кенсел- культура or Канселлинг, the term is almost always kept anglophone and thus made to sound foreign. It's so clearly marked as an import that individual users can take the term for the wildest possible ride and still tell themselves they're within range of the original meaning. As they overapply and overemploy the term with reckless abandon, they can tell themselves that their hand is being forced by others—the young people who "invented" cancel culture, the Americans who coined the term. Their creativity appears to them merely responsive.

"Political correctness" had a German cognate (*politische Korrektheit*), which was however less frequently used. "Cancel culture," by contrast, has none—when in June 2023 the governor of the German state of Saxony complained about a "Kultur des Abkanzelns," this was largely interpreted as an *allusion* to the English term, not its translation.[37] In French discourse, too, where the expression *wokisme* predominates, fear of this new culture is linked to anglicism. The French know the homemade *annuler*, but media and politicians usually rely on terms with a more straightforwardly anglophone origin. Vladimir Putin rarely uses Канселлинг, but instead uses a Russian equivalent, культура отмены, derived not from the English word "to cancel" but from the noun отмена (cancellation, abolition, termination). However, the formula used by the Kremlin is often Пресловутая культура отмены, that is, the "so called" or "notorious" cancel culture.[38] So here too, the speaker is at pains to emphasize that speaking about canceling is the discourse of the other.

Whether in Berlin, Paris, or Moscow, invoking the word "canceling" is supposed to indicate the opposite of what the widespread examples (in space, time, and specific context) would suggest. As described, cancel culture implicitly constitutes a global monolith, and specifically an anglophone monolith. At the same time, someone who complains about canceling signals that talk of canceling is being forced on them from outside, even when they're giddily parroting decontextualized US discourses. The strange intermixing of participatory discussion with the feeling that one is merely mirroring, reflecting, and reacting is one more dimension in which the global reception replicates, on an even less tethered level, the pathologies of the US discourse.

But just who is participating? Who is the diagnosis "cancel culture" for? In September 2020, the Pew Research Center tried to find out how widespread the fear of cancel culture was among US residents. Of those questioned, 44 percent stated that they had heard either "a great deal" or "a fair amount" about cancel culture, 18 percent answered that they had heard "not too much" about the topic, and 38 percent had heard nothing at all.[39] Pew further broke down the results by groups, and indeed awareness of cancel culture was not evenly distributed in the population: 49 percent of respondents who did not have a college degree said they were unfamiliar with the term. The number was about half that (26 percent) for those with college degrees. And 44 percent of women surveyed had never heard of cancel culture, compared to 31 percent of men.

The divergence in terms of gender is particularly striking. It certainly suggests that familiarity with the concept of cancel culture is not nearly as widespread as is sometimes presupposed in the media (a group that is, by dint of their profession, hyperaware). After all, if it were a controversial topic frequently discussed in families, one would have to assume that men and women would have heard about it more or less equally. Besides gender, the factors most correlated with a respondent having heard "a great deal" about cancel culture were age (43 percent of eighteen- to twenty-nine-year-olds had heard "a great deal" about cancel culture), college education (27 percent), and political affiliation (30 percent of self-declared liberal Democrats had heard a lot about cancel culture). What can we infer from this?

First, this discourse is not, or not only, prevalent among those who position themselves politically on the Far Right. Although Donald Trump has repeatedly fomented the cancel culture panic, although it has served as a recurring theme on Fox News, awareness is not particularly widespread among the groups often misinterpreted as Trump's base (conservative-leaning, low-education voters). Similarly, a survey conducted in 2021 by the French *L'Express* together with the demographers at IFOP found that among voters who had voted for Emmanuel Macron in the 2017 French presidential election, 26 percent said that they had heard the term "cancel culture," 14 percent knew what it meant, and 12 percent had heard it but did not know what it meant. Among voters for the Far Right candidate Marine Le Pen, 17 percent had heard the word, 6 percent knew what it was, and 11 percent had heard it but did not know.[40] In general, one can say that although cancel culture, wherever its specter is raised, is castigated in the name of the "silent majority" (Donald Trump), "the people's army" (Nigel Farage), or "La France des oubliés" (Marine Le Pen), it is far more widely invoked when looking *at* those milieus from outside, rather than within those milieus themselves.

Second, if we are primarily concerned with locating the people who are sensitized to cancel culture along the political spectrum, then, as the Pew pollsters themselves write in their analysis of the data, they are to be found both on the Right and on the Left. On the other hand, those who have little familiarity with the topic come from the political center. The critique of an alleged cancel culture is not (or as of 2020 was not) the kind of autoimmune response of the "center" against extremism, as cancel culture handwringers like Yascha Mounk and Thomas Chatterton Williams like to position it. Warnings about cancel culture activate (unfortunately Pew does not ask whether positively or negatively) the political extremes, so to speak.

Third, the authors of the study unfortunately don't address the fact that their findings at least suggest that having heard of cancel culture is not the same as believing in or worrying about its existence as commonly described. Commenting on the Pew findings, the *New York Times* wrote, "However you define cancel culture, Americans know it exists and feel its burden."[41] The second part of that statement is manifestly incorrect. In a second step, Pew asked the respondents who had heard of cancel culture to define it. And the most common answer by far was something utterly anodyne: Cancel culture, according to this majority, meant "actions taken to hold others accountable." This suggests that while many (particularly Democratic voters) were aware of the controversy over cancel culture, they perceived it as something commonplace and unproblematic.

Fourth, one thing those who had heard a lot about cancel culture had in common was access to media. The three groups in which more than half of respondents had heard "at least some" or "a great deal" about cancel culture were under thirty, college graduates, and liberal Democrats—which suggests that awareness was correlated in particular to social media use. As mentioned, the only other group that showed a similar level of awareness of the term were men. So it seems to be about very specific social media. Fox News might be a source of awareness of cancel culture, but as a study in 2021 showed, contrary to common prejudice, 48 percent of Fox viewers are women.[42] Fox News might therefore be less important than other media, especially digital media.

Attempting a first, functional description of cancel culture discourse, we find that it is aimed more at media-savvy, educated people. Those supposedly excluded from the modern woke discourse (the coal miners and truck drivers on whose behalf cancel culture critics like to attack left-wing discourse) seem to be less aware of it. In this respect, the framing of the *New York Times* in its much-cited editorial is interesting. The editors invoked a broad, society-wide fear: People at dinner tables and bowling alleys across America tremble with fear of cancellation. The newspaper merely gave them a voice. The study results quoted by the *New York Times* suggest something completely different: Concern is much more rampant in America's editorial offices than at America's dinner tables and bowling alleys.

The question of how close or how far one has to feel from cancel culture in order for the language games about it to work will occupy us in the following chapters—whether it's about Americans thirty years past their BA but with a lot of opinions about "students these days" or whether it has to do with Europeans uncannily invested in the dietary preferences of Oberlin sophomores. But even in the United States, one has to realize that most ordinary people (people who are not professionally concerned with opinions) do not locate cancel culture in their immediate environment. Whether you're critical of it or don't care, it's happening out there somewhere.

As I mentioned above, in the 2020 study by the Pew Research Center, participants were asked to define cancel culture in their own words. Pew grouped the individual answers under different headings—wokeness, the university, self-censorship; the entire vocabulary of the mainstream press's description of the problem (and of European discourse about cancel culture) was conspicuous in its absence. By far the most common description was, as already mentioned, "actions taken to hold others accountable"—59 percent of Democrats and 49 percent of all respondents described cancel culture in this or a similar way. Fourteen percent proposed something like "censorship of speech or history"—this answer was more popular with Republicans (26 percent) than with Democrats (6 percent). "Mean-spirited actions to cause others harm," said 12 percent (15 percent Republicans, 8 percent Democrats). Nine percent gave the circular answer "people canceling anyone they disagree with." And finally, with 6 percent, was the answer that cancel culture had something to do with "consequences like being fired or boycotted."

That last definition—job loss and boycott—is absolutely central to perceptions in US media, and it is essentially the canonic definition in Germany, France, and the UK. In all these countries' media discourses, warnings of "existence destroying" professional consequences are never far away—which may have to do with the fact that media discourses are shaped by, well, people in media. It's not for nothing that the *New York Times* and Siena College asked about fear of "retaliation," a word that in the United States is primarily associated with being fired. But in the Pew poll, only 6 percent of respondents saw job loss as a key feature of cancel culture (just 7 percent of Republicans and 3 percent of Democrats polled). This likely points to a difference between those who write articles in traditional media and those people Pew interviewed.

The *New York Times* picked up the Pew study and cited it in an editorial about fear for one's job and reputation. To its credit, the piece is also concerned with other issues, such as non-white people afraid of racism and anti-LGBTQ+ laws in conservative American states. But these are excursions, and time and again, the text finds its way back to the practice of "attacking people in the workplace, on campus, on social media and elsewhere who express unpopular views from a place of good faith," which is "the practice of a closed society."[43] It seems two discourses are running in parallel here, with two different concepts: one within the media, in which media people in particular are the target of cancellation, and which is about the destruction of livelihood and job loss; and one in the wider population, where cancel culture is largely defined by specific forms of debate and accountability. Unfortunately, Pew does not further break down the large group that understands "canceling" in terms of accountability practices. But "accountability" almost sounds like it's primarily about celebrities and public figures—about Louis C.K., rather than the student who is afraid to say what he really thinks about Louis C.K.

This disconnect constitutes one of the few genuinely new aspects of the cancel culture discourse compared to the one about political correctness. Political correctness was something people were encouraged to find—and indeed did find—anywhere and everywhere; it was not tethered to prominence at all, though being censored by the politically correct *could* of course make someone prominent. By contrast, cancel culture, which began circulating after, and to some extent in reaction to #MeToo, has trouble deciding whether it is about the prominent or the average. But therein lies its objective correlative: Cancel culture as an idea speaks to the sense—I think the accurate sense—that in our new media world, prominence is distributed along an infinite spectrum. In a world where, thanks to social media, a private individual can have the reach of a small media empire (just without the legal counsel or public relations department that would have traditionally gone along with such reach), the line between important and not-so-important people, events, institutions, and pronouncements is far more difficult to draw.

However, that doesn't mean—and this is something that those interviewed by Pew seem to recognize better than the *New York Times*—that this distinction no longer exists. The discourse on cancel culture is based on the intuition that in the digital world, media power no longer functions quite as hierarchically as in the pre-digital world. However, the idea that this means that there is an absolute leveling—such that the seemingly powerful can suddenly be the real victims—is, quite mysteriously, seemingly more plausible to those with power and privilege in a certain industry than to the outsiders. This is one of the reasons why the complaint about cancel culture is an elite discourse. It succeeds in editorial offices of newspapers and among tenured faculty members. Fixated on the anarchy of the internet, of microblogs, of student activists, cancel culture discourse emerged as a product of American prestige media—and before long it was exported to prestige media elsewhere.

TWO

Word Histories

At Boston College, feminist professor Mary Daly has refused to acknowledge any males who raise their hands in her class on "phallotechocracy" and Star Wars. At Yale last year, a male student objected to U.S. policy in Central America as a "pain in the butt": and was reprimanded for his "latent heterosexism." At Harvard, campus feminists have been known to bring whistles to lectures, so they can "blow the whistle" on oppression. If the professor uses an unacceptable word like "he" to refer to a gender neutral subject, the noise begins.

—EARL RYAN, *Campus* (Spring 1991)[1]

I'm a professor at a midsize state school. I have been teaching college classes for nine years now. . . . Things have changed since I started teaching. The vibe is different. I wish there were a less blunt way to put this, but my students sometimes scare me—particularly the liberal ones.

—EDWARD SCHLOSSER, *Vox* (June 2015)[2]

The cancel culture panic represents a triumph of redescription over continuities of feeling. It relies on our basic trust that a new word reflects a new sets of facts, a change in our world; and that, if it appears more in print and on television, this reflects an objective increase in the phenomena it designates. But in truth descriptions of the cancel culture of our own moment sound an awful lot like supposedly acute problems from ten, twenty, thirty years ago. If the problem cancel culture names is real, it has been real for some time. Alternately, the current language game may draw its energy and plausibility from earlier ones that have been forgotten or repressed. The genealogy sketched in this chapter

40

suggests that the persuasiveness of cancel culture warnings results from the fact that it insists on suddenness while actually drawing on well-established truisms and conventions. Just like the language game about political correctness, cancel culture discourse is discursive shock and awe: The omnipresence of the label and its lack of precision suggest that there must be a massive societal change underway.

Political Correctness

It's easy to forget, but the term "political correctness" burst into public discourse with the same speed and force as the term "cancel culture" did in 2019. The complaint that came to be associated with the label (that groupthink and a thought police had taken over college campuses) was of course older—we will trace its history in Chapters 3, 4, and 5. But as a term, "political correctness" took the United States by storm in the span of just a few years. In his book *The Myth of Political Correctness: The Conservative Attack on Higher Education*, John K. Wilson gathered the following numbers: In 1989 and 1990 the number of newspaper articles containing the phrase "political correctness" was fifteen and sixty-five, respectively. In 1991, it jumped to 1,570, in 1993 to 4,914, and in 1994 to 6,985.[3] Breathless TV coverage followed; the term ended up playing a role in the 1992 presidential campaign, and it influenced legislation and publishing for much of the 90s. Where the cancel culture panic was a refracted reaction to #MeToo and Black Lives Matter, the panic over political correctness (PC) can be understood as a reaction (and backlash to) feminism and the (very, very gradual) diversification of American workplaces and universities.

What most Americans don't realize is that political correctness had a career outside of the United States, but it was a different one. Generally, the emergence of the term was far less explosive than in the United States, where its luster dimmed after some time. But usage in France, Germany, and elsewhere remained fairly constant. This was because there the discourse on political correctness remained, by and large, a discourse about the United States. In most European media, the term remained anglophone, and if a localized equivalent existed, the English version of the term remained dominant. In Germany, for instance, *politisch korrekt* gradually emerged as a broader phrase, basically a term for "boring" and "(overly) uncontroversial," while the English version of the term always carried the far more specific narrative about American left-wing moralism. Eventually, interest in the term cooled in Europe as well. As a half-remembered hodgepodge of factoids and anecdotes about the United

States and its universities, political correctness slumbered in the collective consciousness in Germany, France, the Netherlands, and Switzerland, waiting to be kissed awake by being linked to new fears. This was exactly what happened in the cancel culture panic.

One fact that slid out of view in non-American descriptions of PC was that post-1990 the label was almost never self-applied in US public debates. No one said unironically of themselves that they were "politically correct"; much to the contrary, many proudly claimed the label of "political incorrectness." Almost every year a new television show, comedy special, or book had the phrase in its title. An entire brand of humor—from Denis Leary's standup to Bill Maher's talk show to *South Park*—thrived on ridiculing a vividly imagined Greek chorus of politically correct sticks-in-the-mud. The comedy was funny only if you could imagine their outrage alongside the so-so bit about chain-smoking at a Dunkin' Donuts. They were apparitional; their reactions were whatever the bit needed their reactions to be. Lenient and censorious, powerful and impotent, they contained multitudes, and they were so unifying and entertaining because they didn't actually exist.

Historically, too, the term had never been an affirmative self-description. "Politically correct," as Wilson has shown, did indeed spring from left-wing discourses. It was rarely used, but when it was, it sprang from fringe communist groups and was usually ironic. In his book, Wilson quotes the historian Roger Geiger as saying that "political correctness" functioned as "a sarcastic reference to adherence to the party line by American communists in the 1930s."[4] But, he points out, Dinesh D'Souza, in his 1991 book *Illiberal Education: The Politics of Race and Sex on Campus*, recast that history as follows: "The term 'political correctness' seems to have originated in the early part of this century, when it was used by various species of Marxists to describe and enforce conformity to favored ideological positions."[5] D'Souza and others reinterpreted an infrequently applied and self-deprecating label among fringe Marxists in the 1930s and 1940s as an explicit and unironic program of the American Left. The same would one day happen with "cancel culture": It was a piece of obviously marginal, obviously self-ironic terminology that was repositioned by various grifters as the actual secret and dead-serious core of "the" Left.

By 1991, D'Souza and company were selling old wine in new bottles. His reference to the old Marxists betrayed that fact. At least since the McCarthy era, right-wing publicists and politicians had tried to convince the American public that colleges were riddled with Marxist professors. That wasn't true and didn't catch on. It was a Far Right discourse and openly conspiratorial, too conspiratorial for mainstream consumption. D'Souza was part of a wave that helped the same set of ideas break through into the liberal mainstream. His book was reviewed in the *Washington Post*, the *New York Times*, and in the *New York Review of Books*. An excerpt appeared in the *Atlantic Monthly*, a magazine that until today (as *The Atlantic*) loves a good cancel culture story but that also regards itself as centrist.

D'Souza was no longer concerned with the professors, at least nominally, but with the students. His arguments related to what appeared to be fundamentally American values such as freedom of speech and expression. He no longer positioned the Left as a threat to American power, but rather saw in political correctness a cultural fifth column gnawing at the very foundations of American liberalism. The threat he evoked was no longer creeping Marxism but a more unspecific "totalitarianism." He warned that on college campuses, white Americans were increasingly disenfranchised. The topoi on which he based this diagnosis should be familiar to anyone who has read a few cancel culture texts in recent years: A totalitarian thought police has established a new left-wing orthodoxy; a new left-wing McCarthyism is bent on annihilating any dissent; conservative viewpoints have been artificially suppressed; academic standards are crumbling due to misguided affirmative action efforts; and, instead of better arguments, outrage and identity politics rule.

In 1984, William Bennett, Ronald Reagan's secretary of education—a neoconservative culture warrior who mostly fought against supposedly Far Left tendencies at US universities during his time in office—warned of a "rising tide of left-wing intolerance" at America's colleges. According to Bennett, the campuses were "increasingly closed, increasingly conformist, increasingly insular and in certain instances even repressive."[6] But Bennett's crusade didn't catch on beyond a certain bubble, possibly because it seemed more like state censorship than battling censorship itself when the secretary of education used his bully pulpit to tell schools what to teach. D'Souza, on the other hand, was not a member of Reagan's cabinet, just a relatively unimportant advisor to that administration. He was young, smart, a graduate of Dartmouth University, and he wasn't white. His worries were easier to absorb into mainstream discourse than the spittle-flecked tirades of aging commie hunters.

In order to succeed in the mainstream of 1990, right-wing ideas (and right-wing operators like D'Souza) had to come in the sheep's clothing of centrism. Fortunately for D'Souza and PC, sheep's clothing was in anything but short supply during the transition from Reaganism to Clintonism. By the early 1990s, the Democratic Party under Bill Clinton did not want to leave conservative ideas to Republicans alone. It was a time when many of the Democratic Party's old sacred cows were put out to pasture and often simply replaced by the Republican Party's own sacred cows. Whether it was "soft on crime" rhetoric or concerns about "welfare queens," Clinton's government catered to many of the fears and prejudices that Reagan had relied on for his restructuring of American politics.

This is what made the language games about political correctness so explosively successful at this historical moment. Political correctness (which no one could quite define, but which made everyone mad) offered itself as a bridge: for liberals who flirted with conservative ideas and for Reagan voters who wanted to switch back to the Democrats. George H. W. Bush had warned against political correctness in a 1991 speech to graduates of the University of Michigan. Just two years later, Bill Clinton in turn proclaimed, "The time has come to stop worrying about what you think is politically correct." Clinton said this in a speech in honor of noted neoconservative, Democratic Senator Daniel Patrick Moynihan, in which he rehearsed a long list of conservative obsessions of the Reagan–Bush years: It was a speech about the inner cities, where "very often only the churches are there standing alone against the deluge, and the people in the social services overpowered, and the police outmanned," where "gangs take root as a form of social organization and drugs take root not just as a form of self-destruction but as an economic endeavor."[7] The warning about political correctness was an integral part of the rhetorical arsenal that allowed Clinton's Democratic Party to (selectively) sound like Reaganites.

Another reason both sides of the aisle could agree that political correctness was a problem was that there was hardly anyone who would have been explicitly "pro" PC. In politics, as in pop culture, the politically correct remained phantoms. You imagined their outrage, you put words in their mouths. You didn't have to consult them, yes, you didn't have to identify who they were. Their motivations were always better explained by their conservative victims or their liberal critics than by themselves. In D'Souza's book, and in the famous cover stories that established the term in winter 1990–91, the politically correct rarely, if ever, got a chance to speak. Just as with the "cancelers" of today, there were no famous proponents of political correctness.

What George H. W. Bush said in Ann Arbor in May 1991 will sound familiar to anyone who has read a few anti–cancel culture diatribes: "The notion of political correctness has sparked controversy across the country." The president didn't elaborate on who sparked it, whether it was the term, or what was understood about it that triggered the controversy. Political correctness was an issue because it was an issue. Bush did say that political correctness "declares certain topics off-limits, certain expression off-limits, even certain gestures off-limits."[8] But there was very little detail on which "certain" topics, expressions, or gestures. Instead of naming an incident or pointing out culprits or listing statistics, Bush immediately went to the big, abstract whole—freedom of expression: "Ironically, on the 200th anniversary of our Bill of Rights, we find free speech under assault throughout the United States, including on some college campuses."[9]

Bush's speech criticized a repressive "crusade," criticized "Orwellian" language rules, took aim at "increasing intolerance in our country," bemoaned the "increasing tendency to resort to intimidation rather than reason in settling disputes," complained about a "politics of division and derision" that was "not worthy of a great nation grounded in the values of tolerance and respect." Almost all of Bush's complaints from 1991 recur in present-day descriptions of cancel culture. The other, sharper undertones—Cultural Revolution, totalitarianism, and so on—were notes the president didn't sound in Ann Arbor because he didn't have to. His audience would have heard them anyway. This thanks to *Newsweek*, which in December 1990 described "PC" as "strictly speaking, a totalitarian philosophy," claiming that the "tyranny of PC" reigned on the campus, and that students "censor[ed] even the most ordinary of opinions."[10] Or thanks to the *New York Times*, where Richard Bernstein had bemoaned the "hegemony of the politically correct," a "growing intolerance, a closing of debates, a pressure to conform to a radical program or risk being accused of a commonly reiterated trio of thought crimes: sexism, racism, and homophobia."[11] Or *New York* magazine, which reported in January 1991: "But curiously enough, in the past few years, a new sort of fundamentalism has arisen, precisely among those people who were most appalled by Christian fundamentalism. And it is just as demagogic and fanatical."[12]

Critiques and analyses from the 1990s and our own today sound at times nearly identical. For a description of the present offered with considerable urgency, this diagnosis is surprisingly timeless. It is precisely in this timelessness that the cancel culture discourse has made its home: It warns about the exact same things we were warned about in 1991 using a set of rhetorical exaggerations and conceptual slides that themselves are decades old. We have gotten used to this form of sudden, scary transformation, and we have gotten used to the vocabulary in which to discuss it.

This was true for the United States, but it was even truer outside of it, where, as mentioned, the discourse about political correctness arrived more gradually but established itself far more permanently. Few Americans would be able to recall Bernstein's *New York Times* piece that did its part in establishing the vocabulary of political correctness in the zeitgeist of the early 1990s. But former German President Joachim Gauck in 2019 wrote specifically about the impact the article had on his thinking: The article, Gauck wrote, was "like opening a floodgate."[13] Gauck similarly quotes George H. W. Bush's Ann Arbor speech, an article in *Die Zeit*, and Philip Roth's novel *The Human Stain*. But remarkably, Gauck does not regard the fact that the warning about left-wing intolerance contained in these texts was, by 2019, going on thirty years old as a sign that maybe there had been some hyperbole at work. No, he regarded this long discursive tradition as proof of the validity of the warning. If the cancel culture panic made Americans into amnesiacs, it made Europeans into historians.

From Callout Culture to Cancel Culture

The path of the term "cancel culture" through first US and then European discourse resembles the journey taken by the term "political correctness," but the two paths are by no means identical. "Political correctness" was a marginal left-wing term that was strategically exaggerated and stripped of its irony by right-wing culture warriors. With this trick, the Right managed to convince the liberal mainstream that the problem was new (rather than just the description). Cancel culture, on the other hand, was a topos in online spaces that tended Left, tended young, tended Black. It was appropriated and stripped of its context by institutions and voices of the social and political center. Like political correctness, the canceling in cancel culture started out as an ironic byword among leftists, which was then treated by (mostly white-dominated) conservative and liberal organs as though it were an explicit political project.

By the time the term spilled over into European countries, into Australia and Russia, it had attained new audience support: among right-wing journalists and Fox News. It was their hyperventilating, hyperbolic deployment and tone that was absorbed in German-, Italian-, and French-language discourse. This was helped by a constitutive confusion about the meaning of the word "cancel": None of the translators and importers of the term seemed to know exactly which of the many senses of the verb "to cancel" in English was actually supposed to characterize cancel culture. But instead of tolerating a degree of ambiguity and making it clear that the *New York Times* and Fox News's Tucker Carlson might mean different things by the same label, the media in these countries instead seemed extremely certain they knew what canceling was.

In their certainty, the adapters of the term often didn't realize what they were adapting. The German career of the term makes this clear. In the Austrian daily *Der Standard*, Michael Wurmitzer defined cancel culture as follows: "Publicly boycotting someone, stopping their performances, stopping them from happening, erasing them. The decision [to cancel] is made in the social networks."[14] Claudia Ihlefeld wrote in the *Heilbronner Stimme*: "The term from the English-speaking world describes—literally translated—something outrageous: the practice of erasing something, annihilating it."[15] In other early German-language articles on the subject, we read that canceling means "de-existentialization,"[16] "deletion,"[17] "ripping out root and branch."[18] We read that the term derives from "the pulpit in church," that "the 'cancelli' [were] the bars and barriers that separated the chancel from the nave."[19]

"Erase," "delete," "rip out": All of these are of course plausible senses of cancel. But are they indeed the sense presupposed in cancel culture? Looking over the above German translations, they all suggest that cancel culture has eliminatory intent, which in German activates historical parallels to National Socialism and the Holocaust, even if the American use of the word in no way conveys this. I still would like to hold onto the idea of "de-existentialization," silly though it may be as a gloss on "canceling": As we shall see later, the worry about cancel culture traveled beyond the United States as a way for people with a certain power and prestige to reflect on #MeToo. This is the experiential core of the expansion of the term: If you were to stick to the facts, all that happened was that your buddy lost his job over being a sex pest at work—which indeed happened more often than previously during #MeToo. But it *felt* like what happened to them was so much more than a firing: It was an erasure, a deletion, and, why not, a ripping out root and branch.

Much as in the discourse around political correctness, journalists writing outside of the United States and writing in languages other than English created the impression of a solid, clear, and distinct object well beyond whatever the US term managed to conjure. They evacuated ambiguities and sanded off both the term's sociological origins and its strategic deployment in conservative US discourse. They assumed that what is commonly described with the label simply and straightforwardly existed: There existed something that deserved the label "cancel culture," and this something had to be interpreted. What dropped out was the question of usage. How did this expression come about? Who needed it and for what purposes? In this chapter, I will try to sketch an answer to these questions, but also to explore the distortions that arose in public debate because these questions weren't asked.

Interestingly, the "culture" aspect of the term "cancel culture" came first. It's been thoroughly forgotten, but before the panic about cancel culture, there was a small-bore panic about "callout culture." Callout culture describes the aggressive singling out of bad behavior on the part of celebrities, companies, and institutions. The term "calling out," as media scholar Meredith Clark writes, was part of a whole tradition of African American media practices, more precisely "discursive accountability practices."[20] Before calling out, for example, there was the practice of "reading" or "dragging." All of these were ritualized, often ironized forms of ad hominem criticism. By the time "calling out" became "callout culture," the term actually used by African Americans had already found a broader base of users: progressive, internet-savvy young people.

Callout culture was intended as a description of very specific online behaviors and communities. The expression seems to have established itself primarily on and in relation to the platform Tumblr. It was often about expressions of opinion, communication strategies, and behaviors that were perceived as problematic (usually as sexist, racist, homophobic, privileged, or lacking solidarity). Characteristic of this online culture was the popular Tumblr blog "Your Fave Is Problematic," a compendium of problematic aspects of various fan favorites.[21]

So far, so similar to today's descriptions of cancel culture. But it's important to see what had to be forgotten or suppressed along the short path from callout culture to cancel culture and from Tumblr to the *New York Times* and eventually *Le Monde*. In certain online forums, there is clearly such a culture, leading to a deeply unproductive and ungenerous style of engagement and making those forums deeply unappealing to outsiders. However, many users of these forums also criticize this culture, which is where the term "callout culture" originated: as a kind guardrail by which online communities examine themselves and try to prevent a collective drift into the dysfunctional (or, as they say, toxic). Calling out was never primarily something that social justice warriors (SJWs) do to, say, Donald Trump, but rather an internal mechanism of self-policing in spaces that were generally left-leaning and aligned with identity politics—for instance, in LGBTQ+ spaces or on Black Twitter.

The question is why problematic fan favorites and the Tumblr discourse surrounding them should concern the rest of us, insofar as we are not part of these communities. This is the kind of distortion in the economy of attention described in Stanley Cohen's model of moral panics.[22] If you do not care for it, then callout culture is a perfectly legitimate reason not to hang out too much on queer Tumblr or YA Twitter. But once callout culture made it into the broader discourse, that was never the focus. Rather, the term suggested that *all* of culture was now subject to the dictates of the callout.

Moreover, as it was appropriated and expanded, the term was reframed as a supposed description of the very groups that had originated it. Within these groups it had been an internal designation (legible largely to other in-group members) and was primarily reserved for critiquing their own discursive practices. But as traditional media became aware of the label "callout culture" and made it the subject of more or less panicked articles, a lot of their writing recapitulated what Cohen in his model of moral panics called the "inventory phase." As mass media attempt to interpret a circumscribed local development for a broad audience, they begin applying the term with an inflationary zeal, giving their audience the impression that what is increasing in number are the *incidents*, not just the framing used to describe them.

Even this phase was shaped by those characteristics that were later to make the cancel culture panic so successful in international media, especially print media. After all, reporting on Twitter (X) and Tumblr, without asking yourself how representative the individual posts or tweets really are, is distorting—but also extremely easy. As is almost always the case with a moral panic, the question isn't whether someone has in fact said X, Y, or Z—with roughly 100 million tweets a day there's always someone—but whether and why it is newsworthy that they said it. What the term "callout culture" described was real. But today, if you look for tweets about callouts, it was a couple hundred posts from accounts that had roughly the same 10,000 followers. And even among them, the term was never used affirmatively, but primarily represented an immanent critique of a specific form of public shaming.

The mass media discourse on callout culture in the United States was too short-lived to have made much of an impact outside the English-speaking world. And yet it did leave a trace, and a rather telling one at that. Above I quoted an article from the *Neue Zürcher Zeitung* defining cancel culture. Here is how the newspaper describes the term: "The first stage of 'cancel culture' is called 'call-out': the outcry about a misconduct. If the hordes of Twitter (X) follow the call to premature judgment, then we get a collective attempt at de-existentialization."[23] Another article, this one in Germany's *Die Zeit*, calls "call-out culture" and "shitstorm" "the little siblings of cancel culture."[24] The French edition of *Forbes* describes cancel culture as an "emanation of call-out culture."[25] These articles thus suggest that callout culture was a preliminary stage of cancel culture. In truth, both terms meant pretty much the same thing.

But the misunderstanding shows how European importers of cancel culture vocabulary looked at the evolving US terminology. In reality, callout culture is not an evolution of a cultural phenomenon, but an evolution of the *description* of the *same* phenomenon. The non-English texts misunderstood the attempt by conservative opinion makers in the United States to give the panic a better—read: scarier—label as an evolution on the part of the object they described. One reason why callout culture as a label didn't stick, but cancel culture did, might have been that in "calling out" you can still hear the relative powerlessness of the gesture described (you register protest), while "canceling" is more active and sounds more threatening. But even the sense of threat rumbling in the latter term had to be carefully cultivated. Because the origin of the word in the social networks does not seem particularly threatening at first glance.

Talk of "canceling" people goes back to the 1980s, likely further, though usually it implies something interpersonal—a breakup, for instance. Canceling as a designation of discontinuing a parasocial relationship—no longer supporting, or no longer paying attention to an artist, say—most likely started much later on Twitter. Journalist Michael Hobbes has suggested one possible origin. In March of 2014, the satirical *Colbert Report* tweeted a quote from the show, which comedian Stephen Colbert later admitted had to come across as anti-Asian racism out of context. Then twenty-three-year-old activist Suey Park responded with the hashtag #CancelColbert. Within twenty-four hours it became the most used hashtag in America. Park later said that she was never serious in her demand. Like so many of those allegedly canceled later, Colbert ultimately fared far better than his canceler. Although the TV host sought to shield his young critic from fan opprobrium on his next show, Park dealt with trolls and death threats for years. Colbert's show ended in 2014, when he took over *Late Night* and became one of the biggest names in television. #CancelColbert isn't mentioned once in Colbert's lengthy Wikipedia entry.

As murky as the meaning of canceling would later become, it was clear what Suey Park meant by it in 2014. She wanted his TV show to go off the air. That is certainly how US media at the time reported on the controversy. Colbert himself seemed to understand the hashtag that way; he almost had to.[26] After all, the offending joke wasn't something the real Stephen Colbert had said, but was in fact verbalized by his satirical alter ego, a slightly exaggerated parody of Bill O'Reilly. This character could only be canceled by taking him off the TV schedule. However, in reflecting on the imbroglio, the fictional Colbert also poked fun at the inability to distinguish a satirical statement from a serious one. Why not, he suggested, trend #CancelSwift to punish Jonathan Swift for his "Modest Proposal"? And this may have been the first moment when the talk of canceling people of interest to the public attained wider currency.

It took some time for this language game to fully enter the lexicon. There is a documented spike in online usage of "you are canceled" after the phrase was used on an episode of *Love & Hip Hop* in December 2014, but the usage of "canceling" as part of an interpersonal spat (often, as on *Love & Hip Hop*, a breakup) is quite a bit older. Sometime in 2015, we see calls for canceling of real-life people, but real-life people of some prominence, mostly on Tumblr and Twitter. The tweets followed the formula that "XYZ is canceled," something that can sound ominous in hindsight. But here, too, it is worth taking a closer look.

The talk of someone "being canceled" at this point did not seem to mean that the canceled person should be muzzled or made to disappear. Rather the phrase was an expression of disappointment on the part of fans. And the seeming severity of the verdict had nothing to do with moral absolutism; instead it indicated a healthy dose of irony. It arose from the excessive closeness and identification that fans sometimes develop towards the object they adore; but it managed to poke fun at that closeness in the same breath.

As Meredith Clark has shown, this version of canceling took root above all on Black Twitter. African American users took to Twitter early and were long overrepresented on the messaging service. They transported to the platform many culturally distinctive discursive practices that had established themselves on message boards or in real life—and there they were suddenly visible to the whole world.[27] The sociologist Melissa Brown speaks of these users as "virtual sojourners": They make use of the mechanisms and publics of platforms, even though they are marginalized even in the digital world.[28] There is always a danger that outsiders will appropriate or commercialize their content, that mainstream discourses will use their contributions to stoke prejudice about the community, or that politicians will declare it a problem.

Black media has long existed alongside the white mainstream. Black Twitter transfers this relationship into the virtual world. Roderick Graham and Shawn Smith call this kind of space a "virtual counter-public" and a "digital enclave."[29] It works as a counter-public precisely insofar it is not identical with "the" public, because its codes and conventions are not immediately, and are not meant to be, accessible to all. This constitutively and self-consciously marginal counter-public is where the use of canceling as a targeted withdrawal seems to have first come to prominence. In this language game, the canceler refused to give the canceled person attention or, in the case of artists, money.

When a user cancels a celebrity in these spaces, that act is based on an implicit admission of one's own powerlessness, even marginality. A young woman on Twitter decreed—half angry, half ironic—that in her little corner of the internet some superstar or other was no longer worth thinking about. Canceling was canceling because it was helpless, because it had no consequences, because it had no legal force. As with "calling-out," the "cancellation" is "back talk," as Clark writes—that is to say, it insists on a response, even if the parasocial relationship (between fan and star, for instance) doesn't allow for anything of the sort.[30]

To be sure, one shouldn't automatically credit an online community's profession of powerlessness. Many people tend to underestimate their own power, especially when they jump onto a bandwagon, especially online. They chime in, agreeing with millions of others, and then realize to their horror what they helped, in however small a way, to effectuate. However, when we look at celebrities targeted by the phrase "XYZ is canceled," when that phrase was still new, it's clear that there was no threat of silencing. Only a few years later, newspaper readers in Europe would be told that "canceling" meant encouraging a mob to "destroy" a celebrity, to "wipe out" or "tear him out by the roots." But in these tweets "canceled" meant that a user wanted or expected something from their idol, and that they at the same time felt a little bit ridiculous about being so demanding.[31]

As we have seen, this almost willful misrecognition, whereby something ironic and playful is deliberately taken as straight-faced, was the key to the success of political correctness as a political watchword in the early 1990s. It is how we get the persistent stories about, say, schoolchildren requiring litter boxes, because they "identify as cats." Anyone who has ever spent time around young people can sense the joke behind the meme and—more importantly—can hear the joke being missed by Republican politicians or Murdoch media.

But how did this context get lost in the case of canceling? The answer involves both the blackness and the twitterdom of Black Twitter. Over the last few years, an implicit folk taxonomy has developed with regards to social media statements: We tend to regard posts on Facebook and Instagram as comparatively private statements, while we regard tweets as public opinions. There is some objective basis to this; after all we can in fact see every tweet ever sent, insofar as it hasn't been deleted or Elon Musk's algorithmic tweaks haven't destroyed our ability to search for them. The abysses that lurk in your average Facebook group are hidden from outside view and search engines. X (né Twitter), after all, wants a reaction to these tweets; its algorithms thrive on serving you content with which you are likely to disagree. This means that the platform seeks to divest whatever you put on it of its context and target audience as quickly as possible, and then put your tweet where it does not belong and where it will arouse the maximum outrage—and thus more engagement.

But it's not just about outrage, or even the outrage about the outrage—both of which are the aspects of social media that traditional media seem to care most about. It also, perhaps even mainly, has to do with who is outraged. And in that regard, it's important that the talk of canceling was very closely associated with Black Twitter, although the term wasn't unique to it. The panic about canceling arose from a white gaze cast on a Black online bubble. In the online world (as the offline), Black spaces are both distinct yet never allowed to be *too* distinct—something that is true of Black Twitter as well.[32] In the United States, Black cultural traditions are often the object of a—concerned, controlling, sometimes panicking—view of the (white) state and the (white) majority society and media. How Black people live, how Black people express themselves, what Black people consume—all of this becomes a fodder for observation.[33] "White man makes guns?" the comedian Chris Rock famously joked. "No problem. Black rapper says 'gun'? Congressional hearing." The desire for control is not always this overt, but it is never entirely absent either. This desire, even where it is openly racist, is expressed in tones of concern, fear, and, well, panic.

Essential to this sudden and strategic centering of Black culture and expression is a reversal of center and margin. A marginal phenomenon—for instance one affecting primarily certain groups, like only young people in certain neighborhoods, in certain cities—suddenly becomes the central focus of a national debate. It appears on the evening news, in the *New York Times*, or in the Congressional Record. It usually attains this sudden centrality only once it has been rhetorically demarginalized: It is said to no longer "only" affect young people in certain areas of Atlanta, Long Beach, or Houston, but "now" allegedly threatens the whole country, or at least your suburb, your neighborhood school, your local Kroger's. In that process of demarginalization (as in a moral panic in general), local, situational, and contextual knowledge are explicitly ignored.

One would think that young people would be the best interpreters and explainers of their practices. But as local, bounded practices are ground up for national media panics, young people are often the last to be asked and the least likely to be listened to. The role of guide now falls to middle-aged sociologists, *Washington Post* columnists, or the local police chief. Distance and abstraction are suddenly required for an accurate assessment of the problem.

In the panic over political correctness in the early 1990s, we noted a second important discursive trick that works similarly: suddenly and strategically de-marginalizing the marginal. This trick takes an opinion that seems dominant in some subculture and claims that it actually constitutes a society-wide orthodoxy. Witness how pronouns or trigger warnings went from practices that are certainly widespread at certain college campuses to something that supposedly represents a nationally dominant discourse. In the virtual world, this process is referred to as "context collapse." This is the mechanism by which a discursive practice targeted at one specific audience is removed from its communicative context and experienced by an entirely different audience as directed towards them.[34]

Sometimes such a collapse is an unintended by-product of our sprawling and increasingly varied virtual world. Sometimes it results from clumsiness. But often, context collapse is something that someone actively promotes. In the case of cancellation, what most participating users would have understood as a proverbial tempest in a digital teapot was recast into a verdict on our culture at large, or at least a significant subset of it. This contortion requires a certain amount of melodramatic imagination, one trained on campus narratives that date back to the political correctness panic and, as we shall see, at times even longer. If you knew enough to intuit how ridiculous the fearmongering really was, no one wanted to hear your opinion.

Cancel Culture Before the Panic

It is unclear when the term "cancel culture" was first used on Twitter. The term existed in relation to all sorts of things—the tendency to cancel Uber rides, or TV shows, long before it was used in its contemporary sense. The first tweet that does use it in a way that is at least similar to modern usage dates back to autumn 2016. It refers to the alleged relationship between Drake and Taylor Swift and expresses the worry they would very likely "cancel" each other in song after their split. "Ugh I hate cancel culture until I want to set things on fire," user @unicorninkk wrote.[35] Most likely, she meant by that term the tendency, particularly Taylor Swift's, to devote thinly veiled diss tracks to her ex-partners immediately after a breakup. Two things seem worth noting here. First, that practice would have corresponded exactly to the description of callout culture that was common at the time. And second, @unicorninkk's verdict was explic-itly aesthetic: She simply didn't want to hear any more songs of that type.

Talk about cancel culture, like the word "canceling," originated on Black Twitter, where it was marshaled in defense of various "problematic faves," from

Jay-Z to R. Kelly and Azealia Banks to Erykah Badu. But it was used as a kind of immanent critique of these fan communities and online spaces. When users complained about "cancel culture," they indicated that those who criticized these stars made it too easy on themselves, were too moralistic, too quick to declare someone or something "problematic." Importantly, however, both sides of this debate—those who criticized something as problematic and those who claimed that this critique constituted cancel culture—were part of the same discursive space.

Blog posts using the word in the summer of 2017 are steeped in the vernacular and preoccupations of Black Twitter and of young LGBTQ+ bubbles and largely address users in those spaces. In the few Twitter threads that are still accessible from that time, "callout culture" and "cancel culture" are used interchangeably. If tweets accessible today correctly reflect the development at that time, the number of tweets about cancel culture exploded in November 2017—at about the same time as the rapid spread of the hashtag #MeToo. In the spring of 2018, the term made the leap to gay Twitter when fans of RuPaul Charles, host of reality show *RuPaul's Drag Race*, used the phrase to defend the host against allegations that he had made "problematic" comments about transgender people.

Up until this point, the diagnosis "cancel culture" had been part of a larger critique of what is known as toxic stan Twitter, indisputably an unpleasant aspect of certain online fan cultures. The "canceling" in "cancel culture" was for these critics not an established activity practiced by specific users, but rather a more or less unpleasant aspect of online life, a pattern of behavior we all can fall into at some point—just as in the case of trolling, mansplaining, or gaslighting. The idea that this unfortunate tendency of online discourse suggested something about the broader public, about society at large, seems entirely foreign to this discourse. These users wanted to make their little corner of the internet a better place.

Many tweets from 2016–2018 have since been deleted, meaning that it is almost impossible to say anything with absolute certainty about the early Twitter discourse on canceling and cancel culture. Nevertheless, until 2018, not a single tweet I could find on the subject—hundreds, if not thousands, in the spring of 2018 alone—contained the words "campus," "university," "students," or "freedom of speech."

Cancel culture's big break came in June and July 2018, with Kanye West. For the first time, a "canceled" person complained about being canceled for a mainstream white audience. In addition, West identified a second potential cancellation victim—a man whose ability to present (and regard) himself as perpetual victim is perhaps unmatched in the long history of American thin-skinnedness—namely, then-President Donald Trump. In an interview with the *New York Times*, rapper Kanye West used the word "canceled" seven times. "'I'm canceled," West said. And added: "'I'm canceled because I didn't cancel Trump.'"[36] Here it was, the word from hip-hop fandom, threatening both a white conservative man and his most bizarre fan. The interview appeared on June 25, and the word was soon everywhere—in relation to Roseanne Barr, YouTuber Logan Paul, and Hollywood actor Kevin Spacey.

Three things are striking about the coming out of the term. First, it seems to have entered the vocabulary of the Trumpists only through the liberal *New York Times*. Unlike the term "political correctness," which was a right-wing creation successfully foisted onto centrist publications, the term "cancel culture" was popularized by liberal media. Only in a second step did the right-wingers discover the label as a way of scoring points in the mainstream. "Everyone is canceled," wrote Jonah E. Bromwich in a long article in the style section of the *New York Times* on June 28, 2018—most likely also to explain to readers the specifics of the Kanye West interview, which probably left many of them puzzled.[37]

Bromwich's article drives home a second point: Early uses in the traditional media did not use the term to diagnose anything new. The early coverage did not treat the Roseanne Barr scandal (the performer had defamed a member of the Obama administration as a "mixture of Muslim Brotherhood and Planet of the Apes"), the uproar over Logan Paul (who had filmed and streamed the bodies of suicides in the Japanese Aokigahara Forest), and outrage about Kevin Spacey (whom several young men had accused of rape) as anything new, nor did they suggest that there was something unprecedented about the response to them. In other words, they treated "canceling" as a new buzzword for something altogether familiar. The respective public disputes had either been discussed without the vocabulary for a long time, or they resembled earlier incidents and now reemerged at the same time as the term "cancel culture."

Third, the *New York Times*'s early reporting was entirely without any note of panic. Bromwich's article treated the term "cancel culture" as an online curio. The text clearly referred to internet culture: The author had interviewed academics familiar with the phenomenon, such as Meredith Clark, and seemed to view everything with a healthy dose of irony. And although Kanye West was always worth a headline in 2018, he wasn't exactly known as a trendsetter but rather as an inveterate eccentric. Less than four years later, the same newspaper would warn in a huge editorial about the immense "burden" of cancel culture. Gone was the talk about Kanye West or Black Twitter, gone were the problematic faves or back talk, gone were celebrities and their fans. Cancel culture was now about the language police and about self-censorship, about the fear of being mistaken for racist or homophobic or sexist. The word now evoked the classic topoi of the political correctness panic.

The first definition to appear in the *New York Times* was far more precise: Canceling, Bromwich wrote, was "total disinvestment in something (anything)."[38] In its very first text on the word, the newspaper thus recognized clearly that what stood behind the online discourse was the logic of the market, fandom, and attention. It was a gesture of retreat, not control; of self-empowerment, not of overpowering. The canceler said "don't count on my attention," even if that had no expected effect on the person they were canceling. In the 2022 editorial, the constellation of the individual and the collective imagined by the term "canceling" had rotated by 180 degrees.[39] While in 2018 the canceling party was still imagined as an individual who opted out of the collective, by 2022 the *New York Times* suggested canceling *came from* a collective and *targeted* an individual.

Had things shifted so fundamentally in public discourse between 2018 and 2022 that such a redefinition of canceling became necessary? This seems unlikely, especially since the examples for cancellation often come from 2017, 2018, or 2019. It seems much more likely that in the discursive explosion that followed the first articles about cancel culture in June and July 2018, the outlines of the alleged phenomenon began blurring. Or perhaps better, once alienated from the specific discursive spaces that had developed it, the term was applied to everything and anything, and haphazardly integrated into discourses, old and new. In some contexts, "cancel culture" simply replaced the expression "political correctness"; in others it reactivated the panic about speech codes or gave new shape to a nearly forty-year-old fear of identity politics.

Precisely because its origins had become so thoroughly repressed, "cancel culture" was able mean many different things to so many. It wasn't really a concept anymore; it had become a meme. But it was a meme that wasn't allowed to admit that it was a meme—rather it had to act as though it were (still) a highly precise term denoting an acute and clearly defined problem.

Newspaper readers and Twitter users in the United States witnessed this process firsthand, and many commented on it at the time. What they most likely didn't notice, and what many still don't realize, is that in the midst of this very process, the term spilled over into Europe and Latin America. It had not really made the transition when it was an online-only term, but now it was transferred from US newspapers to German, French, and Italian print media. For instance, the term "cancel culture" seems to have arrived in German-speaking social media at roughly the same time as it hit the German-speaking legacy media—in the summer of 2019.

The term appears in the London *Times* for the first time on April 4, 2019, in an article about Gen Z and the difficulty of marketing to it.[40] The French daily *Le Figaro* mentions the word on June 13, 2019, in the paper's culture section, in an article dealing with Woody Allen as a "victim of the cancel culture rampant there [in the US]"[41] (other examples cited are Bill Cosby and Roman Polanski). The first mention in the *Australian* (Sidney) is a column on September 25, 2019, in connection with a book by the political scientist James Flynn that was canceled by a British publisher.[42] The first mention of the expression "cancel culture" in Germany's center-right *Die Welt* is in the culture section on July 25, 2019. The occasion: "The legendary comedian Louis C.K. masturbated in front of several women—and was banned from the stages. Now he is planning his comeback. Oliver Polak went to Milan to see his idol."[43]

The first article in Mexico's *Milenio* appeared on December 1, 2019, and was about Woody Allen.[44] In Spain, the first article to use *cultura de la cancelación* appeared in *El Pais* on December 6, 2019—its first examples are Kevin Spacey being cut from the Netflix show *House of Cards* and R. Kelly's concerts being canceled.[45] The first mention of *cultura do cancelamento* in Brazilian media appears to have been an article about "virtual boycotts" in *Folha de Sao Pãulo*— while the article names many names, it opens with an anecdote about people picketing the screening of a Polanski film.[46]

Despite the various national differences, these articles make it relatively clear what version of the term "cancel culture" was first exported: It traveled the world as an aftershock of #MeToo, and above all #MeToo in US media and culture. There was, at least at the beginning, no talk of creeping totalitarianism, no spillover of a new spirit of censoriousness from America to wherever the writer was sitting, no fear of a "woke wave" that would later dominate imaginaries from Macron to Putin. Certainly, there were attempts at making these stories locally relevant—for instance, *Le Figaro* reported on Woody Allen because the French public has maintained an exceedingly positive relationship with Allen for years. But the US focus remained.

Also notable is the tendency of cancel culture to become a subject of the culture pages and to attach itself to culture issues. As we shall see, whether in France, Germany, or the UK, the term would make only sporadic appearances in cover stories, in the politics section, or (remarkably, given how US-centric cancel culture articles were then and have remained) even in the foreign affairs section of European newspapers. Rather the topic was always refracted through the prism of culture—it was about authors and philosophers, statues and films, books and performances.

The most striking commonality in these articles is that they treat cancel culture as a given. Unlike Bromwich's 2018 *New York Times* article, which worked hard to define and explicate the term, these newspapers introduce the term quite late in their stories and do nothing to explain it. In the London *Times*, we learn that "cancel culture is really big with [Gen Z]"; in *Le Figaro* we learn that Allen was "a victim of the prevailing cancel culture [in the US]"; in *Die Welt* we learn that Louis C.K. felt the "full force of the 'cancel culture.'" Readers therefore had to work out the meaning of the word from context. This had the paradoxical effect of localizing this phenomenon, even as the articles implicitly made the case that it was, or was in the process of becoming, global.

The entry for "cancel culture" in English-language Wikipedia was created on December 31, 2018; the entries for other languages didn't begin until a year later (the French entry on December 28, 2019) with Spanish, Portuguese, German, Dutch, and Russian entries following for the next year, the Russian entry, for instance, on December 16, 2020. The creation of Wikipedia pages thus lagged considerably behind the deployment of the term in print media. What this means isn't easy to pin down, but it certainly suggests that the term mattered more to offline audiences speaking *about* online phenomena than to online communities themselves. By contrast, the Wikipedia pages for #MeToo show no such lag.

The timespan during which the term established itself in the lexicon in various non-US countries coincided with the greatest definition creep of the term in America, mostly thanks to conservatives attaching it to anything that vaguely fit. In a column for the *Wall Street Journal* in March 2019, former Reagan speechwriter Peggy Noonan played her old hits about political correctness, but this time used the term "cancel culture." The text was illustrated by grim-looking young Chinese women during the Cultural Revolution.[47] Fox News jumped on the trend and discovered cases of cancel culture everywhere. In September 2019, Laura Ingraham told her 3 million viewers that attempts at fossil fuel divestment proved that "cancel culture takes aim at the oil and gas industry."[48]

Cancel culture lost more and more of its erstwhile specificity and became the Second Coming of political correctness. Up until this point, cancel culture had been a panic about Twitter and its users. The role that the small-bore campus anecdote had once played in PC stories had been reanimated into small-bore dustups on social media. But after a brief trip down a few Twitter rabbit holes, the campus strongly reemerged as a focus of attention. This moment of opportunistic reframing was once again misinterpreted by non-English observers as an actual real-life process of a spreading problem or disease. According to an article in *Neue Zürcher Zeitung*, "cancel culture" exists "no longer simply in the US, but also in Europe. And no longer just at universities. It wants to erase anything that doesn't suit a mostly left-liberal majority."[49]

Partially because it had become so broadly applicable, the term also found use across the political spectrum, as the example of Germany indicates. In August 2019, a first text on the subject appeared in the *Tagesspiegel* in Berlin—a left-leaning daily. By September, the right-leaning Zurich-based *Neue Zürcher Zeitung* dedicated the first of many articles to the topic (the specific article was about comedian Dave Chappelle). But that same month, the left-wing *tageszeitung*, organ of the aging 1960s student Left, wondered whether "a cancel culture really was the solution"—the topic under discussion was tenor Plácido Domingo.[50] In October, the center-left *Süddeutsche Zeitung* dedicated a long piece to the topic, written by the paper's film critic. The framing was maximalist, and the newspaper headline read: "Anyone Who Doesn't Suit You Must Disappear," adding: "That's Not How the Rule of Law Works."[51] This two-step pattern would set the tone going forward in Germany: culture pages opining on a supposed crisis concerning the rule of law that the actual politics section of the paper mysteriously failed to address.

The text in the *Süddeutsche Zeitung* shows just how much of the remaining context had been sandblasted away by fall 2019. No longer was cancel culture a problem of online discourses; it was a political problem made in America and now poised to invade Germany: "In the US, there is a longstanding phenomenon of a 'court of public reason'"—the author is likely thinking of the term "court of public opinion"—and "now the phenomenon of 'cancel culture' is arriving in Germany."[52] The writing exemplifies the central misunderstanding of the German-language reception of the American cancel culture debate. Certainly, media like the *New York Times* had discovered cancel culture in 2018 as a (to them) new phenomenon—but that phenomenon was a marginal aspect of certain online fan culture. By contrast, however, the accusation that left-wing discourses posed a threat to freedom of expression was a very old one, which in the intervening year conservative media had opportunistically grafted onto the term "cancel culture." Either cancel culture was a totally new phenomenon (but then it was all about Twitter faves and had nothing to do with Plácido Domingo) or it was a new version of a forty-year-old warning about "McCarthyism from the Left" (but, in that case, "cancel culture" was just an opportunistic change in label).

Outside of the United States, the sudden emergence of the buzzword was frequently understood as an indicator that "American conditions" (usually pretty hazily understood) were suddenly arriving in Germany, France, the UK. Few are the examples from the actual country in these non-US texts. It was the reference to the United States that gave the discourse its relevance. Between July 2019 and July 2022, *Die Welt* published 174 articles that mentioned the term "cancel culture"—only 32 do not mention the United States in some way.

Because the proliferation of the term was equated with the proliferation of the problems it was used to describe, the intensity of the panic in the United States legitimated its European offshoots, rather than calling the problem into question. The fact that Americans were calling everything "cancel culture" was not taken as a sign that the term was overapplied. Rather, it was a sign of how bad things had gotten. Authors largely did not see the *word* as eminently mobile, but rather the *reality* it allegedly named. As we will see, metaphors of a "wave," of an "infection," of a "changing climate" proliferated especially outside of the United States and usually referred to a spread of supposedly specifically American pathologies to unsuspecting new host nations. Outside of the United States, "cancel culture" became a term through which various publics could work out their fraught relationship to the United States and to the sense that—not least through digitalization and social media—they were becoming more American than they perhaps liked.

THREE

The Imagined Campus

> No one of any intelligence who reads both is going to agree that Alice Walker is as profound or artful as Shakespeare, yet it is possible that Walker's black lesbian saga [*The Color Purple*] is now assigned more often in college courses than all of Shakespeare's plays combined.
>
> —THOMAS SHORT, *Academic Questions* (Summer 1988)[1]

> *Inclusive.* It's one of those ghastly, politically correct words that have survived the demise of New Labour. Schools have got to be "inclusive" these days. That means wheelchair ramps, the complete works of Alice Walker in the school library (though no Mark Twain) and a Special Educational Needs Department that can cope with everything from dyslexia to Münchausen syndrome by proxy.
>
> —TOBY YOUNG, *Spectator* (2012)[2]

> In the United States, some teachers refuse to teach the relatively well-known poet William Shakespeare in class. He represents the toxic worldview of white straight men, he is racist and must be replaced promptly by diverse, inclusive poets. This case of cancel culture is particularly remarkable because to this day no one knows exactly who this Shakespeare actually was.
>
> —HARALD MARTENSTEIN, *Zeit Magazin* (March 2021)[3]

If you want to understand the American origins of the cancel culture panic, you can't start in 2018 with Kanye West, with Donald Trump, or with Harvey Weinstein. The discourse around cancel culture extends to a much older one—that about the dangers of political correctness. But even this term only leads further down the well of the past: Before the panic about PC, came the panic about speech codes, campus sex, the disappearance of the Western canon in curricula, and so on. In the beginning, if you can even talk about a beginning, there was a mood: a looming unease about the American college campus and what was happening there. But there was also a persistent interest in what was happening there, beyond whatever interest might have seemed justified. Americans have become strangers to their colleges and at the same time feel they understand them better than ever.

The various panics nestle in the gap between what is happening at US universities and what people can be made to *believe* happens at US universities. The international reception of US discourses about US campuses has filled this gap with further content. If the popular image that most Americans receive of their universities is often quite skewed, cultural and geographic distance multiplies the selective perception. As in a game of telephone, one distortion is layered on top of the other. Tracing this development, one doesn't find outright villains who lied about the state of the universities. Rather, one finds that for decades various moral entrepreneurs tried unsuccessfully to spread certain narratives about higher education among the US public. The moment the term "political correctness" caught on simply marks the point at which a decades-old narrative suddenly broke through into a wider public: the moment many Americans were finally willing to believe the old stories.

The extent to which the US population and academia, the country's thousands of colleges and universities, have grown apart is the subject of frequent handwringing. This is odd, as the opposite should by rights be the case: In 1960, just 7.7 percent of Americans had attended college. By 1990, when fears of political correctness first took hold, that number was 21.3 percent. By 2019, when the cancel culture panic began, it was 36 percent. The number of Title IV educational institutions authorized to award bachelor's or associate degrees (i.e., colleges) also increased during this period—from 3,231 in 1980 to 3,559 in 1990 and to 4,042 in 2019—although the zenith (4,726) was reached in 2012.[4]

Oddly enough, then, narratives of overprivileged, out-of-touch college students took hold at a time when more Americans from a broader range of class backgrounds were studying on an increasing number of campuses. What's more, they enrolled in universities that were supposedly represented by an ever-shrinking subset of those campuses. "The" university we meet in warnings about cancel culture bears little resemblance to the institutions the vast majority of us (or our children) attend. For one thing, the complaints are largely about the Ivy League—although fewer than 1 percent of US students go to even the "Ivy plus" schools. The descriptions of different (non-Ivy) institutions envision them very much as Ivy-like.

Harvard remains a particular fixation. In 2023, President Claudine Gay of Harvard came under fire for alleged academic dishonesty. So did Stanford's President Marc Tessier-Lavigne. Gay was also in the news for her handling of student expression related to the October 7 attack on Israel (see Chapter 5), but everyone involved in the pressure campaign that built in December of 2023 insisted that it was all about academic standards. (They also insisted, unconvincingly, that their attacks had nothing to do with the fact that she was the first Black woman to serve as Harvard's president.) The *New York Times* dedicated dozens of articles written by a handful of reporters to Gay's case, to say nothing of opinion pieces. The situation at Stanford, by comparison, merited only one—once Tessier-Lavigne had resigned. In comparison, of course, Stanford can't exactly complain about receiving too little media attention. But the image of our universities is a kind of inverted pyramid: How many stories from Harvard do you read about, how much does a place like Harvard dominate what people think of as college? And how much are the institutions the vast majority of Americans attend—secondary campuses of big state universities, commuter schools in urban areas, community colleges, to say nothing of for-profit universities—part of our picture of "the university"?

Complaints leveled against these universities focus on the curriculum, but primarily the humanities curriculum and even more specifically history and English departments. This even though the significance of these departments for the larger university has dramatically declined: At the end of the 1960s, BAs in English accounted for almost 8 percent of all degrees awarded; by 1982 that number was down to 3 percent. While it recovered to 5 percent in the mid-90s, it is now back to 2 percent. History underwent a similar trajectory, from 6 percent in 1967 down to 1.5 percent today.[5] The campus that people are mad about is increasingly no longer the campus as it actually exists, but an *image* of that campus we've all grown used to. The panics surrounding campus culture do not stem from the fact that Americans have become alienated from their universities. Exactly the opposite may be the case: The panic is fueled by the fact that Americans think they know their universities all too well.

Someone must have been spreading lies about the American college, because without the campus having changed all that much, one day it found itself declared a bastion of illiberalism. Although "lies" probably overstates matters. Certainly, philippics against US universities have a tradition that goes back almost seventy years. But they only caught on, especially among people who had actually attended one of these institutions, after the university had become a very specific projection screen. In other words, the *kinds* of stories that political correctness and then cancel culture narratives set on American college campuses had to be established as plausible campus stories over the course of decades.

The campus we encounter in the average political correctness anecdote is characterized by a penchant for the melodramatic: upstanding heroes fight against villainous censors; the most absurd cowardice and conformity square off against courageous outsider figures. Extreme sensitivity and grotesque rituals of exclusion are rampant. Everything is black or white. Even when they relate real events, such anecdotes are literary in their imagination. This chapter is about the generations of storytellers who influenced this literary imagination, and the kind of audience these stories have taught generations of Americans to be. The rest of the world took part in this process, but only indirectly, only secondarily. In the United States much of the public sees the campus in literary guise, even if the public doesn't realize that fact. But at least it exists in literary terms. In most of the other countries that became fixated on stories of the reign of political correctness in the United States, the campus is itself a literary import; there are no analogous campuses to tell fictions about, so both the campus imaginary and its narratives are imports. Nevertheless, French- and German-language discourses have eagerly replicated the American process of alienation with respect to the conditions allegedly prevailing at their own national universities. Before we trace this strange translation process, I will first recount the history of these campus legends and show how this form of storytelling achieved its plausibility.

The Groves of Academe

Since the 1950s, campus novels have been a staple of US literature. From Mary McCarthy's *Groves of Academe* (1952) and John Williams's *Stoner* (1965), via Robertson Davies's *Rebel Angels* (1982) and Don DeLillo's *White Noise* (1985), to Chad Harbach and Jeffrey Eugenides (*The Art of Fielding* and *The Marriage Plot*, both 2011, respectively), the North American campus has served as the perfect stage for comedies, small tragedies, crime novels, and much more. Certainly, there are also campus novels in Great Britain, such as Kingsley Amis's *Lucky Jim* (1954), one half of David Lodge's *Changing Places* (1975), or the first volumes of Anthony Powell's *Dance to the Music of Time*. But it's the North American campus—with its brick buildings, central quads, and garrulous students—that dominates the genre. In France, Germany, Austria, and Switzerland, the campus novel genre arrived only slowly and haltingly, if at all. The ones that did were self-conscious imitations of US models.

This is initially an aesthetic phenomenon—the US university is a reliable source of motifs for literature and film—but one that has quickly grown into a political problem. Compared to most European universities, the American campus can appear remote and isolated. Of course, even the most remote rural college is interwoven with its environs by money, class, race, cultural capital—not to mention the cooks, secretaries, and other staff who work there. But for outsiders, it can be difficult to see this intertwining at first glance. Even for the teachers at such a university, it is not always easy to distinguish a secretly rich hippie from a proudly unintegrated child of the working class. And this lack of transparency is not primarily due to the distance. Even the college one highway exit away is another planet; that's how architecturally and culturally self-contained many campuses are.

The limited legibility of these places stands in blatant contrast to the fact that, especially in US culture, they are constantly being offered up for interpretation. How many aging college professors have you encountered in literature? How many impressionable freshmen in Hollywood romcoms and crime series? The university has been a stage for such stories for more than a hundred years—it is simply perfect for stories about maturing, aging, and failure. However, in novels such as Williams's *Stoner* or Nabokov's *Pnin*, the campus itself is seen less as an institution or milieu: It rather represents a kind of lab environment in which certain questions, problems, and tendencies can be presented in perfect isolation. Even though the campus is thus a conceit of these stories more than their topic, these texts are usually called campus novels.

The world they describe is fairly static. Campus novels are social novels that do not have to say that much about society. Adam Begley notes, "On every campus in every decade, there's the urgent need for new funds, issues of academic freedom, worries about hiring and admissions quotas, petty jealousies, endless inter- and intra-departmental squabbles."[6] The students on this literary campus are, according to Begley, "elemental, as unvarying as earth and fire."[7] Which is to say, in consuming literature about campus life, we collectively fictionalize the student body. When another wave of panic about *actual* events on college campuses hits our newspapers, it almost always draws momentary plausibility from this constant. This is one reason why the supposed suddenness of the phenomenon at issue can feel oddly timeless.

But even beyond the sociological invariants, the campus novel as form transports other prejudgments that, after almost seventy years, can be difficult to notice as such. The literary scholar Jeffrey Williams distinguishes between "campus novels," in which the student body is in the foreground and professors and administrators are part of the backdrop, and "academic novels," in which the constantly changing students recede into the background noise in favor of the deeper rhythms of campus life.[8] When the campus becomes literature, no matter how the respective authors decide to tell their story, the picture is always necessarily partial. Either teachers or students are consigned from the first sentence to mere flitting shadows, ancillary factors in the experience of others. And we as readers have to make peace with that.

As a genre, campus novels tend to be comedic—more specifically, they fall under the rubric of a comedy of manners. But precisely because they grapple with the absurdity of human existence through academic convention and infighting, "most campus novels . . . simmer with barely concealed feelings of anger and even despair."[9] This too contains a sort of covert lesson. What happens on campus can never *just* be funny; campus literature rather encourages us to identify something existential, even demonic, behind apparent comedy, behind patent absurdity.

Take a more low-rent kind of campus fiction as an example. In nearly sixty seasons of *Law & Order* (counting its reboot and some of its offshoots *Special Victims Unit (SVU)* and *Criminal Intent*), dozens of murders happen at the fictional Hudson University, a college that has pretty much anything the plot requires (Pervert professors! Students moonlighting as escorts! A nuclear reactor! A murdering dean!). Of course, this fake university only exists because the producers wouldn't get permission to film if they set fictitious murders at real institutions. The episodes are usually filmed on the campuses of several New York institutions—Fordham, NYU, Columbia, Union Theological Seminary, and Yeshiva University. Hudson University is a kind of distillation of all universities, perhaps even of "the" university itself—an idea that we as audiences have come to accept.

This fantasy university, where murders happen all the time, is still relatively easy to see through as a construct. With other caricatures, this is much more difficult, at least for some viewers. In the 2014 film *God's Not Dead*, a tyrannical philosophy professor stands in front of his students at the beginning of the first lecture—behind him is a blackboard with names like Michel Foucault, Bertolt Brecht, and Ludwig Feuerbach—and asks them to sign a declaration that states "God is dead" or otherwise receive a failing grade. A single student refuses, much to the displeasure of his godless classmates. It's unclear how seriously the film takes this scenario, but the political message behind it is nevertheless potent: This is how many Republican representatives in state legislatures see universities today—and they control the finances of many such institutions.

But beyond the fact that the campus we've learned to inhabit is structured mostly through fictions, there is another problem: the uniformity suggested by these fictions. There are many different types of colleges in the United States, and they have become if anything more diverse over time. But their fictional image is shockingly uniform. If this were just a matter of aesthetic clichés like ivy-covered neo-gothic buildings or charming, rundown fraternity houses, it wouldn't be particularly dangerous. But campus fictions also flatten the image of students and teachers. And that is an invitation to distortions that are deeply politically relevant. Once the students at a community college are portrayed as pampered snowflakes who live in enormous comfort in their ivory tower, one sees how the icon "college" fatally occludes and distorts the much more diverse reality.

Unfortunately, this distortion has long been ideologically motivated and politically desired. There is now a cottage industry that shapes campus narratives. By that I don't mean Netflix shows or Philip Roth, but rather political groups and publications funded by think tanks or conservative foundations like the Smith Richardson Foundation (founded 1935), the Bradley Foundation (founded in 1942), or the John M. Olin Foundation (founded in 1953, dissolved in 2005). In the 1970s, the American Enterprise Institute began to take aim at universities. In the 1980s, they were joined by the neoconservative members of the Reagan administration, among them Bill Bennett and Lynne Cheney. In the 1990s, it was renegade leftist David Horowitz who compiled lists of radical professors and students, as well as co-publishing a magazine called *Heterodoxy*, a "samizdat publication inside the gulag of the PC University."[10] Today organizations like Turning Point USA, the Young America's Foundation or Fox News continue this work. Campus narratives have become propaganda that we do not reliably classify as such.

Horror stories of campus life have become explicitly politicized. But also democratized. From early on conservative groups asked students and professors for stories about alleged censorship and oppression. When you look through early publications of the Intercollegiate Studies Institute or Accuracy in Academia, they almost always start and end the same way: They open with various tidbits of campus leftism run amok, and they close with an address, an 800 number, or (later) a website through which a reader could find other similar stories and, importantly, submit stories of their own. These organizations spent tremendous resources packaging and distributing tendentious campus anecdotes in a way that would maximize media attention. But they also appealed to each individual reader as a potential teller of campus stories.

And where the relevant anecdotes wouldn't come, there were ways to prime the pump: The same groups linked conservative speakers with campus groups

intent on causing controversy. Theirs was, in other words, an enormous incitement to produce discourse, a diagnosis that encouraged participation. Not
everyone could write a campus novel or an episode of *Law & Order*. But thanks
to the campus arm of the right-wing noise machine, anyone could help turn the
campus into a caricature they could then criticize.

The fact that the stories of this conservative narrative tradition are becoming more and more entrenched (in a 2023 Gallup poll, only 19 percent of the
Republican voters surveyed had "a great deal" or "quite a lot of" confidence in
the country's universities; for Democratic voters that number was at 59 percent,
but it had been 68 percent just eight years before[11]) has less to do with the target
group's lack of education and more to do with the virtual remoteness with
which the university exists for most Americans. In a way, the college campus
also symbolically belongs to everyone and to no one.

Over 40 percent of Americans (94 million) have attended some type of college, have memories, impressions, and associations even if they may be decades
old now. Campus novels, films, and TV series are always popular in the United
States. Once Americans graduate from college, they probably spend more time
on fictional campuses than real ones. That wouldn't be so bad—if this fictional
campus weren't repeatedly treated as real in politics and journalism. In the
media—not just US media—we are constantly asked to evaluate what is happening at US universities. We simply aren't allowed to be indifferent to what
happens there. Within the framework of McCarthyism, arch-conservative
groups warned against communists in the faculty. Ronald Reagan was elected
governor of California in 1966 on two promises: reduce welfare and "clean up"
the University of California, Berkeley. Since then, taking aim at university students has become *de rigueur*, especially for Republican politicians.

But perhaps there are completely different experiences of alienation lying
behind this willingness to help construct fictional college campuses. The campus
is full of young people who, for the first time, are developing their own rituals
and discourses relatively independently of adults. The most important contact
that people of a certain age have with universities is when they drop their off-
spring off on campus—and over the next four years have to watch their dear
child grow into a full-blown adult. It's not always a pleasant process; it's deeply
eerie and certainly also depressing for parents. In this scenario, the moral concerns associated with the tradition of the campus narrative coincide with a widely
shared emotional experience. The fact that adult readers think they understand
the campus better than they in fact do likely draws its power from another relationship. Many of those adults have children who have begun to strike out on

their own. And they are perhaps torn between the feeling that they know better than those children and the sense that they no longer understand them at all.

Since the 1960s at least, this intergenerational aspect—the fact that, whatever else it is about, it is also always about ungrateful youth—has given this conflict its enormous power. When Reagan launched his attacks in the mid-1960s, the university had a far more central position in US society: Professors were more present in the media than today, and the point of college was far more self-evident—between the space program, the military-industrial complex, and the GI Bill. In a liberal welfare state, academic perspectives were a natural part of public discourse. In the last fifty years, the university has at least partially lost this position, but the belief that one can infer what the Left is up to in the United States, based on the activities of a handful of professors and students at a few elite universities, is more deeply rooted than ever. The panic over Marxist professors never really caught on outside of conservative circles—in the end college professors were just not that important. But when the politics of the students themselves became an issue with the advent of the worry over political correctness, when prejudice against the university campus was linked to a generational conflict, a modern American mythology was born.

But even that overlay took time. And while the story of the virtual campus begins with Mary McCarthy and John Williams, this other kind of campus narrative begins with William F. Buckley's *God and Man at Yale*, published in 1951.

Also a Campus Novel

In the shadow of the campus literary canon, which today could still appear on a syllabus in American Studies, a second one has been flourishing since the 1950s. It did not present itself as literature; it presented its claims as facts rather than literary inventions. But all the same, it weaved tales and established a mythology. This mythology centered the campus experience of a very different set of stakeholders: donors, trustees, and parents. "In the last analysis," we read in *God and Man at Yale*, "academic freedom must mean the freedom of men and women to supervise the educational activities and aims of the schools they oversee and support."[12]

William F. Buckley, Jr., published *God and Man at Yale*, when he was all of twenty-five years old. Along with Russell Kirk's *The Conservative Mind* (1953), Buckley's book in many ways sparked the modern American conservative movement—and it articulated itself through a confrontation with the college campus.

"The" college campus meant—as it would in the next seven decades—a very specific kind of campus, from which Buckley cheerfully generalized to hundreds of other institutions that couldn't have been more different. Yale might be in the title, but as Buckley wrote in the foreword, he suspected "that what is amiss at Yale is more drastically amiss in other of our great institutions of learning."[13] So what was the matter with Yale? Buckley himself had studied at Yale from 1946 to 1950, a time when the university was keen to present itself as anti-communist. President Charles Seymour publicly declared on Graduation Day 1949 that the university "knowingly hire a communist to the teaching faculty."[14] The question of whether this was compatible with academic freedom was the subject of heated debate at the university.

Young Buckley saw this as a sham debate. He had no problems with commie hunting, but beyond that he felt that the university itself didn't actually honor the values it claimed to defend. Academic freedom appeared to him a chimera that universities like Yale didn't practice and that they "can't even believe themselves." To start with, Buckley felt that this freedom did not extend to everyone: The faculty was upset about the firing or investigation of communists, but, Buckley wrote, "I should be interested to know how long a person who revealed himself as a racist, who lectured about the anthropological superiority of the Aryan, would last at Yale?"[15] Secondly, Yale violated the autonomy of its students, because the university, according to Buckley, indoctrinated its pupils. Most of the teachers were not communists; however, the staff, according to Buckley, was out of step with the rest of the country in a more fundamental way: They were deeply anti-Christian and anti-individualist.[16]

In God and Man at Yale, Buckley went through the individual departments one by one—a deeply gossipy, detailed, impressionistic stocktaking. The chairman of the Philosophy Department was "a distinguished scholar and a distinguished man," but also "an earnest and expansive atheist."[17] Several professors were clergymen, but always the wrong type of clergyman, from the wrong denomination, with the wrong attitude. There was a large Christian student association with an influential journal of its own—but "membership on its staff requires no profession of faith in even the most attenuated dogmas of Christianity."[18] Buckley's survey was sweeping, respectful in tone, but deeply idiosyncratic. It reads like a bit of a time capsule today.

What makes God and Man at Yale an early forerunner of the books that would establish stories about campus political correctness in the popular imagination in the 1980s was Buckley's reasoning: He accused the university of cutting itself off from American society. Buckley warned that "under the protective label of 'academic freedom'" universities had "produced one of the most extraordinary incongruities of our time": The university drew "its moral and financial support" from "Christian individualists," but saw as its job "the task of persuading the sons of these supporters to be atheistic socialists."[19] The university did not train its pupils for the world, but almost against it. "But if the recent Yale graduate, who exposed himself to Yale economics during his undergraduate years, exhibits enterprise, self-reliance, and independence, it is only because he has turned his back upon his teachers and texts."[20] *God and Man at Yale* gave the self-sufficiency and insularity of the American university campus, the fact that it was so obviously non-contiguous with the world around it, a demonic note.

Buckley established conventions for a particular genre of campus criticism that have now become so self-evident that they hardly catch the eye. For example, from a specimen of the species "university" that is unusual in every respect, such as Yale University, the author thinks he can, indeed must, infer things about "the" university as such. Buckley repeatedly refers to the exceptional character of Yale, but then he compulsively generalizes. This trick—that one can never say exactly how specific these campus narratives are meant to be—was to accompany the genre through its many changes. Even a work as dissimilar at first glance as Allan Bloom's *The Closing of the American Mind* (1987)—a book that calls for the distance between campus and society to be greatly expanded—constantly speaks of society and "the university" but really only means specific elite institutions.[21]

Likewise the way in which the university becomes synonymous with the humanities, and the humanities with English and history departments, was to become a theme of university criticism over the course of the next few decades. John Taylor's 1991 article in *New York* magazine, which along with others unleashed a discursive tsunami about political correctness, makes this clear. For Taylor used the sociolects of very specific lines of research to characterize "the university" and "the campus" as a whole. The magazine's cover asked: "Am I misogynistic, patriarchal, gynophobic, phallocentric, logocentric?" Taylor claims that "the new fundamentalists" are "an eclectic group" including "multiculturalists, feminists, radical Marxists, and New Historicists."[22] It is somewhat comical that Taylor's list, alongside fairly broad movements such as feminism and Marxism, also includes "New Historicism," a theory that while very popular in some English departments in the 1980s and 1990s, would at that time have been no more than a footnote to a footnote.

This strange tendency to accept an ever-dwindling set of embattled-to-moribund subdisciplines as a *pars pro toto* for the university, indeed society, has persisted since Buckley. Some authors, such as Allan Bloom, had theoretical reasons for this: They regarded the humanities as the crown jewel of the universities. For others, it was probably more the fact that the authors themselves were, well, authors and had attended mostly classes in English and history while in college. But as time went on, there were ever fewer students who came into sustained contact with this particular part of the curriculum.

The face of the average college student, the average college course, and the average curriculum have all changed fundamentally since *God and Man at Yale*. Yet when Roger Kimball's *Tenured Radicals* sought to expose the "institutionalization of a radical ethos in academia" in 1990, it raised few eyebrows that the book mainly consisted of a laundry list of English professors and historians.[23] While the subtitle said that "politics has corrupted our higher education," Kimball's "diagnosis of the tragedy that has befallen academic culture"[24] is based almost entirely on a description of disciplines that were already becoming increasingly marginal in his day—a dissonance that is also evident in the cancel culture panic of today.

The distortions in fundamentalist propaganda like *God's Not Dead* are obvious and unintentionally funny. Every detail seems to have sprung from some kind of fever dream. But instead of mocking the open insanity of *God's Not Dead*, it's worth reflecting on how little realism it takes to make even serious contemporaries nod along with a similarly fantastical campus story.

Homeschooling activist Jeremy Wayne Tate tweeted in 2022 that his friend's son was "a senior at the University of Michigan," and "in his four years at Michigan he has never been required to read anything published before 2016."[25] Reactions fell into two camps. Many users expressed their outrage at academic faddism; and teachers replying to his tweet made fun of the claim, which was immediately recognizable to them as an obvious falsehood. These were instructors familiar with canon lists and coverage worries, with having been handed required syllabi that probably hadn't been updated since 2016, let alone containing texts from then. Tate's lie was screamingly obvious to those familiar with higher education in the United States—and deeply plausible to many who were not.

Consider just how long otherwise well-informed contemporaries have been fooling themselves into believing some classic (Shakespeare, Plato, or Homer) is "no longer" taught at "the university." "The old teachers who loved Shakespeare or Austen or Donne, and whose only reward for teaching was the perpetuation of their taste, have all but disappeared," lamented Allan Bloom in 1987.[26] "Out goes Homer, as well as Darwin and Dante" harrumphed no less august a publication as *Time* magazine when Stanford University had the temerity to change an introductory lecture sequence in 1988.[27] "Shakespeare, Aristotle, Adam Smith, Max Weber, James Madison, Cicero, and the Bible" are being replaced on mandatory reading lists, complained Les Csorba of the conservative nonprofit Accuracy in Academia (also 1988). According to Csorba, these stalwarts had been replaced by "Caldicott, Sagan, Dewey, Keynes, Galbraith."[28] For the modern reader it is fairly obvious that the death of the canon couldn't have been all it was cracked up to be—if for no other reason than that the new-fangled authors allegedly prescribed in the new curricula are identifiable today only via vigorous googling, but the supposedly exiled classics are identifiable even without Wikipedia.

In 1991, *Campus* magazine, published by the conservative Intercollegiate Studies Institute (ISI), noted: "At a recent conference of the Modern Language Association, Catharine Stimpson, a leading feminist academic, was asked to give an example of a book that exhibits patriarchy. She couldn't—or wouldn't."[29] A modern reader of the anecdote can almost hear Professor Stimpson's exasperated silence over what we would now call trolling. The article's author, on the other hand, seems to be assuming his reader will hear something completely different: namely, that a leading English literary historian (whose most recent book at the time dealt with Virginia Woolf, and who could presumably have simply responded with the two words "Virginia Woolf"[30]) could not think of a literary example of patriarchy. And finds that idea plausible.

In hindsight, the claim that Alice Walker's *Color Purple* was "now assigned more often in college courses than all of Shakespeare's plays combined,"[31] which crept up in a good number of early PC scare stories, sounds more than a little far-fetched. But even though the claim now feels historic—about as 80s as a Duran Duran mixtape in a Walkman—that didn't prevent it from being trotted out again and again. In 2012, *Spectator* columnist Toby Young fantasized about (British!) schools that had "the complete works of Alice Walker in the school library (though no Mark Twain)."[32] The transatlantic game of telephone amplified this distortion. The stories of curricular change that barely had any relationship to the facts in the United States got wilder in the international retelling. Consider an article that appeared in the *Süddeutsche Zeitung* in 2000 that describes a curricular overhaul at Stanford in the 1980s. Students, the journalist notes, were not concerned with "putting Mozart and Beethoven, Shakespeare, Goethe and Molière . . . in the Orcus [to be] banished (if they had any idea of their existence, which we shouldn't assume)."[33] Note the strange switch between supposed detail and sheer speculation: The journalist imagines a campus where students haven't heard of Mozart, where they sort of seem to want to banish Shakespeare but also don't. What is clear to him, by contrast, is what is poised to replace the classics: "the study of 'ethnic cultures'" (a term he presents in English, thus apparently giving an opinion on an academic field he can't accurately name). The journalist might have known better in 1988, but that he did not know better in the year 2000 is itself deeply telling. German writers and their readers were simply too inured to this version of the US university campus to question it—or to look up the term "ethnic studies" before publishing an essay.

Marc Fabian Erdl once called this the "triad of German cultural reporting on 'political correctness': fetishism of the classics, anti-intellectualism and ignorance of details."[34] After more than thirty years of such claims, Harald Martenstein was able to strike the same note again in *Zeit Magazin* in 2021, this time as a "case of cancel culture":

> In the United States, some teachers refuse to teach the relatively well-known poet William Shakespeare in class. He stands for the toxic worldview of white straight men, that he is a racist and must be replaced promptly by various, inclusive poets.[35]

After decades of habituation, the acceptance of such a claim requires two things. Inclined readers must be able to brush aside the obvious unreality of such stories. And readers must be able to forget that they've been fed similar stories for decades.

The Late 60s: A Kind of Caesura

The Cow Palace is a multipurpose venue in Daly City just south of San Francisco. Throughout its history (the building opened in 1941), the San Francisco Warriors played basketball there, the Grand National Rodeo took place there, and the Beatles (1964 and 1965) and the Rolling Stones (1966) performed there. In 1964, the Republican Party held its national convention at the Cow Palace, in which, after a bruising primary and a contentious nominating process, arch-conservative Senator Barry Goldwater from Arizona prevailed as the presidential candidate. Goldwater was defeated by incumbent Lyndon B. Johnson in a landslide victory, and the Republicans were trounced in the Senate and the House.

Only two years later the Cow Palace witnessed a sort of Republican rebirth. Ronald Reagan was running for governor of California. On May 12, 1966, the

Hollywood star appeared in front of thousands at the Cow Palace and gave a speech that went down in history as the "Morality Gap" speech. Reagan had been traveling the state since 1965 with a promise to "clean up the mess at Berkeley." The most famous campus of the University of California had been in turmoil since 1964. Students had objected to administrators' attempts to restrict campus protests by civil rights activists and had launched the Free Speech Movement. In 1964, students occupied Sproul Hall, and in 1965 came the first mass demonstrations against the Vietnam War, which was only a few years old at the time.

In the mid-1960s, the university was new to right-wing politics. The word "university" had not appeared once in Goldwater's campaign book, *The Conscience of a Conservative* (1960). This despite the fact that the ghostwriter of the book had been none other than L. Brent Bozell, Jr., Buckley's roommate at Yale and co-founder of the *National Review*— thus not exactly a blank slate when it came to universities. Goldwater, by contrast, had never attended college, and the conservative milieu he was addressing was more concerned with the local school system and the supposed brainwashing done by high school teachers. But by 1966, Reagan sensed that conditions at American universities could also be politically exploited. In an autobiographical text, he wrote: "I don't care if I'm in the mountains, the desert, the biggest cities in the state, the first question is: 'What are you going to do about Berkeley?' and each time the question itself would get applause."[36] The myth of Ronald Reagan was created by the actor staging himself as an antagonist to another myth: that of Berkeley.

Reagan proved highly adept at telling stories about college during the campaign. The future president didn't just talk about the well-documented student riots. He wasn't content to demonize the Free Speech Movement as a "filthy speech movement." He wasn't content to simply call for discipline and consequences. His culture war against Berkeley was possessed of a kind of feverish imagination of the campus; he shared with his listeners an entire mythology of sexual perversion and drug abuse on campus. He played on the puritanism of his audience with the same skill as he played on their voyeurism.

"You heard about the report of the [California] Senate Subcommittee on Un-American Activities," Reagan told the Daly City audience. (The report alleged that the Berkeley campus was a hotbed for communists and an epicenter of sexual misconduct.) Reagan said he hadn't read the report himself, but he had here—Reagan then pulled a piece of paper from his pocket—"a copy of a report of the District Attorney of Alameda County. It concerns a dance that was sponsored by the Vietnam Day Committee [and] sanctioned by the university as a student activity." Reagan said, "the incidents are so bad, so bla-tantly contrary to our standards of human behavior, that I couldn't possibly recite them to you here from this platform in detail." Then Reagan proceeded to recite them here from this platform in detail:

> Three rock'n' roll bands were in the center of the gymnasium playing si-multaneously all during the dance, and all during the dance movies were shown on two screens at the opposite ends of the gymnasium. These movies were the only sources of lights in the gym proper. They consisted of color se-quences that gave the appearance of different colored liquids spreading across the screen, followed by shots of men and women on occasion, shots with the men and women's nude torsos on occasion, and persons twisted and gyrated in provocative and sensual fashion. . . . Sexual misconduct was blatant. The smell of marijuana was prevalent all over the entire building.[37]

Reagan knew his audience well. His speech script included the sentence, "There were indications of other events which cannot be mentioned here."[38] In his speech Reagan devoted much time to discussing eloquently what he claimed he couldn't discuss. If the report he was referring to is identical to the one later included in the Senate inquiry into the incident in the California state legislature, the truth is that Reagan had kept almost nothing from his audi-ence.[39] Screens, three rock bands at once, the smell of marijuana! Reagan knew communism and anti-war slogans were one thing. But to activate the instinc-tive disdain and secret fascination his listeners felt for the radical students, he had to deliver sex, drugs, and rock 'n' roll. Reagan's Berkeley Tales are master-pieces of collective projection. As he himself noted, he had not seen the Senate report—after all, Reagan was still a private citizen in 1966. But it was precisely this distance that made Reagan the perfect medium—precisely because he, like his listeners, didn't know the details, he could imagine, and react to what he imagined, alongside them.

A later investigation by UC Berkeley revealed that the descriptions of the party at the university involved a lot of imagination. Reagan's listeners at the Cow Palace and his voters probably didn't care. In November 1966 he defeated the Democratic incumbent Pat Brown with 58 percent of the vote. With Rea-gan's speech, a tacit agreement had been established between conservative poli-ticians and their target group: Stories about universities didn't necessarily have to *be* true, but they had to *feel* true.

As a political orator, Reagan relied almost obsessively on small anecdotes and pop mythological parables, often obscuring or simply forgetting whether they were from a movie, real life, or modern folklore. "Reagan," according to Garry Wills, "used anecdotes and moral examples" without "regard for niggling little details about the source or accuracy of his stories."[40] Moreover, this type of rhetoric only worked if the listener did not question what was being said. John Patrick Diggins mentions a story frequently repeated by Reagan about two bomber pilots in World War II and their conversation as their plane went down. Repeated inquiries (from movie star Warren Beatty, among others) as to how the conversation between two men who ended up dying could possibly be known Reagan brushed aside with his customary nonchalance.[41] Most of the Gipper's anecdotes had to do with sports and the military, but in moments like the "Morality Gap" speech, the university became part of Reagan's mythmaking. Perhaps it's no coincidence that the anecdote-heavy mythology of political correctness in university life took hold just as Reagan, with his half-invented but vividly meaningful stories, rode off into the sunset.

But Reagan's tales of the university also made a tangible offer to the consumers of his anecdotes: They were allowed to be concerned about what young people were doing on campus because it was patriotic and a sign of their own seriousness; they were not just sticking their collective noses into the intimate lives of young people. The more schematic the horror stories were, the better. Because if you had to contextualize and explain details, you were already on the defensive rhetorically. As Frederick Dutton, then a member of the University of California Board of Regents, put it, Democratic Governor Pat Brown, "the person who had the responsibility," had to "see the problem more in grays . . . . Pat had the grays, Reagan had the black and whites."[42]

But contrary to conventional wisdom, the 1960s do not seem to have been the turning point in everyday Americans' relationship to their universities. For the popular opinion about college students, the important decade was the 1980s. To be sure, certain segments of the intelligentsia began souring on the universities—in particular that segment of the intelligentsia that would later come to be called neoconservatives. What Reagan did in the 1960s was prove that a long-held conservative unease about the universities could also be used to motivate voters who didn't understand themselves as conservative. In 1969, as governor, Reagan sent police officers to clear student-occupied People's Park in Berkeley; a young man was shot dead during the operation. Reagan then sent 2,700 National Guard soldiers to Berkeley, and the city was occupied for 17 days. None of this hurt Reagan: He was re-elected in 1970 with 52 percent of the vote.

Reagan's particular mode of creating legends about colleges and the students and teachers there has had a tradition since the 1950s. Until the 1980s, however, it was a discernibly conservative tradition. *God and Man at Yale* was published by a conservative publisher and took a deliberately cantankerous, partisan tack when it came to the university. Buckley himself was to become famous in the following decades, above all through positions mostly on the right flank of the Republican Party: He published an apology for Senator Joseph McCarthy, defended segregation, and supported the regimes of Franco and Pinochet. While he swam in a conservative mainstream, he would never have been mistaken for a defender of liberalism.

Although Reagan's culture war slogans anticipated the panic of the 1980s, there are also significant differences. The Gipper had concrete proposals to combat the problems he identified at Berkeley: Cut the university's funding and mobilize the police and military against the students. By contrast, when negative campus narratives experienced a renaissance in the late 1980s and early 1990s, it was never clear what the authors wanted to have happen. Certainly, budget cuts were always part of the answer, as was increased precarity for instructors. But even Charlie Sykes—whose book *ProfScam* blamed all the university's structural problems on lazy and seditious college professors—stopped short of clear demands as to what was supposed to be done about the miscreants. Rhetorically at least, disapproval was enough.

Of course, in the United States of the Reagan era and beyond, one no longer had to demand anything beyond budget cuts—cuts became the *lingua franca* of moral displeasure. The wide proliferation of stories about campus political correctness participated in this language game of Reaganism—after all, it coincided with a massive state disinvestment from universities. Financial disinvestment and moral overinvestment were entwined: Politicians could use tales of political correctness to justify budget cuts to voters. But the campus you encounter in the average political correctness anecdote—where dismissal is easy and existence is precarious—is one characterized by the early foreshocks of a casualized workforce, which changed full-time tenured and tenure-track positions to adjunct, part-time, or contingent lecturer positions. As disinvestment intensified, the number of tenured professors declined, and the number of easily terminated contingent faculty increased.

Reagan still mostly condemned the chaos at Berkeley from the perspective of the taxpayer. It was probably no coincidence that he attacked the liberal consensus by demonizing a state-funded public university, rather than, say, Stanford, which was riven by similar turbulence in the 1960s. In the 1970s, California experienced a major tax revolt—especially suburban voters rebelling against perceived excessive taxes and the programs they funded. As the historian Lisa McGirr has shown, it took a surprisingly long time before complaints of this kind, which have since become a *basso continuo* in American politics, sparked a response among voters, even in conservative Southern California.[43] The culture war surrounding UC Berkeley during Reagan's 1966 campaign offered an early opportunity to bring together unease about certain subcultures with an as-yet unarticulated concern with having to share your money with others.

By the 1980s, the tax revolt had seized first California and then the entire country. But the concern with the university persisted. Those who warned about political correctness no longer made any distinction between private and public universities, between elite and mid-tier. In the early years of the political correctness discourse, conditions at Stanford, particularly the aforementioned reorganization of the introductory humanities course sequence, were a more important point of reference than conditions at Berkeley. The old rhetoric of "not with our tax dollars" had given way to a new understanding of why what happened at some faraway campus mattered to everyday Americans. Reagan had stopped short of attacking private institutions, probably precisely because they were private. But by the 1980s, a university's status as a private entity no longer rendered it immune to conservative—or indeed liberal—attack. This was because the detour via tax dollars was no longer necessary. Colleges, their students, and what they were taught there were the general public's business, one way or the other.

Finally, Reagan's success was an explicitly conservative success. His attacks on the university, "embarrassed and weakened California liberals."[44] The mere gesture of pulling a prosecutor's report out of his jacket pocket at the Cow Palace in 1966 likely was intended to evoke memories of Joe McCarthy, who in an infamous February 1950 speech produced a "list" of names of "communists in the State Department." At the Cow Palace, Reagan operated within an explicitly anti-communist tradition.

In contrast, the culture war rhetoric of the twilight years of the Reagan presidency lacked such explicit references to anti-communism. In Kimball's *Tenured Radicals*, the word "communist" appears four times, and the word "radical" appears on every other page. In Dinesh D'Souza's *Illiberal Education*, "communist" is mentioned six times, "radical" forty times. In 1965–66, when Reagan spelled out what he (allegedly) expected of universities, he had sounded authoritarian, presenting himself as an openly conservative challenger to a liberal consensus. By the time conservatives once again targeted universities, during and shortly after Reagan's time in the White House, they claimed to represent liberalism on the defensive. Of course, if you listened carefully, you could hear that the solutions they were suggesting smacked of illiberalism and censorship. But it was an important part of the PC discourse that the quiet part generally stayed quiet.

When Harvard donor Bill Ackman demanded in January of 2024 that "Harvard must create an academic environment with real academic freedom and free speech,"[45] he was celebrating the resignation of Harvard's president, which he had in no small measure orchestrated. And he was calling for the members of Harvard's board to step down, especially if they shared Gay's "politics and views about DEI." He called for the shuttering of Harvard's Office of Equity, Diversity, Equity, Inclusion & Belonging: "the staff should be terminated." His quest for academic freedom seemed, in other words, largely to involve the silencing and firing of people who disagreed with him. Ackman was drawing on a blind spot that campus culture critics have been exploiting since *Illiberal Education*: In intellectual background Dinesh D'Souza was a theocratic paleoconservative, but in his book he presented himself as liberalism's savior. In the language game of political correctness, it was always the other side that was illiberal and authoritarian.

FOUR

The Neoconservative View

> Anecdotal horror stories from today's politically correct campus are legion, and the cases are endlessly absurd. But the darker aspect of the vast, Vichy-like capitulation of the academy lies in the cowardice and opportunism revealed. For the most shocking aspect of the transformation of higher education really is that it was not resisted, but welcomed. There's an Us and Them, all right, and We were not so much conquered as sold out. Why?
> —DOUGLAS FOWLER, *Heterodoxy* (October 1992)[1]

> Until a few years ago, almost everyone agreed that while our schools might not be performing as well as they should, our colleges and universities were institutions we could point to with pride. Now, however, there is growing awareness that our colleges and universities are in trouble.
> —LYNNE CHENEY, "Telling the Truth" (1992)[2]

There is another way of describing Reagan's performance at the Cow Palace: By conjuring up the threat posed by Berkeley, the Great Communicator was able to reunite the conservative camp in the wake of the Goldwater catastrophe of 1964. Panics about campus life would grip a broader electorate with some regularity over the next few decades. Exactly when such a panic broke through had less to do with the specific activities of students or with supposed excesses of campus culture; rather, it was tethered to the right wing having another identity crisis.

William F. Buckley, Jr.'s attack on the universities can be understood as a harbinger of a project that would mediate between very different, almost incompatible forms of political reaction. After all, he simultaneously accused Yale of not being traditionalist enough and not being individualistic enough, which managed, by fixating on Yale, the trick of positioning religious fundamentalism and liberal individualism as related conservative projects rather than as fundamentally opposed. Buckley's *National Review* soon came to embody a "fusionism" that combined Christian values of conservatism, libertarianism, and anti-communism.[3] In this project, the fixation on universities constituted an important unifying force.

I said earlier that the late 1960s do not appear to have been the major turning point in everyday Americans' relationship to the universities. Typical readers may have regarded the events at Berkeley as anomalous and not as a verdict on the university as such. But the major impact of the late 60s was on a sort of time release. By then, what Reagan had pointed to had clearly spread: Anti-war protests, civil rights protests, and SDS activism held many campuses in their grip. In 1968 students at Columbia occupied the university president's office, and in 1969 Cornell saw armed protestors take over Willard Straight Hall. A large group of intellectuals later cited these events as the beginning of a slow turn against the university and against a certain kind of liberalism that they thought it represented.

Neoconservatism commonly denotes a specific configuration of political positions, but it of course also denotes a specific generational experience. Figures such as Norman Podhoretz, Midge Decter, and Irving Kristol initially saw themselves as left wing and gradually drifted to the right from the late 1960s. Figures like Jeane Kirkpatrick and Allan Bloom saw themselves as liberals until 1968, after which they began to identify more and more with conservative positions.

Only some of these renegades—Allan Bloom, Donald Kagan, Werner J. Dannhauser among them—were university academics. Most—such as Irving Kristol, Norman Podhoretz, and Midge Decter—had studied extensively and were shaped by the universities, but they set up shop within literal shouting distance of these institutions. Their collective accusation was that the university had gone off the rails—not just the students, not just the professors but both these groups in an intergenerational tangle of dysfunction. For Decter, Bloom, and Dannhauser were not just disgusted by the Black Panthers on the campus; they were perhaps more disgusted by the majority of colleagues who expressed some measure of understanding for the Panthers, those colleagues who coddled the young American minds.

In the opening to her 1975 *Liberal Parents, Radical Children*, Midge Decter addresses "My Dear Children" as follows:

> What your admiring professors did not tell you was that your attitude to the university was helping to reflect and deepen *their* sense of *them*selves.

In your challenge to the value of their work they found the echo of some
profound bad conscience.[4]

There was a way knowledge and values were supposed to be handed down from
one generation to the next; the modern family and the modern university had
turned that transmission itself pathological.

The rest of Decter's book was, as she put it, an exercise in "fictionalized
sociology,"[5] meaning that she invented stories ostensibly based on real observations—about liberal parents, their excessive deference to their young, and
again and again about the universities that aided and abetted their dysfunction. From the beginning, the neoconservative attack on the university was
also an effort in collaborative storytelling. Most importantly, it invited its audience, which would grow with each decade, to join in the production of campus
stories that felt perhaps truer and more representative than they were.

Generally, as in Decter's case, the neoconservative disaffection with the
institutions of higher learning was in the service of those very institutions.
The neocons' point wasn't (or wasn't yet) that college was useless; it was that
college—in the hand of softhearted liberals and "angelheaded hipsters" (Allen
Ginsberg's phrasing)—was at risk of *becoming* useless. In Barbara Ehrenreich's
acerbic description:

> Looking at the student movement, they foresaw cherished institutions in
> flames, and beyond that the threat of a radically egalitarian future in which
> education and intellect would be valued no more than, say, the skills of a me-
> chanic or the insights of the downtrodden.[6]

This constituted, as Ehrenreich put it, a turn against their own class and a turn
against the very institutions that had defined them as intellectuals. But they
were defectors from these institutions who nevertheless thought of themselves
as saving those institutions. "The neoconservatives steered clear of attacking
the central sources of middle-class authority: professionalism and expertise."[7]
They simply questioned whether the universities as presently constituted—
insert here various and rotating cavils about affirmative action, radical professors, abandonment of the classics, overreliance on theory, underreliance
on theory, over-professionalization, under-professionalization—could legitimately confer that kind of authority.

When the conservative movement took over Washington with Reagan in 1981,
paleoconservatives and neoconservatives within the Reagan camp quickly clashed
over various appointments. One seemingly marginal post that nevertheless

generated immense infighting was that of the head of the National Endowment for the Humanities. Reagan had decided to nominate the literary scholar Mel Bradford for the post, a paleoconservative who openly lamented the defeat of the southern states in the Civil War and who had even compared Abraham Lincoln to Hitler. The neoconservatives—who had little interest in southern nostalgia, were huge admirers of Lincoln, and were largely apostates from East Coast liberalism—rose up against Bradford's nomination in droves and were successful.

Bradford was replaced by William Bennett, who was supported primarily by the neoconservatives around Kristol and Podhoretz. Bennett, as head of the NEH, would present the report that can be seen as the starting signal for the panic about allegedly threats to freedom of expression at the university ("To Reclaim a Legacy: Report on the Humanities in Higher Education," published in 1984). At the end of a bruising political fight within the right wing lay a kind of palace truce: They might not agree about Lincoln or Jefferson Davis, but they did agree on English professors at UT Austin.

When, at the end of the presidency of George H. W. Bush, conservatives from Pat Buchanan to Ross Perot went on the warpath against establishment Republicans, one central way to bridge the multiple divides was to focus on campus culture: It unified everyone in contempt. Whenever conservatives in the United States were at odds—whether after the Goldwater debacle, or in the disputes around fusionism, or in the clash between paleo- and neoconservatives—colleges and universities became an easy rallying and unifying point. And thus, since Buckley, the conservative movement has produced its own campus literature, though of course it doesn't call itself that. It is written almost entirely by a particular type of author: a highly educated conservative who is disillusioned with the institution but who never really gets away from it either. They usually aren't on the faculty but work in a think tank or at a magazine where all they do is occupy themselves with universities.

It shouldn't come as a surprise that the PC panic and this form of campus literature experienced a renaissance after 2016—that is, at the moment when the Never Trumpers (who were often the neoconservatives of yesterday[8]) broke with the rest of the conservative movement. Anti-Trump dissidents like David Brooks and Trumpists can still agree on their hatred of Harvard.

The books that started the political correctness panic in the 1980s were fusionist in the broadest sense. It didn't matter whether they came from neoconservatives like Allan Bloom or from theocrats like Dinesh D'Souza: They were able to flatter contradictory constituencies simultaneously. Even the most incompatible forms of conservatism could appear coherent when reflected in the fun house mirror called college campus. More importantly, by the 1980s, liberal America was willing to believe their stories.

More than the neoconservative political project, the neoconservative generational experience of disaffection had become quite recognizable to a broader swath of the public. Neoconservatives had begun telling the story of their own dissidence from liberalism, their disillusionment from the university and elite media, and these narratives were available to others as a template. What made the neocons—who consisted, after all, of rather exclusive circles of East Coast literati and academics—effective as a template was the mediatization of their experience. In their stories of apostasy from liberal orthodoxy, they painted a picture in which millions could recognize their own aging process, their own changing priorities, their relationship with the next generation—and could see all of these reflected as politically informed and philosophically profound.

The World Bloom Made

When neoconservatism reached the general public in the 1980s, it posed a certain difficulty for traditional media. They didn't know how to classify these characters. There was a traditional conservative sound and habit, schooled in anti-communism, conspiracy thinking, and Christian fundamentalism. But when neoconservatives complained about the university, they complained in the tones of liberalism. They weren't outsiders convening hearings; if anything, their complaints were insider-y to a fault: Someone had been mean to them in the faculty lounge, a student group had torn down their posters, an activist had disrupted their class.

This shift is probably best encapsulated by Allan Bloom's 1987 bestseller *The Closing of the American Mind*. Unlike Reagan, Bloom was an expert on the university, as well as its near-lifelong inmate. He wrote that when he first saw the University of Chicago at sixteen, he "somehow sensed that I had discovered my life."[9] He would go on to receive both his BA and his PhD from Chicago, under the supervision of Leo Strauss. After stations in France, Germany, Yale, Cornell, and the University of Toronto, Bloom returned to the University of Chicago in 1979, where he taught on the prestigious Committee on Social Thought. Bloom met the novelist Saul Bellow, who convinced Bloom, who had hitherto mostly made an impression as a brilliant teacher and highly learned translator, to share his views on the university, the modern world, and the "soul of the students" in book form.

The Closing of the American Mind was published in 1987 and sold hundreds of thousands of copies. The book was translated into French as

L'Âme désarmée ("The Disarmed Soul," 1987), into German as *Der Niedergang des Amerikanischen Geistes* ("The Decline of the American Spirit," 1988), and into Dutch as *De gedachteloze generatie* ("The Thoughtless Generation," 1988). It made Bloom a frequent guest on talk shows, as much at home on Oprah's couch as lecturing to packed auditoriums in Europe. Both Bloom's book and its media echo would have a major impact on the virtual campus that Americans thought they knew so well.

Bloom's starting point was diametrically opposed to Buckley's *God and Man at Yale*. Buckley regarded the university's remoteness from society at large as its major problem; Bloom—as an ardent defender of the liberal arts, a teacher oriented towards pedagogic eros—diagnosed exactly the opposite. What Buckley feared—that Yale would turn Christian individualists into agnostic sociologists in four years—was essentially the seigneurial right Bloom was claiming for the university.

"I speak on behalf of a disadvantaged group," Bloom said in a 1987 interview on PBS: "A certain kind of student in America who has philosophical longings and I think is being deprived of the atmosphere" in which they could fulfill them.[10] This criticism applied to the natural sciences as much as to business schools, management courses, and early professionalization. But part of the "atmosphere" was also the identity politics pursued by feminists and African American students. This is what made Bloom's book so influential. On the one hand, Bloom was a defender of a university that even leftists could like—one where money wasn't everything, where there was time for precision and for daring thinking. And on the other hand, in April 1987, he could appear as a guest on Buckley's television show *Firing Line*; there he went on primarily about the "self-isolation" of Black students and about the "unnaturalness" of feminism. Here the "wrong" students were completely different; they weren't business majors but the English professors who no longer wanted to teach Shakespeare. In his book, Bloom wasn't necessarily more cautious, but he was more Socratic—he wanted to provoke, unsettle, challenge, and encourage better thinking. In the media circus surrounding *The Closing of the American Mind*, this subversive element dropped out almost entirely.

Bloom's book was received with interest in Europe, but in comparison with the attention German and French newspapers would later devote to campus anecdotes, it wasn't really understood as a critique of the university but rather as a broader critique of a trend in US culture. This changed over the next few years, as a whole wave of outrage bait flooded the American book market. These largely followed exactly Bloom's peculiar alchemy—English professor

Edward Jayne in 1991 referred to these works collectively as "the neoconservative view of the American university."[11] Reagan-appointed education officials in Washington had started things off. William Bennett spearheaded the collectively written report "To Reclaim a Legacy," which appeared in 1984; reports by Lynne Cheney (wife of the future vice president) appeared in 1988, "Humanities in America," and in 1992, "Telling the Truth." Bennett and Cheney had each headed the National Endowment for the Humanities. After Bloom came E. D. Hirsch's *Cultural Literacy*, Russell Jacoby's *The Last Intellectuals* (both 1987), Charles Sykes's *ProfScam* (1988), Peter Shaw's *The War Against the Intellect* and John Silber's *Straight Shooting* (both 1989), Page Smith's *Killing the Spirit* and Roger Kimball's *Tenured Radicals* (both 1990), and finally Dinesh D'Souza's *Illiberal Education* (1991).[12]

Sykes's *ProfScam* at one point quotes "dissident academic" David Berkman with the sentence: "The only thing we [academics] can't criticize or investigate is ourselves."[13] This sentence sounds more than a little bizarre amid a veritable deluge of academic and nonacademic investigations on that very topic, to say nothing about the periodicals solely devoted to it, from David Horowitz and Peter Collier's *Heterodoxy* to the NAS's (National Association of Scholars) *Academic Questions*. In those years, anyone, academic or not, who wanted to reach a maximum audience, didn't have to do much more than yell publicly about professors, students, or preferably both.

D'Souza's *Illiberal Education* was by far the most successful among this crop. D'Souza synthesized Buckley's and Bloom's perspectives, either not caring or not noticing that these were incompatible. For D'Souza, the university was elitist and egalitarian, relativistic and moralistic, too attached to tradition and overtaken by new fads. However, *Illiberal Education* became influential precisely because of this rhetorical trick. D'Souza's book simply did not decide between an elitist defense of the liberal arts à la Bloom (i.e., a university that, precisely because it is removed from the everyday problems of the polis, can most effectively shape tomorrow's elite) and the populism of *God and Man at Yale*. Through this trick, conservative university critics were suddenly able to position themselves as defenders of the liberal arts—Yes!—as defenders of liberalism as such. "In short, instead of liberal education, what American students are getting is its diametrical opposite: an education in closed-mindedness and intolerance."[14]

This merger gave the panic over political correctness in the United States its explosive power. With the highly artificial and selective gaze that books like D'Souza's cast on the university, liberals and neoconservatives could in principle be united. As Jayne wrote in 1991: "All in all, it is easy to agree with the diagnosis of neoconservatives that much is very wrong in academia, but it is more difficult to agree with either their explanation of its cause or most of the remedies they propose."[15] Contradictions, of course, remained. Was the university's autarky from broader society a problem or the solution? Was the decline of the American university a result of its fear of being elite or of its elitism? These contradictions could be papered over during the PC panic with two maneuvers: First, simply recite the old demands that Reagan had routinely placed on the university (although what the glut of neocon "academic jeremiads" demanded was never made clear), and second, never explain exactly how political correctness was to be countered. At their most facile, this crop of books instead indulged in a self-pitying and retrospective look towards an allegedly rosier past.

Too much precision could only do harm in this context—clear demands or simply a too-specific answer to the question of when things were supposedly still okay at American universities could only spoil the liberal-conservative unanimity. So instead of demanding things of the campus, the new university scolds were content to tell an endless string of apocryphal campus stories. Buckley's Yale stories were still reasonably motivated: "Yale" was in the title, and Buckley's dissatisfaction with the venerable university stemmed from his specific experience there and his particular biography. But since Reagan at the latest, a Manichaeism had snuck into the campus anecdote: In one corner you had the bizarre customs and political crackpottery of the cloistered inmates of academic institutions (who showed up in example after example, but weren't usually themselves consulted about any of this); in the other you had Reagan and his voters, who looked on with a mix of amusement, concern, malice, and anger. Campus anecdotes had become a genre suitable for the masses. And they could, as D'Souza proved, be offered in service of two diametrically opposed critiques of the educational system.

Unlike Bloom's book, D'Souza's was received in Europe not as a sobering look at the state of American society and thought, but rather as a source of anecdotes about the American university. Although *Illiberal Education* does not appear to have been widely translated, the book found a warm reception in the culture pages of newspapers and magazines—and with it the American campus had found its niche in European print media. The *Neue Zürcher Zeitung* gives us a good idea of this shift. When Bloom's book had come out in 1987, the newspaper had gone out of its way to note that "Bloom does not just present another book of criticism of the American educational system"; rather, "he takes on the whole evil spirit of the time."[16] The *Neue Zürcher Zeitung* thus had clarified for European readers that for Bloom university culture was not as important as the zeitgeist beyond the campus. This was why readers outside of the United States should care.

But four years later, in June 1991, the same paper devoted a whole page in its weekend edition to D'Souza's *Illiberal Education*—featuring a relatively balanced review and a long text, which mostly repeated D'Souza's main theses as facts. In October of the same year, a multi-page essay by Daniel Hofmann appeared in the same newspaper reciting D'Souza's examples and quotations.[17] In the time that elapsed between Bloom's book and D'Souza's, German-language readers had learned to care about the US campus environment for its own sake. What's more, the German readers did not seem to try to contextualize the American discourse but merely accurately reproduce it. In this strange hovering between facts and feelings and the tolerance for fiction, the second set of articles belonged recognizably to the same genre as D'Souza's book. The D'Souza of *Illiberal Education* was treated in Europe like the hero of a novel who exposes the madness of the campus world.

We Other Neoconservatives

The campus of the PC panic was a literary creation shaped by two generations of storytellers—from William F. Buckley and Ronald Reagan, through Allan Bloom and Dinesh D'Souza to Saul Bellow and Philip Roth. Which is not to say that everything they wrote on the subject was invented. But they did teach several generations of Americans what aspects of campus culture to pay attention to, how to talk about them, and how to infer broad national trends from quirky and insulated campus rituals and debates. This was especially true when it came to questions of diversity, race, and gender. Since the 1980s, that perspective—though born of specific generational and political configurations—has become broadly suffused throughout the political spectrum and available around the world. When it comes to campus stories, we've all become (or all have the option of becoming) neocons.

Caroline Fourest is a French journalist whose *Génération offensée* appeared in 2020 and was quickly translated into several languages—if you read Spanish, you can read *Generación ofendida*, in German *Generation Beleidigt*, in Italian *Generazione offesa*, and for the Danish speakers in your life there's *Generation krænket*. What doesn't exist is *The Offended Generation*, or whatever an English edition would be called. Which is too bad, as Fourest's story of an easily offended woke generation of leftists, who are obsessed with identity politics and constantly want to cancel all those who disagree with them, would fit in nicely in the United States. The book recapitulates a very particular and deeply recognizable way of observing the United States, and above all, of observing US campuses.

Consider a passage where Fourest describes how identity politics has transformed the university campus. Fourest recalls walking into a cafeteria at Hollins University in Roanoke, Virginia:

> The partition of the tables in the dining hall reminded me of the mess hall from the prison show *Orange Is the New Black*. The lesbians stayed with their own kind as much as the trans or the Black students. The Black students told me in confidence that they didn't dare express their opinions about the topic of homosexuality.[18]

This passage confidently entwines a pose of acute observation with a pronounced indifference to what is right in front of the writer. There is something remarkable about the clarity with which Fourest feels she was able to diagnose what ailed this American campus dining hall. That she was able to gain the confidence of "the Black students" to such an extent that the young women shared with the visitor from faraway France their true feelings about the topic of homosexuality that they didn't dare share with their classmates. I don't mean to ridicule Fourest's report—for all I know this really did happen—but I think any American reader would have spotted the fact that these tropes are by now exceedingly well-worn: We know the separate tables from high school movies and, well, *Orange Is the New Black*. We wince at a visitor who wanted to know about homophobia and thought, oh good, a table of Black people.

Fourest uses these clichés to indict a new (and American) spirit of wokeness that threatens to invade France, but they clearly come from the "just-so" campus literature of the political correctness panic. They emerge, for better or for worse, from the neoconservative gaze onto the college campus: a gaze that wants to be disappointed by what it sees, that seems excited at the idea that the university is in the grip of a crisis, that thrills at even the hint of liberal hypocrisy.

Compare a passage from *The Closing of the American Mind*, written a full thirty-two years before Fourest published her observation:

> [Students] pretend not to notice the segregated tables in dining halls where no white student would comfortably sit down. This is only one of the more visible aspects of a prevailing segregation in the real life of universities—which includes separation in housing and in areas of study, particularly noticeable in the paucity of blacks in theoretical sciences and humanities.[19]

A year after Bloom's book came out, Richard Bernstein, two years before he introduced readers of the *New York Times* to "the hegemony of the politically correct,"[20] wrote in the Gray Lady that at Berkeley "floors in the undergraduate library are, in practice, segregated by race, and rarely does a single white or two comfortably join a dining room table occupied mostly by blacks."[21]

Here is a passage from an essay by Dinesh D'Souza from 1991: "Students at several universities have remarked on the widespread phenomenon of 'black tables' at the university dining hall, where groups of African-American students insist on eating meals by themselves and regard white students who join them with undisguised antagonism."[22] In 1995, it was Peter Thiel's and David O. Sacks's turn to worry about how "many dining hall tables become self-segregated, as students eat their meals with others they have come to know from the same race."[23] In 1999, National Public Radio's *All Things Considered* reported from the cafeteria at Boston College, which "looks like many student dining halls across the country. African-American, Hispanic and Asian students are sitting at separate tables. A group of foreign students of different colors are sitting at another."[24]

Fourest emphasizes that she's presenting firsthand insights into the state of identity on American campuses. Yet those firsthand insights turn out to be tired observations identical to those made in decades' worth of campus reports. And they yield an identical diagnosis: Identity politics leads to division, to self-isolation, and to a betrayal of the liberal founding ethos of America's educational institutions.

Depending on who proffers the argument, this self-segregation is said to be politically dangerous (and thus remarkable in the first place) insofar as it stands for a general sorting tendency in society (as though the communities from which students come to college had not been segregated until Berkeley decided to institute an African American theme house). It is said to be dangerous for the students because the university does not adequately prepare them for "real life." And it is said (by Greg Lukianoff and Jonathan Haidt in their 2018 repeat of this thesis, *The Coddling of the American Mind*) to be detrimental to the cognitive development of young people because it does not adequately confront them with opinions and values that diverge from their own.[25]

Why does it matter that Fourest's report from a small Virginia university rehashes over thirty years of similar reports? One reason is that there is a hidden narrative to the description of the problem. These narratives imply that there really was a time when things were different, when college really was a place where you met all kinds of people from diverse backgrounds. Now, this has been lost, and with it our liberal democratic patrimony. Given this narrative, it is of course relevant that between Bloom's diagnosis and Fourest's report, thirty-three classes graduated from the offending American universities. (Bloom's description appears to refer to the 70s, so it may well be fifty classes.) The students Bloom was concerned about are now at least in their mid-sixties. The coddled young minds Haidt and Lukianoff were so worried about are at least thirty now, and probably your tax accountants or your doctors.

Secondly, it is important to emphasize that the available data suggest that the phenomenon described here is quite limited. It does exist, but its potency as an icon of campus dysfunction seems to derive from selective perception. As education scholar Julie J. Park has noted, there are plenty of all-white organizations on college campuses, some explicitly so (certain fraternities and sororities, for instance), others just for sociological reasons. These are self-segregated, visibly so—but we do not tend to see the self-segregation.[26] In 1994, a University of Michigan study surveyed 6,000 students at 390 colleges and found that non-white students were far more likely to eat, study, live, and go out on dates with people from other ethnic groups than white students.[27]

What makes the phenomenon of separate dining tables so enduring in the popular imagination is the immense significance texts like Bloom's and D'Souza's have attached to it. We have all been taught that it exists and what it means. The fact that Fourest's first association when walking into the Hollins dining hall is with a fictional analogue (the prison canteen in Netflix's *Orange Is the New Black*) is a telling slip: Her report understands itself as relaying immediate impressions, but it in fact regurgitates long-mediated and standardized images of American campuses.

While data may not bear out Fourest's observations, there is an almost visionary sharpness to them. The passage cited above presupposes that the university campus is eminently readable and eminently representative for society at large. Young people sort themselves according to ethnic groups when eating, and Bloom, Bernstein, D'Souza, Thiel, Sacks, and Fourest can, firstly, recognize this fact and, secondly, interpret it precisely. My own experience is that the lives of my students are fairly alien, and becoming more alien to me with each passing year as I get older and they stay—scandalously—the same age. The idea of walking onto any campus, striding into a dining hall, and offering a full-throated analysis of what is happening there strikes me as absurd.

The gaze cast by these observers on the university campus is a phantasmatic one, schooled in film and fiction, and only finds on campus what it projects on it in the first place. Fourest claims to have seen "the lesbians" sitting only with other lesbians, and "the trans" students with other trans people?[28] What does a lesbian table look like? How do you recognize a table full of transgender students? Hollins University had seventy-six African American students in 2020—approximately 8 percent of the student body. One wonders how an ethnically monolithic dining hall table could even be managed with such a small group. Most likely Fourest *did* notice some sorting among the students—anyone who has taught at a university will have noticed something along these lines. But the sharpness and the clarity of the divisions seem largely owed to the visitor's imagination.

In that imagination, the students' actions and choices unfold with the clarity of a religious revelation. Most interestingly, understanding them usually doesn't seem to require actually talking to the students. Neither Bloom nor D'Souza nor Fourest seems interested in why students should self-segregate. There are very good studies on this question, but they do not seem to matter to these authors.[29] After all, they know what they see and they know what it means. The gesture in these passages—almost forty years apart—is one of titanic confidence in not having to ask.

It is precisely this hallucinatory proximity that is intensified in the European reception: When he wrote *Closing of the American Mind*, Bloom had spent almost three-and-a-half decades as a denizen of the educational institutions he was describing. Fourest requires but a short reading tour for comparably sweeping judgments about "the" American university. European discourses on cultural appropriation, identity politics, and wokeness feed on a strange mixture of identification and exoticism: The United States is incredibly different from Europe, these observers invariably point out. But by the same token, they find this difference extremely easy to interpret.

Behind this mixture of exoticism and identification there is of course an identity politics all its own. Why is Fourest reporting from the Hollins University dining hall in the first place? Because she sees it as a harbinger of developments that are now inevitably coming to Europe—what French newspapers call "the woke wave" (*la vague woke*).[30] That is to say, the interest in the American campus is undergirded by (a) the notion that American cultural trends have a way of traveling the globe and dominating other cultures, and (b) the sense that these ideological imports from the United States threaten something homegrown and vulnerable. Fourest doesn't seem to notice the irony that her book is actually mostly a recycling of American anti-PC discourse. But conversely, the differentness of what is observed in the United States is primarily an incentive to articulate an alleged (French? European?) special path. At the end of

Fourest's American warning about the danger of fixating on one's own identity, Fourest calls for a return to European identity.

It's likely no coincidence that in 2020 Fourest would take us into a dining hall to observe specific identity groups separating from the other students, where the other students are imagined as somehow "normal" (white, cis, straight, etc.). In the 80s and 90s, the fear of political correctness in the United States emerged from an unease with US universities becoming less monocultural—not necessarily more diverse, mind you, but less full-throated in their endorsement of a dominant culture and identity. Especially in Europe, the cancel culture panic is oriented in a very similar way. Those stoking it may be, like Fourest, self-identified leftists, but the data points on which they fixate at US colleges, the things that scandalize them and those that pass without notice, are those of the neoconservative generation. As is their basic trick: using stories about the university to stage a drama of disaffection with, and perhaps even a defection from, positions on the Left.

FIVE

The Will to Melodrama

> **CARTOON CRIME:** The locksmith of the University of Northern Arizona was recently fired by Affirmative Action police in the administration for having a newspaper cartoon on his office wall. The cartoon pictured three dogs in an alley watching a cat, tail in the air, saunter in their direction. The caption: "She's looking for trouble."
>
> —THE EDITORS, *Heterodoxy* (October 1992)[1]

Here is how Dinesh D'Souza opens his chapter on "Tyranny of the Minority" in his 1991 book *Illiberal Education*:

> On February 9, 1988, Stephan Thernstrom, Winthrop Professor of history at Harvard University, opened the campus newspaper to read the headline, 'Students Criticize Class as Racially Insensitive."[2]

The story of Professor Thernstrom was a mainstay in the torrent of articles and books on the tyranny of political correctness that swept across the United States from 1991 onwards. And as the PC discourse spread around the world, Thernstrom's story, as told by D'Souza and others, spread along with it: an easily encapsulated, easily recycled example that required—or seemed to require—very little additional context.

It is important to note that the story of Stephan Thernstrom traveled as a story, prepackaged and polished by repeated use. Leaving aside the facts D'Souza presents for the moment, let us concentrate first on the kind of story he tells using these facts. Because D'Souza's lurid presentation of the incident is deeply indebted to the tropes of fiction. We follow Thernstrom as he unsuspectingly flips through the newspaper over his morning tea, sees the headline, and then discovers that the course mentioned is his "The Peopling of America." Three Black students had taken offense at several statements he had made in class about slavery and the Jim Crow era. They "took their complaints to Harvard's Committee on Race Relations, an administrative committee set up by President Derek Bok to arbitrate such matters." Thernstrom, we are told, was shocked: "I was absolutely stunned when I read this," D'Souza quotes him as saying. "None of the students had come to me with their complaints." Many of his Harvard colleagues were equally astonished because, as D'Souza tells us, Thernstrom had "a good reputation as a progressive."[3]

Thernstrom himself is quoted describing his treatment as "McCarthyism of the Left" and comparing himself to a rape victim. What is striking in hindsight is not the heated rhetoric (our present moment is hardly immune to heated rhetoric); it is that the framing that dominated the Thernstrom story exclusively belonged to Thernstrom. In dozens of accounts, we do not hear from the three students, we do not hear from President Bok, we do not hear from Thernstrom's allegedly astonished colleagues. In the rare instances that we do, they are trotted out dutifully to say their piece in articles that—from the word go—accept the story Thernstrom told of his cancellation.

More interestingly still, writers ran with the story Thernstrom told and further embellished it—usually in the direction of heightened literariness. In a breathless dramatization of the professor's plight at Harvard, John Taylor in *New York* magazine described a harried Thernstrom, an unassuming everyman whose world crumbles around him from one instant to the next:

"Racist."
    "Racist!"
    "The man is a racist!"
    "A *racist!*"
Such denunciations, hissed in tones of self-righteousness and contempt, vicious and vengeful, furious, smoking with hatred—such denunciations haunted Stephan Thernstrom for weeks. Whenever he walked through the campus that spring, down Harvard's brick paths, under the arched gates, past the fluttering elms, he found it hard not to imagine the pointing fingers, the whispers. Racist. There goes the *racist*. It was hellish, this persecution. Thernstrom couldn't sleep. His nerves were frayed, his temper raw. He was making his family miserable. And the worst thing was that he didn't know who was calling him a racist, or why.[4]

Even the venerable *New York Review of Books* ran with Thernstrom's story. In his review of *Illiberal Education*, C. Vann Woodward adopted D'Souza's account so closely that a few sentences found their way from the book into the essay almost unchanged.[5] Woodward's Thernstrom was D'Souza's Thernstrom. As was the version that Maarten Huygen reported in the Dutch *Handelsblad* in 1991, as an indicator that "minorities threaten academic freedom at American universities."[6]

The story also had an echo in European countries—a time-delayed one, but one that is all the more durable. The Thernstrom case, which American media fixated on for about four or five years, made appearances in non-US media for several more decades. In Switzerland's *Neue Zürcher Zeitung*, he appears in one of two anecdotes in a 1992 essay, both retold from *Illiberal Education*—D'Souza's "cool and controversial reportage on the politics of racism and sexism on the American campus."[7] As late as 1997, *Le Monde* felt it couldn't introduce the work of Cornel West and Henry Louis Gates without briefly reminding its readers about Harvard's "political correctness scandal."[8] And in 2002, Jan Fleischhauer was still citing "the case of Harvard historian Stephan Thernstrom" in *Der Spiegel* as proof that a "self-appointed political police" was running rampant on US campuses.[9]

Telling Lies

Fleischhauer described the Thernstrom episode as a "case." In doing so, he failed to notice that Thernstrom had come to him not as a set of facts, but as a story, and that each retelling over the years seemed to layer on more fictions rather than more facts. Just in case anyone misunderstood the meaning of this episode, D'Souza opened the chapter on Thernstrom with a quote from Kafka's novel *The Trial*: "Somebody must have been telling lies about Joseph K., for without having done anything wrong he was arrested one morning."[10] Fiction was thus never far from the Thernstrom story.

It should come as no surprise that much of this breathless melodrama was far from true. The historian Jon Wiener reconstructed the events in detail, using a research method that D'Souza and Taylor had not thought of: asking anyone other than Professor Thernstrom.[11] What he found was the following: The three students insisted that they *had* approached Thernstrom before speaking to the campus newspaper. In fact, they had approached him directly after the lecture they found objectionable. The students had *not* labeled Thernstrom racist. Wendi Grantham, one of the students, stated explicitly in a letter to the editor of the *Harvard Crimson*: "I do not charge that he is a racist."[12]

The story at the *Crimson* hadn't come about because the three students had gone to the newspaper. Rather, the newspaper had gotten wind of discontent in Thernstrom's class and had solicited opinions from African American students who were enrolled in the course. Several of those the *Crimson* had spoken to had indicated that the content of one of the lectures had made them uncomfortable. The sociologist Orlando Patterson, whom one of the three students had asked for advice, recalled trying to mediate: "I told her I was sure Steve wasn't a racist, and suggested she go talk to him about how she felt. She did. They had a long talk, shook hands, and that was the end of it. But the *Crimson* made it into a political issue."[13] The Committee on Race Relations D'Souza mentions was not a disciplinary body. As the *Crimson* explained at the time, students "discussed the problem" with a panel of faculty members and administrators, after which students agreed to "compose a written statement detailing their criticisms," which they would then send to Thernstrom.[14]

To be sure, you don't have to credit the account given by these people and institutions any more than Stephan Thernstrom's. But none of them ever appears in any of the articles that used the case as the linchpin for a grand narrative about political correctness run amok. And it is remarkable how much collective memory and how many inconvenient facts you have to actively ignore in order to embrace Thernstrom's version of events as fully as Taylor, D'Souza, and later Fleischhauer did. In order for Thernstrom to become the hero of this story, the community that surrounded him had to fall silent.

Opinions may differ on the questions underlying this episode. Are students right to raise objections about teaching material? To what extent should instructors take students' feelings into account in their teaching? At the end of the day, *l'affaire* Thernstrom was a marginal intermezzo at an Ivy campus. Its only real consequence, if you can call it that, was that a well-known professor in a fit of pique—either justified or unjustified, depending on whom you ask—decided to no longer offer a once-popular course. Not only were there no disciplinary consequences for Thernstrom, but there was not even a disciplinary procedure nor the possibility of one. There was an exchange of views, albeit a fairly contentious one, in the pages of the *Harvard Crimson* and the *Harvard Independent*. Perhaps the students were wrong and overreacting; or perhaps the professor had been too sensitive in responding to respectful, if critical, reactions to his teaching.

But I'm less concerned with the episode than with what became of it. D'Souza's Kafka reference already points to the fact that his Thernstrom is at heart the protagonist of a novel. Utterly unsuspectingly, he picks up the newspaper one morning and finds himself in an absurd situation not of his making. In John Taylor's article, he stalks the familiar pastures of the campus like a hunted man, as though a protagonist in an Ibsen play or in Arthur Miller's *Crucible*. In actual fact, no one had whispered about Thernstrom; he knew full well which students were unhappy with his lectures, and his sleep was unaffected too. So alarmed was Thernstrom by Taylor's poetic license that he later clarified that the opening scene in Taylor's article (including the whispers of "The man is a racist!") was pure fabrication.

This is not to debunk the anecdote but just to point out that, as it traveled, it was distended, always in the direction of greater literariness. This enrichment by literary devices and tropes clearly represents a form of complexity reduction—the story could travel so well because, in the telling, it became so seemingly obvious and straightforward. At the same time, this simplicity generated its own complexity down the line. The episode made its way into various publics over the span of decades and was drafted into a variety of causes. This is why I don't think it's worth debunking the story; instead, I think it is imperative to understand the uses to which it was put. The Legend of Stephan Thernstrom circulated alongside a whole genre of campus anecdotes, which collectively taught people how to think about facts, details, and interpretations, and the relationship among the three, when passing judgment on campus politics.

D'Souza and Taylor both go out of their way to present Thernstrom as a hapless everyman. This is not because they necessarily have to, but probably simply in deference to fictional conventions. In spite of a left-wing past, by 1988 Stephan Thernstrom was valued as an influential conservative voice. His wife, the social scientist Abigail Thernstrom, was an early conservative critic of affirmative action and in 1987 had published a critique of the Voting Rights Act (*Whose Votes Count? Affirmative Action and Minority Voting Rights*), which was, according to Adam Shatz, "a virtual bible among conservative jurists."[15] A few years after the imbroglio at Harvard, the Thernstroms made news as the joint authors of *America in Black and White*, published in 1997. That same year they were part of a group of prominent conservative intellectuals invited to several events at the White House by President Bill Clinton in an attempt at bipartisanship.

In *America in Black and White*, the Thernstroms claimed that neither government programs nor the civil rights movement had really helped advance the lot of African Americans. But thanks to the aftereffects of World War II, the economic boom, and a steady decline in white racism in the 1950s, the Black population was now (in 1997, for those playing along at home) well-off enough to make redress measures, such as affirmative action, unnecessary. Since the 1960s, the Thernstroms argued, there had been a change in "the balance of power in racial confrontations"; "black anger" now found its complement in "white surrender."[16] Even in the 1990s, claiming that affirmative action was no longer necessary and that "black anger" was the main obstacle to racial harmony in the United States wasn't generally considered a left-wing position. In her 2020 obituary in the *New York Times,* Abigail Thernstrom was termed as a "neoconservative."[17] Stephan described himself that way in an interview with Todd Gitlin—in 1991.[18]

Not—as Jerry Seinfeld would say—that there is anything wrong with that. But why was D'Souza so dead set on presenting these garden variety neocons as "progressives"? Why did John Taylor's article in *New York* magazine likewise emphasize that Thernstrom was "mainstream"? Their everyman, who wakes up one morning to find his good name tarnished in the campus newspaper, wasn't allowed to be what he quite clearly was in real life—a conservative. The reason why has to do with narrative more than political logic. D'Souza, for one, wanted to emphasize the irony of the situation, a progressive being attacked by other progressives. If even a Stephan Thernstrom isn't safe, who is?

But, just as in later tales about political correctness and contemporary ones about cancel culture, D'Souza's hero is supposed to be purely reactive. Like Franz Kafka's Josef K., but also like Kingsley Amis's Jim Dixon and later Philip Roth's Coleman Silk, he is a fictional character to whom things just sort of happen. As Saul Bellow describes the associate professor Artur Sammler in *Mr. Sammler's Planet,* he is a "registrar of madness."[19] Whatever rhetorical and affective excesses he is himself guilty of, they are in truth desperate reactions to the madness others deposit on his doorstep. If D'Souza had decided to position Thernstrom correctly politically and socially, he would have had to admit that, in this case, a person who thought that the defining problem of race relations in the 1980s was "white surrender" to "black anger" had perhaps responded disproportionately to an expression of the same. Thernstrom's passivity is a literary motif with a political dimension.

As literary scholar Elaine Showalter notes in her book on campus novels, this lethargy is one big difference between the professors we meet in fiction and the ones we meet in a faculty lounge: "Fictional professors do not imitate their real brethren in one crucial detail: seeking legal counsel."[20] Go through Showalter's specimen, and you indeed notice this curious pattern: Professor David Lurie in J. M. Coetzee's *Disgrace* (published 1999) refuses to dispel the false allegations against him. Professor Ted Swenson in Francine Prose's 2000 novel

The Blue Angel would rather drink himself into a stupor than prepare for a vital hearing that will decide his future. Coleman Silk in Philip Roth's *The Human Stain*, also from 2000, quits in anger rather than refute the charges against him. And in Jonathan Franzen's 2001 novel *The Corrections*, Chip Lambert prefers writing an impenetrable screenplay to defending himself against the (at least half-false) allegations against him.

Showalter suggests that fictional professors do not take disciplinary measures seriously, because college disciplinary processes aren't particularly dramatic and do not lend themselves to the plot of a good novel. But perhaps there is more to it than that: Accused academics in American fiction (and the authors who tell their stories) seem to conceive of the banal and low-stakes grind of disciplinary proceedings almost as something metaphysical—the accusation calls their entire existence into question. They have to justify far more than an incautious word or an ill-advised affair; they have to give an accounting of the totality of their lives. In real administrative procedures, of course, the stakes are usually far more mundane—a few hearings, probably resulting in mandatory training, or, at worst, a strictly worded warning from the dean—so focusing on them would deflate things dramatically.

The other reason D'Souza's version of Thernstrom has to be a horrified progressive rather than a conservative is that this version of Stephan Thernstrom isn't supposed to think like this from the start; rather, he has to *learn* the evils of campus radicalism, of "black anger," over the course of his story. It constitutes, in a sense, the moral of the story. Whether it's via Allan Bloom at Cornell in the 1960s, Philip Roth at Princeton in the 1970s, or Stephan Thernstrom at Harvard in the 1980s, we reliably meet the figure of the professor accused of racism or sexism by nameless and faceless agitators. And the narrative invariably presents his story as a lesson in something that was, in fact, its premise. Through the tales of life-long lefties hauled before brutal latter-day struggle sessions, long-held prejudices are given the sheen of hard-earned life experience.

Stories like the Thernstroms'—of how they slowly found their way from Left to Right— abounded in those years, as neoconservatism gained increasing traction on American campuses and as the media began to notice. Indeed, it is striking that many who reviewed Bloom's and D'Souza's books positively in the liberal press were already well on their way along the same path. C. Vann Woodward, for example, originally specialized in the history of progressive America, but was, by the 1980s, notable mostly for diatribes against communist professors and his membership in the conservative National Association of Scholars.

In their own telling, the moment at which the Thernstroms converted to conservativism had a funny way of adjusting to fit the narrative at hand. They emphasized their left-wing roots and acted as if their conversion had been quite rapid. In a profile in the *New York Times* in 1998, the two are described as "affirmative action's unlikely foes" because, among other things, Abigail attended an "elementary school for children of a leftist community in Croton-on-Hudson, N.Y.," "sang songs with Pete Seeger," and voted for George McGovern for president in 1972.[21] The Thernstroms were fond of telling interviewers about when exactly they had first voted for a Republican for president, although the date was never the same. The 1998 profile of the Thernstroms' says the two "acknowledge that in recent years they voted for Republican Presidential candidates for the first time in their lives—Stephan in 1992, Abigail in 1996."[22] Stephan Thernstrom told Adam Shatz in 2001 that he had first voted for a Republican presidential candidate in 1988, and a 2020 obituary for Abigail claims that she had voted for a Republican for the first time in 1992.[23] The legend of the Thernstroms drew on the fact that they had supposedly been liberals until just before the tape started rolling on their current interview and that only very recent events had finally turned them into conservatives.

Speech Codes

Once upon a time, students at the University of Illinois, were required to attend a morning service in the university chapel, listen to a faculty member read "a portion of the New Testament," "repeat the Lord's Prayer," and "sing religious hymns." A student named Foster North objected to this practice; the university (a state institution) expelled him. North sued, but in March 1891 the college prevailed before the Illinois Supreme Court.[24] Until the late 1960s, a decision like the one for the University of Illinois was regarded as constitutional, due to a doctrine called *in loco parentis*. The university, the reasoning went, related to the students as parents relate to their children. As the Illinois Supreme Court wrote in its judgment against North, the university asserted that it "had the lawful right to adopt all reasonable rules and regulations for the government of the university, and in pursuance of that right did adopt the rule in question."[25]

The rules universities could frame by invoking *in loco parentis* were almost limitless and frequently bizarre. Until 1970 women students at Whitman College in Walla Walla, Washington, were forbidden from "spend[ing] the night in a motel or hotel without special permission from their parents or college officials."[26] Other colleges banned jeans, Sunday dancing, blasphemy—or political activities. Stanford University mandated "quad attire" (no pants) for female students on its main quad well into the 1960s.

The beginning of the end of *in loco parentis* came with the civil rights movement in the 1960s. The US Supreme Court ruled in 1961 that a public institution could not expel students for taking part in a protest. The Free Speech Movement in Berkeley, which Ronald Reagan demonized in his speech at the Cow Palace, was in part an attempt to counter the paternalism of *in loco parentis*. The notion that American universities are, or once were, precincts of perfect freedom of expression that have since lost their way relies on a considerable amnesia. And bizarrely, it wasn't until after the abolition of *in loco parentis*, Sunday dancing bans, and quad attire—roughly since the 1970s—that public discourse in the United States became fixated on supposed threats to free speech on campus.

On February 18, 1988, about a week after the article about Stephan Thernstrom appeared in the *Harvard Crimson* and a day after Wendi Grantham's letter became public, Fred Jewett, then dean of Harvard College, published an open letter to the students and the professors. Among other things, he wrote: "While such incidents may not require formal college discipline, they should elicit from appropriate college officials and from the community warnings and clear messages about the inappropriateness and insensitivity of such behavior."[27]

Jewett later told Jon Wiener that the open letter was not connected to Thernstrom (whom the letter indeed did not mention). "As I recall, it was distributed in registration envelopes at beginning of term, a couple of weeks before anything about Thernstrom became news."[28] You can doubt the wisdom of Jewett's letter, but again it is important to see what he said versus what D'Souza made of it. Even if, as D'Souza assumed, the sentence quoted above referred to Thernstrom, Jewett had been very clear that he was talking about speech that might (and perhaps should) arouse objections but that had no disciplinary relevance. Here's how D'Souza parsed the letter: "In short, far from coming to his defense, Jewett appeared to give full administrative sanction to the charges against Thernstrom."[29] Fred Jewett expressly bracketed disciplinary processes. D'Souza put them right back in.

D'Souza—not just in the case of Stephan Thernstrom—compulsively cast incidents that would be best categorized as differences of opinion in language that suggested that they were legalistic processes. Thernstrom defended his practice of reading from the journals of southern plantation owners. D'Souza renders this fact as "he pleaded guilty to the charge of quoting from Southern plantation journals."[30] The students' letter of complaint was an "accusation."[31] Even the *Crimson* lapsed into this reinterpretation from time to time: "Thernstrom waits for charges" was one headline in the university newspaper about a month after the first Thernstrom article.[32] What he was actually waiting for wasn't an indictment from the university. The university committee had asked the students for a more detailed explanation of their criticism, which would then be forwarded to the professor. Thernstrom was waiting for that letter. In the latter *Crimson* article, Thernstrom further confused matters by using the phrase "given the seriousness of the charges"—a phrase that you are most likely to hear at bail hearings.

It is striking how automatically campus anecdotes drift into the vocabulary of the legal system. Harvard had asked the students to document their problems with Thernstrom in order to then mediate between the two parties—a strategy that seems to have been consistently torpedoed by the fact that both the professor and the students were highly intelligent, articulate, convinced of their cause, and kept running to the *Crimson* to make statement after statement. The university administration didn't comment in those same articles, which left the field to Thernstrom's framing, especially as far as the semantics were concerned.

Portraying the inner workings of a university through judicial metaphors isn't necessarily nefarious. Above all, it is about complexity reduction. The campus ecosystem is contradictory, fragmented, opaque; our judiciary vocabulary, by contrast, is good at turning messy lived reality into easily digestible fact patterns. So if D'Souza and others presented Thernstrom as the protagonist of a bildungsroman, a comedy of manners, or a fable of subversion, many texts also presented him in another well-worn narrative—a victim of a miscarriage of justice. Today still, using the language of the justice system can inflate unimportant campus anecdotes into great dramas. It is also almost magically suited to blurring the specifics of the campus environment, leaving behind only grand principles: the First Amendment, academic freedom, individualism, conformity, and something called "the American mind," which is hard to describe but which can be closed, coddled, and—canceled.

Historically, this became very clear in the panic around "speech codes": language rules against harmful or hurtful speech. Many universities, wrote the author Jonathan Rauch in his 1993 book *Kindly Inquisitors*, "are doing exactly what a university, of all institutions, should not do: defining offensive speech as quasi-violent behavior, and treating it accordingly."[33] The debate about such supposed speech codes ran alongside the panic around political correctness, though it never broke through in the mainstream the way PC did. But it certainly got a lot of press. *Time* magazine famously claimed that "nowhere is the First Amendment more imperiled than on college campuses."[34] And Lynne Cheney's 1992 report "Telling the Truth" opened with the following quote from Yale President Benno Schmidt: "The most serious problems of freedom of expression in our society today exist on our campuses."[35] This fear found its expression in legislation. A Collegiate Speech Protection Act was proposed in Congress, but it never passed. California, on the other hand, enacted the Leonard Law in 1992, which prohibits private universities from punishing students for statements protected by the First Amendment. It (of course) exempted religious institutions.

The problem, however, was that the whole debate was based on a deliberate distortion of university practices. The debate assumed that universities had let their students and professors say all sorts of things for centuries and now were suddenly imposing narrow limits on campus discourse—all in the name of feminism and anti-racism. As we have seen, the first part of that story is incorrect—US universities have sought to curtail campus speech for centuries, and in far more draconian ways than today. But the second part of it also turns out to be bunk. As John K. Wilson wrote in 1997:

> No one really knows how many colleges have speech codes for the simple
> reason that no one has ever defined what a speech code is. If a speech code
> means that colleges have the authority to punish students for certain verbal
> expressions that are threatening or abusive or offensive, then every college
> has a speech code and always has had one.[36]

So what gave rise to the impression that such codes were suddenly appearing and were a relative novelty at universities? Essentially, one Herculean effort to impose differences where they didn't exist. There were plenty of traditional rules on the books, and they were tacitly accepted as irrelevant or baked in; they didn't seem to merit reflection or media attention, but were simply part of how colleges had always run. Meanwhile any attempt to clarify or change existing rules was treated like the passage of laws. Many of the colleges that we read about in articles from the 1980s had not really created speech codes so much as simply rewritten outdated codes of conduct. Out were the arcane holdovers of *in loco parentis*; in came rules that brought the university into compliance with Title IX.

Many of the old rules, and many of the new ones, were never enforced. But the criticism of the new speech codes in the media and in conservative legal circles very often reverted to what-if scenarios: what *could* be captured, what *might* be prohibited, who *might* be ensnared, what *might* no longer be sayable. This mode of storytelling became a mainstay of the various college panics— from David Sacks and Peter Thiel warning that students could get expelled for using the "n-word"[37]; to psychologist Jordan Peterson, who rose to prominence in 2016 by claiming a new law in Ontario, Canada would "elevate into hate speech" his misgendering of students;[38] all the way to the winter of 2022, when media worldwide ran with the story that Stanford University would punish students or faculty for using the word "American."[39]

Certainly the attempts to adapt the old rules of conduct to the requirements of a modern university (and the end of *in loco parentis*) were not without problems—some of the updates were ridiculous, ham-handed, or ill-considered. Nevertheless, from the late 1980s and onward, media reports deliberately misunderstood the processes of decision-making and conflict resolution at universities. Once again, the public conjured up a virtual campus, not unlike Reagan's. Only in this case it was not modeled on a hippie commune, but rather was something like a Bizarro World version of the American judicial system.

Many of the most commonly cited excessive rules on colleges campuses were withdrawn immediately by the colleges themselves, quashed by the courts, or were drafts that were never implemented. In the folklore surrounding political correctness, however, they continued to be treated as actually existing and applied regulation. What's more, as Wilson writes, critics did not distinguish between pronouncements of values embraced by the university and university requirements for students.[40] Just because a college described a particular word as hurtful did not mean that its use would result in disciplinary action. And finally, critics were happy to fudge who exactly counted as "the university" that "prohibited" or "mandated" certain kinds of speech.

The conservative intellectual Roger Kimball wrote about one such regulation in *Tenured Radicals*:

> At Smith College, a brochure is distributed to incoming students rehearsing a long list of politically incorrect attitudes and prejudices that will not be tolerated, including the sin of "lookism", i.e., the prejudice of believing that some people are more attractive than others.[41]

Notice the expression "at Smith College." It looks innocent enough, but it's actually part of an elaborate shell game. In the fall of 1990, the Smith Office of Student Affairs had put out a pamphlet, intended as a guide for first-semester students. This pamphlet was Kimball's source.

An American university consists of a huge number of deans offices, vice provosts, countless student groups, a mad thicket of campus offices and proliferating titles, in which even locals easily lose their way. All these offices are constantly busy generating emails, memos, and guides; planning activities; inviting speakers and sometimes uninviting them too. They constitute a cacophony of competing voices, some committed to pedagogy, some to harmonious coexistence, some to reducing the legal exposure of the university, yet others to compliance with federal standards. That some of the endless stream of text spewed forth by these hundreds of thousands of outlets will occasionally contain nonsense isn't that surprising. That critics manage to pick out and distill—from this mad tangle of opinions, guides, and policies—a single rule, admonition, or metaphor and then present it as though it were to be understood as a legal mandate would be impressive if it didn't also distort reality so badly.

In anecdotes about political correctness, there was always the moment when the real university—with its various more or less well-functioning departments, more or less overburdened administrators, more or less independently acting student groups—disappears and suddenly "the" university emerges as a single monolithic entity. "The" university says, forbids, or commands. "The" university demands, dictates, defines. This, too, is a form of fictionality, a kind of user interface that students like to refer to just as much as the press and politicians. As with the equating of disciplinary procedures on campus with legal processes, this vagueness serves two purposes: It brings highly multifarious, local, and parochial events into some kind of overall gestalt; and it more clearly structures the campus narrative.

To use the Smith example, the staff of the Office of Student Affairs, in the words of Smith College's current (at this writing) website, "helps students access a variety of services, programs, and activities."[42] This isn't "the" university, this isn't the president, the faculty senate, the dean of students. If we want to be glib, these folks are—please don't cancel me—pedagogically sophisticated camp counselors. Their words carry about as much legal force as that of the assistant university librarian. Kimball's book reframes a well-meaning and overeager suggestion as a commandment handed down by the university administration that made "lookism" a punishable offense. Similarly, who was behind Stanford's supposed prohibition of the word "American"? Not the president, not the provost, not the faculty senate: It was the IT department that had drawn up a list of *possible* terms to avoid or to replace on official Stanford websites.

Speech codes were and remain therefore unreliable indicators for the actual state of freedom of expression at American colleges and universities. Writers drew on them because through them they could give the college campus and its conflicts the flavor of the courtroom. At the same time, colleges do talk about "hearings" and "counsel," seemingly inviting the inaccurate comparisons to the legal system. Universities, too, like to pretend that these are mini-trials rather than simple disciplinary and mediation processes. The critique of supposed speech codes could fall back on a folkloric understanding of the justice system honed by decades of television series from *Perry Mason* to *Law & Order*.

One thing that has made this fixation on speech codes so potent politically is that there is no way to get the speech question right: If universities are seen restricting speech, they will come under fire for illiberalism; if universities are seen as not restricting speech enough, they will come under fire for moral relativism. In early December 2023, the US House of Representatives held hearings with the presidents of three universities—Harvard, Penn, and MIT—about their efforts to combat antisemitism on their campuses. The hearings went poorly. Two out of the three presidents stepped down, one a day later; the other, Harvard's Claudine Gay, a few weeks after the hearing—after national media, above all the *New York Times*, had run dozens of articles either directly critical of her or mostly about people critical of her. The hearings themselves were long, but the clip that attained infamy featured the three presidents unable to say whether a "call for genocide of Jews" would run counter to their anti-harassment policies. Their answer, notoriously, was "it depends"—an "it depends" that, as Congressman Ritchie Torres put it, showed "that our college campuses are lacking in moral common sense."[43]

You may think the answer "it depends" is unsatisfactory, that it substitutes technocratic legalese for a moral compass. But there are two things to note about this answer. First—and most obviously—the answer is correct. The kinds of slogans that Representative Elise Stefanik, who was running the hearings, had offered up might indeed run counter to a university's code of conduct—something that would have to be determined with a hearing and a fairly involved disciplinary process that would almost certainly come to involve the actual legal system. This frustrates many within the academy, but it ought not to have frustrated the politicians questioning the presidents—for they helped make this a reality.

After all—and perhaps less obviously—the reason "it depends" is the right answer is that for decades now universities have bent over backwards to accommodate themselves to the periodic freak-outs over free speech controversies on their campuses. The lax rules about speech have nothing to do with antisemitism, but rather with the wide berth universities are—sometimes by law—required to give to student speech. Private universities do not have to permit all speech that conforms to the First Amendment, but any time they (or, at least, famous, nonreligious, and supposedly left-leaning ones) deviate from it, they can be assured of a torrent of public opprobrium. In California, they are explicitly barred from putting any daylight between their own speech policies and the First Amendment. Congressman Kevin Kiley, who suggested that Claudine Gay, the soon-to-resign president of Harvard, was hedging on what speech was punishable on her campus because she regarded "the forces of antisemitism" as a "constituency," had it exactly backwards.[44] It was because of people like Kevin Kiley. After years of charging universities with moral rigorism, colleges and universities had positioned themselves as always erring on the side of free speech. But the same actors who had excoriated them for their censoriousness then turned around and chided them for their lack of censoriousness.

What remains in each case is the moral fervor. Faced with campuses muddling through competing impulses and competing stakeholders, faced with administrators who aren't actually trained to be administrators, the one thing no one seems to be able to see is the haplessness, the myopia, and the timidity of these places. And anyone who points this out is accused of making excuses. In Reagan's successful campaign against Berkeley, those who understood the university well enough to see the wobbly and tendentious campus environment as it really was were insiders and were not usually believed. Distance from the campus world, on the other hand, came to be seen as a sign of moral clarity in assessing developments there. Whether Kiley or Stefanik, whether Fourest or Reagan, whether Taylor or D'Souza, whether David Horowitz or Philip Roth— audiences in the United States and beyond have been taught collectively not to look too closely and not to ask precise questions about campus controversies; instead they identify broad strokes and a looming danger. They zoom out impatiently from the most small-bore anecdotes to supposed global threats to the Enlightenment and democracy.

For all these reasons, there is no contradiction in having attended an American university and still believing stories like D'Souza's. Although the number of people getting to know college as it is today may be greater than comparable numbers forty or seventy years ago, there will of course always be more and more Americans who see the institution in the rearview mirror. At that point, the generalized nostalgia of the aging meets a well-stocked cultural reservoir of prejudices about supposedly ever-declining standards, lower quality of teaching, the various faults of "millennials" or whatever generation we are worrying about this week. The last forty years have managed to transform the American view of college (and the international adaptation of this view) into a wholesale triumph of nostalgic retrospection, of mediated perception. In short, an extraordinary triumph of the virtual campus.

Perhaps it was inevitable, then, that a group that can hardly be farther, at least in distance, from the American college campus felt a particular compulsion to opine on it: European journalists, intellectuals, and politicians. In a language game where local knowledge makes you suspect, and where the more abstract your principles and the broader your strokes the more seriously you're taken, campus stories became immensely successful export items. French, German, Spanish, and Italian observers have convinced themselves that they understand these campuses, these episodes, even though all of them have trickled into the culture and opinion pages through an absurd game of telephone.

On a Supposed Right to Live with Fictions

Joachim Gauck, a former Lutheran pastor and East German dissident, was president of Germany from 2012 to 2017. The German presidency is a largely ceremonial post, and German presidents have traditionally sought to offset this constitutional nullity by giving vague national pep talks about the zeitgeist. This made it perhaps inevitable that at some point a German president should gravitate towards worrying about political correctness and the increasing narrowness of what is sayable in public discourse. And of course, it was just as inevitable that he would do it using an example from an American campus. Here is a passage from Gauck's book on tolerance (written in 2019, after he had left the presidency):

> Political correctness has all too often been associated with a certain pitilessness. Not just traditionalists and conservatives complained about this, so did liberals. In his novel *The Human Stain*, Philip Roth describes a respected professor of literature who is deprived of his entire life's work because of one thoughtless statement. He had flippantly described two female students who were regularly absent from his lectures as "dark figures who shy away from the seminar light." What the professor hadn't noticed was that the students were black; his ironic statement was interpreted as racism. Humiliating hearings followed, and the professor finally gave up in exasperation. Not only did he lose his job, he also lost his wife. The literature professor was convinced that she had died of a stroke as a result of him being hounded.[45]

Outside of the United States, the discourse on political correctness or cancel culture at American colleges nearly always includes the fate of Coleman Silk (the character in Roth's novel). Since the cancel culture panic came to Europe in 2019, Silk has found his star once again ascendant in the French and German press. What Gauck does with the story is instructive, because it gets at the heart of the strange virtuality of the American campus in European discourse, how it haunts discussions on political correctness and cancel culture: Because there is something bizarre in the former president seriously using a fictional text as a straightforward illustration of American culture. The curious decision to render the novel's plot in the past tense, perfect, and past perfect is not owed to my translation, but is in the original. It is almost as though Coleman Silk were a real person and as though the "dark figures" incident (it's the German rendition of the word "spooks" in Roth's novel) actually happened.

Gauck is by no means alone in this strange interweaving of fact and fiction. The American Studies professor Claudia Franziska Brühwiller wrote in the Swiss *Neue Zürcher Zeitung*: "In his novel *The Human Stain*, US author Philip Roth shudders at the 'spirit of branding.'" Today (that is, in 2021), "a kindred spirit of branding haunts those who wield the spears of the so-called cancel culture and thereby endanger their own goals."[46] In *Le Figaro*, the recently deceased political scientist Laurent Bouvet said, "Strictly speaking, this novel from 2000 is not visionary, because it basically only says what has been happening in American universities, especially in the literature and humanities faculties, for years."[47] And *La Tercera* in Chile opened an essay about the "Harper's Letter"[48] about the ravages of cancel culture with a novelistic retelling of how "in the second semester of 1998, Prof. Coleman Silk fell in disgrace."[49]

The Human Stain is thus invoked quite explicitly as a cancel culture anecdote *avant la lettre*, proof of the existence and danger of witch hunts on American campuses. The fact that it is a novel is not dismissed entirely but never seems to matter. Much like David Mamet's proto-#MeToo play *Oleanna*, it's a 1990s artifact that, in the hands of contemporary writers, has a funny way of always seeming to herald what is happening at the precise moment they're writing.

But the entwinement of fact and fiction in *The Human Stain* is more complicated than one might think. Roth's narrator positions the novel as a commentary on the "ecstasy of sanctimony"[50] that he sees sweeping American politics in the late 1990s. However, after the book was published, Roth began to emphasize that his novel was in fact based on a true story that happened to his friend, the sociologist Melvin Tumin, at Princeton University. Behind the fictional campus anecdote was a real one. In 2012 Roth wrote an "open letter to Wikipedia" (which the *New Yorker* reprinted), requesting a correction to the entry for his novel in the online encyclopedia. Wikipedia (or rather someone editing it) had claimed that Roth had modeled Coleman Silk on literary critic Anatole Broyard. In truth, Roth explained, Silk's story was inspired by "an unhappy event" in Tumin's life. "One day in the fall of 1985," Roth claimed, Tumin made that faux pas with the "spooks." "A witch hunt ensued during the following months," Roth went on, "from which Professor Tumin—rather like Professor Silk in 'The Human Stain'—emerged blameless but only after he had to provide a number of lengthy depositions declaring himself innocent of the charge of hate speech."[51]

Roth's account claims to be factual and is indeed supported by facts. Nevertheless, the novelist seems to not be able to help himself—from the "one day" to the "witch hunt" and the insistent juridical metaphors, he lapses into fictive flourishes in recounting what are supposed to be the facts *behind* the fiction. What we know is this: Roth and Tumin knew each other very well. Copies of several pieces of correspondence related to the "spooks" episode are in Philip Roth's estate. However, they also make clear that Roth's retelling in his open letter omits some details. According to Roth's biographer, the two students had not only complained about the "spooks" remark, but also about the fact that Tumin had suggested to them in a condescending manner that they might want to drop his course. So it wasn't just about a single misunderstood word. The "witch hunt" described by Roth doesn't seem to have gone very far either. The documents in Roth's possession attest (at least in the description of his biographer) to the university's concern for impartiality. It is unclear whether there was ever any threat of actual consequences. Finally, in Roth's attempt to make sure Wikipedia got the facts right, he got the decade wrong. According to Roth's documents (again, assuming his biographer is correct), the episode occurred in 1976, not 1985.

To be sure, there is absolutely nothing wrong with a novelist transforming a real event into a literary work. It is interesting, however, that Roth later became so keen to emphasize the real events that informed the fiction. Sometime between the writing of the book and the 2012 open letter, Roth seems to have changed his mind about whether what he described in *The Human Stain* represented an invariant of American life or whether it was diagnosing a specific zeitgeist. This does not affect the novel as novel, but it does affect the book's role as evidence, in particular the kind of evidence that readers like Gauck and Bouvet see in it.

In the last years of his life, Roth repeatedly positioned his literary work as a description of an extra-literary phenomenon. In an interview with *Le Figaro* in 2012, Roth said the novel was "not at all polemical about political correctness. It is representative."[52] But "representative" of what? What sort of a university is one representing in a factual account from 2012, looking back on a book from the year 2000, which draws on events purportedly from 1985 but that actually transpired in 1976? The factual basis for the diagnosis recedes ever further into the past and is only supposed to be more incisive for it.

If we read—as Roth does in later interviews—*The Human Stain* as a campus anecdote, the temporality of its central conceit changes. These kinds of anecdotes matter because they are supposedly signs of the times, are indications of what is to come, are symptoms of the present. In this respect it is astonishing that Roth's anecdote has, so to speak, no present. It is of course absolutely understandable that Roth was no longer precise about the facts of the episode after so many years. Indeed, in his novels, this is frequently Roth's narrative principle. In an interview with David Remnick, editor in chief of the *New Yorker*, Roth said in 2003: "And I thought, treat '98 as though it were '48, treat '98 as though it were '68. You see? See it, if you can, as history."[53]

Strange, then, that an episode that is supposed to afford a sharp diagnosis of a specific historical moment flitters unsteadily through the decades and somehow always fits as a sign of whatever time we choose. Does the novel really chronicle, as Showalter writes, "a heroic act of civil disobedience in the face of political correctness"?[54] Or is it perhaps rather an indication that the college campus has long been an intense pressure cooker with a wide range of quirky personalities, young ones and old ones, whose meeting releases a certain nervous energy?

Somewhere in the transition between literary exploration and political diagnosis lies a danger zone. When someone like Bouvet pretends that Roth's novel constitutes political analysis in literary guise, when Roth insists that the central story in *The Human Stain* happened to Melvin Tumin just as described, then the issue is not what literature is allowed to do, but rather what it means to teach an audience that it doesn't matter whether a certain type of event is real or fictional. We live with the aftereffects of this enormous indifference, which Bill Buckley and Ronald Reagan exploited as much as Allan Bloom and Dinesh D'Souza. We persuaded ourselves, and let ourselves be persuaded, that when it comes to American universities and their ways, the fact that an assertion is incorrect does not detract from the ambitious diagnosis based on it.

Roth demonstrates for readers (one almost wants to say for *users*) of this genre how to deal with events like those that happened to Tumin. This paraliterary pedagogy is intended to appeal to an audience who (like most Americans who read books by Philip Roth and Allan Bloom) may have gone to college but (again, like most Americans who read Philip Roth and Allan Bloom) probably left the campus a while ago. More to the point, these readers are probably learning about the campus of their moment mostly via their children, who are becoming increasingly alien to them. The fact that these readers, despite all the obvious fictionalization, attach more validity to the stories of a Philip Roth than to the stories of their own children is less an inconsistency than the point of the exercise. After all, only then can college once again be the arena in which their generation's life experiences (this time in the guise of the aging professor) are negotiated. And just like that, it is once again their generation and its experiences that are the focus of the campus stories rather than—the horror!—the lived reality of a new one.

SIX

The Techniques of a Panic

Anecdote, Subscription, Essayism

But joking isn't allowed! Even the most harmless, lighthearted remarks can lead to virulent denunciations. In October, Roderick Nash, a professor at the University of California at Santa Barbara, pointed out during a lecture on environmental ethics that there is a movement to start referring to pets as animal companions. (Apparently, domesticated animals are offended by the word *pet*.) Nash then made some sort of off-the-cuff observation about how women who pose for *Penthouse* are still called Pets (and not *Penthouse* Animal Companions). Inevitably, several female students filed a formal sexual-harassment complaint against him.

—JOHN TAYLOR, *New York* (1991)[1]

One tactic of political correctness is to follow the Orwellian Newspeak approach of trying to eliminate thoughts by eliminating the words, or even unintended associations. Handicapped turns to disabled, black market to shadow market.

—ANTHONY BROWNE, *The Retreat of Reason* (2006)[2]

In a twist worthy of Mark Twain himself, a St. John's University professor has been fired for reading a passage containing the N-word from Twain's anti-slavery novel "Pudd'nhead Wilson" in her "Literature of Satire" class.

—DANA KENNEDY, *New York Post* (2021)[3]

Over the course of forty years, the American public has learned to live with a very specific type of anecdote, one generally adduced to support sweeping reflections on supposedly broad cultural trends. Alongside concepts like political correctness and cancel culture, this type of anecdote has also become an export item that can travel surprisingly far and endure surprisingly long. There is a decent chance that a story like the Oberlin sandwich kerfuffle will be familiar to readers of *O Globo, Le Figaro,* or *Die Welt.* In 2015, a story about Oberlin students allegedly outraged by "cultural appropriation" in their dining hall—specifically a bánh mì sandwich—made the rounds in countless media. The story turned out to be distorted in the way these anecdotes often are—but that didn't stop it from traveling far. We find it mentioned in newspapers in Germany and France, and we find it in Caroline Fourest's book, which I discussed in a previous chapter. Fourest derisively imagines the students making the bánh mì "their 1968."[4]

The anecdotes with which I have been introducing the individual chapters of this book are based on the conventions of the campus novel, even if they are no longer set anywhere near a university campus. But they have also developed their very own syntax over the past few decades. Paradoxically, repetition has made us worse rather than better readers of such anecdotes. We have become so used to certain aspects of this genre that we no longer perceive them as aspects of a genre. And in spreading them, we acquiesce to certain formal conventions that likewise no longer become visible as such.

For instance, we agree to listen to certain tales and to trust certain tellers. These anecdotes usually make clear that the author repeating the account hasn't checked the story personally but is repeating someone else's version. When an anecdote opens an article about political correctness, then we know the author will only stay with it for a paragraph or two and will wind up anywhere but with the original case. Such anecdotes aren't really allowed to be specific; they have to stand in for the broad trend. They aren't allowed to be mere curiosities and aren't meant to elicit amusement. They are meant to send shivers of foreboding and recognition down your spine, even when dealing with a single incident on the other side of the world ten years ago. They are, to paraphrase Marx's famous quote about commodities, "born levellers and cynics," always ready "to change not only the soul but also the body" with every other anecdote of this type.[5]

My argument in this chapter is twofold. First, the anecdotal is not a quality that comes accidentally to polemics about cancel culture. The moral panic surrounding cancel culture succeeds because a very specific mode of anecdotal storytelling has come to seem plausible. Second, the cancel culture panic also proceeds by making other forms of anecdotal evidence less plausible. This second part can be easy to miss: The same newspapers and magazines that teach their readers how to extrapolate from campus flyers, from undergrad soundbites, and from random tweets to arrive at blanket statements about the United States, the West, the young, the Left also teach their readers to be skeptical when a woman speaks up about pervasive harassment or a person of color shares an experience of racism on X (né Twitter). What they grant almost instinctively in one case suddenly becomes an issue in the other. Granting plausibility, limiting plausibility—these are two mutually dependent discourse practices.

Anecdotes

In 2018, a video by psychology professor Jordan Peterson went around the world, cementing his reputation at the time as "the most influential public intellectual in the Western world" (as David Brooks described him via Tyler Cowen in the *New York Times*[6]) and as the "dazzling internet star of the Intellectual Dark Web" (as the *Neue Zürcher Zeitung* called him[7]). The occasion for his nearly two-hour video was the amendment of an anti-discrimination law in the Canadian parliament. The law would add transgender people to the Canadian Human Rights Act as a vulnerable group. But for Peterson the bill (also known as Bill C-16) sought to impose a politically correct orthodoxy, forcing him to apply pronouns he didn't want to, and punishing him should he refuse.[8]

That was not what the law said. But when university students confronted him about his position, Peterson emerged from the confrontation an icon of the very censorship he had decried. The hitherto relatively unknown Peterson became famous in one fell swoop—the first celebrity of the cancel culture era. This meant that, like many others later on, he became famous for what he was supposedly not allowed to say, but nevertheless kept saying; like many others, he was allegedly censored, even though the censorship actually didn't bring him anything except more fame, more money, more readers, and more listeners. In Peterson's case, he has, as of this writing, 5.1 million X (Twitter) followers, hundreds of millions of views on YouTube, bestseller status for his book (*12 Rules for Life: An Antidote to Chaos*) in Canada and the UK, as well as selling hundreds of thousands of copies in the United States. The translation rights to the book were sold for forty different languages.

That immense success had very little to do with his actual cause (his warnings about Bill C-16 turned out to be nonsense); it had to do with Peterson's self-portrayal as a silenced prophet: He dared to say openly what supposedly nobody else dared to say, namely that political correctness had—you won't believe this—run amok. "The citizens of your great country," he warned US readers in *The Hill* "and ours—and of our allies across the Western world—are at risk. Careless, ideologically-addled legislators are forcing us to use words we did not freely choose."[9] It was this mix of prophecy and victimhood that fueled Peterson's immediate success. Over the next six months, *The Atlantic* dedicated several big articles to Peterson, which were only occasionally about his ideas and much more often about how enraged "the Left" was about those ideas. One such article, entitled "Why Can't People Hear What Jordan Peterson Is Saying?," lamented that left-wing observers saw something in Peterson that he actually wasn't. Criticism of Peterson was part of an "epidemic" "of exaggeration or hyperbolic misrepresentation" endemic to the Left—the author doesn't use the word "cancel culture," but the description clearly anticipates the moniker.[10] There was something circular about Peterson's public persona: He was supposedly "demonized"[11] by political correctness because he had the temerity to warn of political correctness. The English *Daily Mail* wrote that he was "a martyr for free speech."[12]

Peterson's warning consisted mainly of well-known anecdotes. This is what he reported in his first viral video:

> I'm a clinical psychologist. [Political correctness] is starting to affect my clients, I've had three clients in the last two years who have been and—and—who have been driven near the point of insanity by politically correct occurrences at work. One of them was a bank employee. What—what finally did her in, fundamentally, was—she sent me a very long email chain referring to a—a ser—a series of discussions that happened in—in this Bank internally about whether or not the word "Flip chart"—you know referring to those large p—pads of paper that you put up on a stand you can flip forward and draw on, kind of an archaic technology now—whether or not the word "flip chart" was pe—pejorative and racist. And the reason for that was that—apparently the word "flip" can be used pejoratively to refer to Filipinos—which was something I didn't even know and I suppose a Filipino could conceivably take offense to having a pad of paper named "flip chart" although it's hard to imagine the circumstances under which that might arise or at least once it was hard to imagine that. Anyways, she gave me access to a string of email conversations about that particular topic and the—the bank did eventually agree to stop using the term "flip chart." I don't know what they replaced it with.[13]

Speaking in 2016, Peterson did not refer to the term "cancel culture" (he used the earlier term "political correctness"), but nevertheless this anecdote is prototypical for the stories that writers and editors have used to introduce articles about cancel culture since 2019. Peterson speaks from a position of authority—he's not some random guy; he's a psychologist reporting from clinical practice. He claims to be able to document the incident of political correctness that brought his patient "near the point of insanity": His patient showed him the internal emails from the bank where she worked.

As always with these types of stories, one cannot absolutely rule out the possibility that this happened. But on the face of it, it seems unlikely that a business in the mid-2010s would weigh in on their employees' use of the word "flip chart" one way or the other. Peterson's story has two characteristics that, on closer inspection, many cancel culture anecdotes possess. (1) On the one hand, it is clearly located in the now (the patient in question had the experience in the "last two years"), but on the other hand it has a patina that suggests the story might be showing its age—as Peterson himself admits, the "flip chart" is "essentially an archaic technology these days," an odd target for censorship in the mid-2010s. A listener who wants to believe Peterson's story has to be able to ignore this friction to some extent. (2) The anecdote's evidentiary value is extremely flimsy, but the threat conjured by it is quite visceral. This mismatch seems to increase the effectiveness of the anecdote rather than reduce it. If we're willing to believe that a Toronto bank in 2015 was talking about flip charts in any way, shape, or form, then we're also ready to swallow the rest of the story.

It is characteristic of this type of episode that its purveyor presents it as an indicator for a recent wave of political correctness, and that, on a second look, it turns out to have a long history. Because the story that Peterson referred to in 2016 had been circulating for decades, especially in chat forums and chain emails. We can find the flip chart example on the website of a certain Lenora Billings-Harris, who seems to have offered her services as a self-employed diversity coach. The website appears to have been launched in 2001 and updated for the last time that same year.

In a 2005 book on conflict resolution, author Suzanne Ghais tells an anecdote very similar to Peterson's: A young woman moderates a panel about gangs under the auspices of the city's mayor. The group consisted of citizens, officials, and several gang members. At the beginning of the first meeting, the young woman directs everyone's attention to the flip chart. A Filipino gang member angrily explained that the word "flip" can be an ethnic slur against Filipinos and that she "had no business leading the group if she didn't know that." One panel member reports that "the facilitator agreed in a tone that could be construed as condescending and apologized profusely."[14] When did this conversation take place? In which city? How did the writer learn of the incident? The book doesn't say. Ghais writes that she learned the story from a member of the panel, but when asked about it in 2022, Ghais could not remember exactly how she met this panel member. She doesn't even recall the city in which this story took place.[15]

On the blog of the Philippines-based American John McCrarey, there appeared in 2010 a version of the anecdote that even more closely resembles what Peterson's patient supposedly told him: "A bank" asked its employees to avoid the word "flip chart"—as with Peterson in the context of a diversity training.[16] On Twitter I was able to find a tweet from Lorna Page (one like) and one from Lauren Elyse (five likes): "My friend worked for a company that banned the word 'flipchart' because Filipino's might get upset :/ [sic]."[17] In a 2017 blog post by a certain Phil La Duke, he reports that he "used to work with a woman" who "forbade us from using the term 'flip chart.'"[18]

You get the idea: This is a story that has happened everywhere and nowhere, that (almost) always happened to others. As an example of what's happening "now," it's quite long in the tooth. What remains is a constant core of meaning: People are too sensitive, and the self-censorship that political correctness demands takes on increasingly bizarre forms. The episode, as is so often the case with anecdotes, signifies more than it documents. There is no consensus as to whether this attempt at censorship ever took place and, if so, when it happened; however, there is a clear consensus on what it means.

After some digging, I was able to find one even earlier version of this form of censorship. But the story differed substantially from the fairly repetitive versions I just outlined. Two Navy veterans in Philadelphia, Ray Burdeos and Nestor Enriquez, who are themselves Filipino, reported to Eliseo Silva (and Burdeos repeated the story in his self-published memoir) that their non-Filipino friends in the service decided not to use the word "flip chart" as a sign of respect. Neither Burdeos nor Enriquez explains when exactly they experienced this act of voluntary self-censorship, but they would have likely served in the mid-1970s. (Burdeos has passed away and attempts to contact Enriquez proved unsuccessful.)[19]

By using a story that has been circulating in various media since the 1990s as evidence of a worsening situation, Peterson falsifies not only the anecdote's relevance, but its meaning as well. If Burdeos is right in his description, then the flip chart example has nothing to do with a recent, increasingly authoritarian political correctness that, as Peterson rather pathetically puts it, has driven his clients "near the point of insanity." Rather, it suggests a fairly durable phenomenon, owed perhaps to the fact that people in a multicultural country like the United States have long been trying to be considerate of one another's feelings and that they are perhaps sometimes overcautious or clumsy in doing so. What's noticeable in his framing is that Peterson tries to precisely avoid this obvious possibility: namely, that this form of politesse has existed for a long time and expresses clumsiness rather than censorship. The enemy of the anecdote is normality, business as usual, the *longue durée*.

Anecdotes as a literary genre can carry significance whether or not they happened. They attach to historic persons or impart little lessons in a space somewhere between fact and fiction. We use them when they feel perfect for a situation, knowing full well that the perfection is likely a sign that the story has been fictionalized in its travels. On the other hand, anyone who uses them to venture a broader diagnosis of their own time should care whether a particular anecdote happened, when, and to whom.

For all its reliance on them, the cancel culture panic has a deeply conflicted relationship to the history of its anecdotes. On the one hand, its mode of anecdotal evidence is effective precisely because any particular anecdote's consumers have been living for almost fifty years with strikingly similar anecdotes that supposedly prove excessive sensitivity, taboos, and speech codes. A new story invoking censorious Toronto bank executives falls on fertile ground because we've lived with very similar stories making very similar points for decades. On the other hand, the sheer weight of its past presents a problem for these anecdotes, because the fact that we've been living with them for so long seems at odds with their ability to prove a mounting crisis at this exact moment. The purveyors of such anecdotes have found a workaround, however: They forget the past in order to be able to repeat it. Peterson's flip chart example may be an extreme case, but these anecdotes generally wear the garb of the recent past even when they have been around for years. This is particularly noticeable when it comes to language change, and things you are "now" "no longer" allowed to say. The language police, which is always felt to be particularly oppressive at the present moment, seems rather to be a constant part of democratic coexistence.

Some of the alleged language curtailments are entirely folkloric—the rightwing press in the UK becomes periodically convinced that some "loony left" local council or other is looking to ban "black bin liners" (trash bags), the term "black coffee," or the nursery rhyme "Baa Baa Black Sheep."[20] These kinds of "language myths" date back to the 1980s but have had vibrant afterlives—researcher James Curran found the nursery rhyme appeared as an example in tabloid articles well into the late aughts,[21] and Anthony Browne opens his 2006 anti-PC pamphlet *The Retreat of Reason* with the bin bag example.[22] All of this is in spite of the fact that no one appears to have ever attempted to ban any one of those words.

But such is the internationalization of these discourses that audiences are being asked to react to language change in other countries and foreign languages. German newspapers have chronicled the disappearance of the n-word from US discourse with great interest, usually with the implication that this is a quite recent phenomenon. When in 2011 a small US publisher (NewSouth Books) put out an edition of *Huckleberry Finn* without the n-word, German newspapers devoted upwards of sixty articles to that fact.[23] But while sheer distance may explain how Germans can mourn the disappearance of the same words over and over again, the relationship to language change modeled for them by US discourse clearly informs domestic debates about changing language as well. Here too linguistic changes that take place over decades are insistently framed as new and sudden.

Take the fate of the German *Zigeunerschnitzel*, a pork schnitzel with a spicy tomato sauce, whose name literally means "gypsy schnitzel." The word *Zigeuner* is considered (and indeed is) a slur, and the word has been gradually falling out of use. Its disappearance has been treated in cancel culture texts in German media as an example for the new speech codes. But in fact, the fate of this schnitzel has been a mainstay in debates over free expression for decades. In October 2023, the *Neue Zürcher Zeitung* commented—on the occasion of an opera premiere—that we are living "at a time when there are heated ideological arguments about cultural appropriation, and a *Zigeunerschnitzel* is not allowed to be called that."[24] Similarly, the news magazine *Focus* warned that the specific name of the schnitzel was in danger of succumbing to a new onslaught of "PC German"—the article appeared in February of 2003.[25] In October 1996, an essay in the *Frankfurter Allgemeine Zeitung* by the demographer Elisabeth Noelle-Neumann used the same word (*Zigeunerschnitzel*) as a case study to explain the term "political correctness" to the paper's readers.[26] And in June 1992, the schnitzel showed up in a litany of "Brave New Words" then supposedly rejiggering the German language.[27] Germany has been mourning this word for over thirty years. And has been using it constantly in the process.

The examples and the framing of the cancel culture panic demand that consumers constantly experience them as new and without precedent. It is quite possible that the fast pace of daily newspaper journalism favored this constitutive amnesia. But even in the United States—where the first wave of PC panic left its mark primarily via books by Bloom, D'Souza, and Sacks and Thiel—the memory of the earlier turns of this spiral are extremely vague. We forget past panics in order to allow ourselves to be freaked out all over again.

SERIOUSNESS

There is a quip usually attributed to the Viennese humorist Alfred Polgar: "For the Prussian the situation is serious, but not hopeless. For the Austrian, the situation is hopeless, but not serious." Just how serious a danger is cancel culture? Just how hopeless is the situation? From the historical comparisons and the hyperbolic descriptions alone, you would think those who warn of it think the situation is dire indeed. But in fact, despite all the apocalypticism in the retelling of political correctness and cancel culture, the articles themselves frequently aren't all that serious. In fact, if one confronts an author about their text—pointing out that events didn't transpire as related or that they don't support the article's conclusion—one is often told to lighten up, to take things with a certain sense of irony.

But it isn't a matter of seriousness *or* irony. Irony and seriousness are in fact intertwined in PC and cancel culture stories. Think about the language game according to which a politically correct censorship brigade polices language and ultimately thought. In practice, this language game works as follows. Critics of supposedly increasing censorship compile a list of new and onerous language rules. They gather either established expressions, which the "politically correct" want to get rid of ("Indian"), or new ones, which the critic feels are faddish and restrictive ("intersectionality").

At best, these collections say that *someone somewhere* wanted to change the way others speak—meaning they are largely silent about how widespread the attempt was or how successful the intervention. Francis Fukuyama reports in his book *Identity* that "manholes" are "now" being relabeled as "maintenance holes"—presumably because they are exclusionary to women.[28] How representative was this demand? With how much emphasis was it put forward? By whom? Fukuyama fails to provide answers, because likely such details would hurt rather than help the anecdote.

In other cases, however, there is no someone somewhere. For in a second step, the critics of PC language almost always get creative and ask: If this, why not that? In the long discourse about speech codes, there is often confusion between anecdote and parody. At the beginning of the PC panic, one German article from 1992 reported that it was "now" "politically correct" to describe potted plants as "botanical companions."[29] If pressed on that point, would the author have said that they were joking? Quite possibly. But it is remarkable that the line between straightforward reportage and parody, between diagnosis and invention, is hard to draw in the litanies of examples in PC and now cancel culture texts.

Especially in the international transmission of these stories, there is a fatal tendency to confuse joke and reality, metaphor and literal reality. Again and again, writers seem to imagine a literal "court" in session where there is only social disapproval; they clearly think there are literal "safe spaces" built into American dorms, beckoning twenty-four hours a day with pillows and pudding for all those triggered by the vicissitudes of adulthood. They think the classics are literally no longer taught on American campuses. Perhaps these writers know better, and their writing is just unclear. But two things seem remarkable: that respected newspapers would print articles that do not clarify whether the phenomenon they describe is a real occurrence or a metaphor; and that readers by and large seem to accept this fact.

This is because this form of storytelling is ultimately creative. People report examples, but they also spin possible scenarios of their own, which, with enough time, can become the examples for the next wave of the panic. Since the 1990s, comedians, politicians, and writers of letters to the editor have reported speech rules that fall somewhere between fact and fiction. Are they reporting literal changes in the way people talk, or are they making a joke? The strange irony is that the more the discourse escalates and the more oppressive language rules are felt to be, the more incentive there is for unseriousness. Collective memory is even worse at distinguishing between the serious and the non-serious. Many an anecdote has gone down in the annals of political correctness that actually originated as a joke by those who opposed it. These reports seem so perfectly ironic because they were never real to begin with.

When *New York* magazine described political correctness in early 1991, one example it raised on its cover was: "Do you say pet or animal companion?" As John K. Wilson wrote a few years later, there is no evidence that anyone anywhere ever demanded this nomenclature: "Do people really say 'animal companion' instead of 'pet'? Does anyone accuse those who use the word *pet* of being a 'speciesist'? Would anyone take them seriously if they did?"[30] No one in any position of influence has ever demanded that the term "manhole cover" be replaced: It is a parody attributed to the people parodied.

"Freedom of speech," Umberto Eco once wrote, also means "freedom from rhetoric,"[31] the right to see the facts undisguised by rhetorical intensification and embellishment. In complaining about an ever-recent narrowing of discourse, often enough we are living with yesterday's hacky jokes and narrative embellishments as though they were facts.

STRUCTURE

The Bancroft Library at UC Berkeley houses the Diamond Collection, a deep-core sample of the arctic shelf of campus stories. While working on her dissertation, *Right-Wing Movements in the United States, 1945–1992*, Sara Diamond seems to have subscribed to every right-wing periodical, newsletter, and speaker service she could find. Her collection ends—as did her dissertation—at the moment when the term "political correctness" entered the American lexicon. But, in a way that makes the dozens of boxes an even more interesting time capsule. Not one of the pieces collected in them likely contains the term "political correctness"; not one contains the term "cancel culture." But to read through her collections is to stumble again and again over stories and articles that could appear today exactly as they did in 1985, 1980, 1975.

We read about a speaker at Harvard being shouted at and are told about the serious questions the incident raises for campus free speech—in 1987.[32] We are warned of "oppression studies" "where the point of view is always the victim's and the 'victimizer' is always wrong"—in 1988.[33] And we read about the lecturer at the University of Pennsylvania who "was required to undergo 'racial sensitivity seminars' and was suspended from teaching for one semester . . . after calling a black student an 'ex-slave'"—in 1985.[34] The sense of déjà vu starts with the mode of storytelling—article after article rehearses the same baubles of campus Sturm und Drang, often years old even when they were cited in the early to mid-80s. Whether it's the Intercollegiate Studies Institute or Accuracy in Academia, the Foundation for Economic Education or the Young Americans for Freedom (which for forty-two years had Ronald Reagan as its honorary chairman), by and large these outfits did not so much produce policy proposals or solid scholarship; they produced an endless deluge of anecdotes.[35]

But what Diamond's boxes also document is the immense effort involved in creating this genre and keeping it in circulation. In the 1950s, a conservative publishing ecosystem emerged that focused on the college campus, with presses and institutions such as Regnery Publishing and Frank Chodorov's Intercollegiate Studies Institute (ISI), whose first president was William F. Buckley. The group was financed by J. Howard Pew, the founder of Sun Oil.[36] Then there was the Olin Foundation's Institute for Educational Affairs (IEA). The foundation's president Bill Simon described the organization's pitch as follows: When it came to the university, "the inmates have taken over the institution." IEA was supposed to be the "counteroffensive."[37] Well before Allan Bloom or Dinesh D'Souza could get rich off campus exposés, this ecosystem pushed collegiate stories, albeit initially mostly to true believers.

There were books like *Educating for Disaster* (by Thomas B. Smith) or *Poisoned Ivy* (by Benjamin Hart)—books for the right-winger in your life, unlikely to be reviewed in the mainstream press, unlikely to be stocked in your neighborhood bookstore. There were the more or less glossy magazines put out by various right-wing outfits—Accuracy in Academia's *Campus Report*, ISI's *Campus*, the David Horowitz Freedom Center's *Heterodoxy*, or the *New Guard* published by the Young Americans for Freedom—many of which opened their issues with a paragraph-each roundup of what *Heterodoxy* calls in its slogan "articles and animadversions on political correctness and other follies." "Squeaky Chalk" is what *Campus Report* called this section: Did a political science survey course at Arizona State University overemphasize "fears of nuclear war, power and weapons"? Accuracy in Academia was ready with a press release. Did the Yale president attend the opening of a gay and lesbian studies center? "Squeaky Chalk" was there to cover it: "So much for God and Man at Yale."[38]

The most frequently used word in these sections may well have been "reportedly." Outfits like Accuracy in Academia had a few full-time staffers, but it relied mostly on a very large campus reporting network. "Reportedly" simply meant that a student, faculty member, or staff from the particular university had gone to the event and sent in a few quotes to the home office. Accuracy in Academia started operating in August of 1985, and by September it told the *Phoenix*, the now-defunct San Francisco State student newspaper, that it had recruited 5,000 members across US campuses.[39] Longer pieces usually drew on one of the hundreds of new conservative campus magazines that conservative foundations were busy seeding at various college campuses (among them the largely Olin-funded Collegiate Network[40]). Writing for one of this new crop of publications could launch careers in the right-wing grift machine (Dinesh D'Souza got his start at the *Dartmouth Review*) or open more rarefied doors (PayPal founder Peter Thiel, co-author of "The Diversity Myth" with David O. Sacks,[41] was a founding editor of the *Stanford Review*).

Any campus anecdote could thus be written up by a local conservative student newspaper and then be picked up by *Campus*, *Campus Report*, *The Freeman*, the *New Guard*, *Heterodoxy*, or another of an ever-rotating set of periodicals. But these periodicals were not simply anecdote-gathering operations;

from the beginning, they also strayed into the *production* of anecdotes as well. Groups like ISI recruited both faculty and student "campus representatives" whose jobs included: "publicizing ISI through writing articles and letters to the editor in campus newspapers" and "arranging lectures, seminars, and debates on campus."[42] One part of the right-wing anecdote machine could invite a speaker to campus—say, Major Andy Messing, executive director of the National Defense Foundation (each campus representative would have received an annual directory of ISI-affiliated academics from which to choose); another part could pay for it in full. When, as happened at Dartmouth in 1987, the speech got disrupted (by two students, as far as I was able to tell), the editor of the Olin-funded *Dartmouth Review* could file a complaint with the college's Committee on Standards, and *Campus Report* could publish an account of the complaint.[43]

Laying out the right-wing campus report biotope in this way can sound conspiratorial. The point isn't that this was particularly nefarious—at least some of these organizations were ineffectual and mostly existed to provide a tax shelter to right-wing billionaires with axes to grind. The point is rather that anecdotes, and the work they do, depend on the uses to which they are put. The real legacy of this at times rather comical and buffoonish set of actors consists of the mechanics of repetition and escalation they pioneered. Even Americans who had never cracked open *Campus* magazine came over time to expect a particular form of anecdote that would illustrate the PC problem, and came to accept it as evidence. In a kind of accidental side effect, newspaper readers the world over, who probably had no idea who William F. Buckley was, grew comfortable with the same kind of stories.

We readers, in the case of the cancel culture anecdote (and the PC anecdote before it), are urged to understand its perfection as an expression of something else: It is absolutely ridiculous, its meaning is patently clear, and it makes the blood boil—because the phenomenon of which it is a part is so clear and unequivocal. We are not, in other words, primed to think of the perfection of the story as an effect of several layers of selection and smoothing, a sign that the anecdote may be more fact than fiction by the time it gets to us. The way cancel culture anecdotes are told makes it difficult to understand them as a product of a chain of transmission. Something seemingly outrageous happened at a tiny college in the United States. Now we read about it in *Der Spiegel*. How did an anecdote from a Virginia cafeteria end up in a French bestseller? Almost no one writing about the cancel culture panic bothers to even suggest an answer to that question. This is a pact any reader makes with cancel culture anecdotes:

We agree to treat them as self-sufficient, self-referential objects, intact as they pass like a coin from hand to hand—and not as a literary form with lots of authors.

What makes a useful anecdote for this kind of circulation? What sort of stories does this machine, and those standing downstream from its ceaseless production, select for?

1. *Focalization*: The former *New York Times* columnist Bari Weiss quit the newspaper in 2020 over concerns about cancel culture.[44] She excoriated the paper for being beholden to Twitter activists: "Twitter is not on the masthead of The New York Times. But Twitter has become its ultimate editor."[45] To establish her independence from online mobs, Weiss started a newsletter on the online platform Substack—the newsletter was first called Common Sense but is now The Free Press—and promised "honest news for sane people." The "honest news for sane people" from the beginning contained mostly stories of cancel culture, wokeness, and supposed censorship. The platform Substack may be new, and the money Weiss was able to make off it unprecedented, but the format has a long tradition. These stories are no different from what *Campus Report* or *Heterodoxy* would have sent out twenty or thirty years ago, and so is the pose of heterodoxy that just barely covers the obvious conservative grievance politics.

As in these publications, the anecdotes Common Sense sent out always described events from one perspective, namely that of the "canceled person." This is significant. In a conventional newspaper piece, the other side—be it the institution, the employer, other employees, or simply the people who criticized the cancel victim—would have had their say as a matter of routine. In cancel culture stories, they generally don't say anything because they're generally not asked.

Anecdotes are almost by necessity focalized in this way. These little stories work so perfectly because they report from a single point of view and do not have to adopt an opposing one, or even mention it.

2. *Information asymmetry*: When, in the course of a cancel culture article, institutions such as universities do get a word in, they are usually quoted as saying that they "have a policy of not commenting on personnel matters." Many cancel culture anecdotes take advantage of information asymmetry: a lopsidedness with regard to who can talk freely, who can present the most straightforward and attention-grabbing version of events. The story of the silenced, beleaguered individual is simply a better story than the patchwork of omissions, heavily lawyered institutional pronouncements, and dissonant details that a complex institution like a university almost necessarily produces.

It is also worth noticing that as these anecdotes travel the globe, their solo-ism is amplified. The vast majority of anecdotes in Spanish, German, or French texts about cancel culture come from the United States, as do the facts of the anecdote and any relevant quotes about it. The writer has usually consulted one or two US sources or received the information via an op-ed or a newsletter. At times, this is literally so: Germany's *Die Welt* frequently publishes trans-lations from Bari Weiss's Substack newsletter as op-eds. Non–fact-checked opinion pieces wind up in non–US newspapers with the imprimatur of major news publications. Those who effectuated the supposed cancellation are often silenced twice through this international game of telephone. European readers will learn about a professor beset by latter-day left-wing McCarthyites—from the professor, and then from a sympathetic op-ed writer. They will not hear from the students who criticized the professor—unless their self-styled victim reports their criticisms. What's worse is that readers can, of course, tell. And in being able to tell, they learn a valuable lesson: We (meaning author and reader) understand the cancelers' discourse better than they do. The cancelers weren't worth asking. The medium—point of view, the single source, and conversely who is not being allowed to speak—is the message.

This asymmetry increases in hindsight, especially as we look back from the digital age to an analogue one. As they age and are forgotten, anecdotes become fossils of power differences. They are themselves the product of power, and even the most critical recipient may forget this with time. Anecdotes bear witness as to who was able to make themselves heard back then, who was allowed to speak freely, and who was not. Who had a name that could be looked up in an archive, and who remained a footnote. Or even less than that: a nameless student, a member of a faceless inquisition. In 1993, the feminist scholar Jane Gallop was accused of sexual harassment by two female graduate students. The episode survives today as an anecdote, mostly in two books by Gallop herself—*Feminist Accused of Sexual Harassment* (1997) and *Anecdotal Theory* (2002),[46] part of an impressive CV. The accusers' side of the story survives mostly through the writing of the person they accused, otherwise only in the deep recesses of the Internet Archive's Wayback Machine—and, ironically enough, in old issues of David Horowitz's *Heterodoxy*.[47]

3. *Irony:* "If you google 'bleeding heart liberal,'" one cancel story on Weiss's Common Sense newsletter began, "Maud Maron might well turn up as the first hit."[48] "A lesbian professor is the object of hate from transsexuals," was the title of an article in *Neue Zürcher Zeitung* about the English philosopher Kathleen Stock.[49] A good PC or cancel anecdote is ironic, not so much in tone

but in its dramatic structure. "In a twist worthy of Mark Twain himself," the *New York Post* explained in 2021, "a St. John's University professor has been fired for reading a passage containing the N-word from Twain's anti-slavery novel "Pudd'nhead Wilson."[50] The last person you would expect is canceled. For Dinesh D'Souza, Stephan Thernstrom was known all across campus as a progressive who was absurdly accused of racism. Philip Roth wrote about the Melvin Tumin incident at Princeton University: "A myriad of ironies, comical and grave, abounded."[51] And because the existing ironies were not enough for him (Tumin explored questions of race, he was progressive, he was Jewish), Roth went further in his fictionalization of the Tumin episode in *The Human Stain* and made the person accused of racism secretly African American.

There are interesting downstream effects to organizing a PC/cancel culture anecdote around a central irony: The irony comes to govern all the details in the story. As a rule, most campus anecdotes emerge out of complicated, de-cades-long processes; they reflect messy interpersonal conflicts, institutional turf wars, and often enough astonishingly petty grievances. All this must dis-appear in favor of the stark, headline-grabbing irony—"feminist accused of sexual harassment!" The irony is a signal that there is a literary imagination at work in a text, and the irony is a signal to a reader of that text that they shouldn't read or think too deeply into the events described. After all, add more and dissonant detail, and the central irony dissolves.

4. *Surface heterodoxy:* This may go without saying for a reader who has made their way through the dozens of examples cited so far in this book, but it is worth noting that these stories have a recognizable gestalt. We are told the beginning of a new story, and we can intuit at least a range of possible punch lines. Cancel culture and PC anecdotes resemble jokes: They follow a structure of setup and resolution; they seem predestined (and are, in fact, often premanufactured) for easy circulation and constant repetition. Have you heard the one about the sand-wich at Oberlin? About the word "American" at Stanford? About the feminist accused of sexual harassment? And like jokes, these stories represent a strange interlacing of heterodoxy and orthodoxy. On the one hand, jokes are where our normal everyday logics and vocabularies are undercut and estranged. Jokes can speak truth to power. But at the same time, jokes of course only circulate when they on some level appeal to the shared sensibilities of the majority.

Something similar is true for PC/cancel culture anecdotes. They often enough present themselves as little nuggets of sanity in a world gone mad. But they are not-so-secretly invested in the status quo. Their unspoken moral, after all, is that the professor did not deserve to be accused, that the feminist could not have committed sexual harassment. As is typically true in cancel culture discourse, anecdotes seem to contain something analogous to Nietzsche's critique of "slave morality": The weak in society have banded together to defame and tear down the great. Most anecdotes feature a singular Gulliver tied to the beach by thousands of faceless Lilliputians. Their irony is an irony of the powerful. It celebrates the sovereign individual and looks askance at collective or institutional remedies. "The university administration was no help," we read in many such stories. "His colleagues wouldn't speak up."

Subscription

I have made throughout this book the point that it's impossible to disentangle the impact of cancel culture discourse from the simple fact of how much there is of it. There is something stultifying, enervating, and obnoxious about the same tired clichés, comparisons, and anecdotes being trotted out time and again. Repetition is a structural principle of the texts in which these anecdotes eventually find their intended home.

There is a tendency to think of PC/cancel culture writings as clickbait: There will be those who agree with the premise of the text, and there will be libs "triggered" by the same—both sides will click the link, see the ads, populate the comments, retweet with a snarky comment. But the era of cancel culture discourse is in fact dominated by an altogether different attention economy. Cancel culture became a widely discussed topic in 2018–19, a moment when most publishers and editorial boards had given up on making clicks from (then) Facebook and (then) Twitter the foundation of their business model. Instead, they were in the process of transitioning to a model based on subscriptions.

Certainly, no editor will disdain hundreds of thousands of views of an article, but the advertising business model associated with clickbait has either collapsed (advertising revenue is declining) or is too insecure to be able to manage it sustainably. After all, a single tweak in an algorithm in Palo Alto and the number of eyeballs, and the advertising revenue associated with it, collapses. At least in Germany, the most interesting metric for an editor has been who takes out a subscription in order to read an article. And when it comes to subscriptions, cancel culture texts perform extremely well, according to several editors for German-language newspapers I interviewed. Yes, these stories get clicks, but above all they net subscribers.

Subscription plays a significant and underappreciated role in the international genesis of the cancel culture discourse. Even if we don't fork over the money, we are subscribed to these stories. Cancel culture discourse is a discourse of repetition: It rehashes older discourses, it proceeds through structurally analogous anecdotes, it works primarily by telling the same old stories again, by breathlessly repeating old warnings as new. But even its repetitiveness is a cover version.

Heterodoxy magazine was first published in April 1992 by professional PC hunters David Horowitz and Peter Collier. Ads for the magazine described it, as noted above, as collecting "articles and animadversions on political correctness and other follies." Looking back today, in the age of the internet, the pitch seems even stranger than it was back then. It's hard to picture someone seeing the ad, enthusiastically calling an 800 number, and ordering a magazine ($2.50 plus postage) just to enjoy campus anecdotes and anti-PC "animadversions" month after month. It's almost touching how much trust Horowitz and Collier placed in the fervor with which certain readers longed for more PC anecdotes from Swarthmore College or Louisiana State University. It's hard to say whether Horowitz and Collier were right, whether there really were that many of this imagined type of reader, because *Heterodoxy* was never dependent on subscriptions. But the magazine ran for ten years and was only discontinued in 2002—after Horowitz and Collier increasingly relied on the internet to publish their anecdotes.

The insatiability, the astonishing tolerance when it comes to repetition and uniformity, have remained a main feature of this discourse. Whether it is political correctness or cancel culture, the anecdotes, the comparisons, the warnings seem to become more abstract the more they are repeated; the information you gain with each new text is exceedingly small. The one thing that's changed since the days of *Heterodoxy* is that the discourse network has accelerated: When it came to stories of political correctness, downright geologic periods elapsed between the cycles of repetition—people may have read the same articles a few times a year. Today, the internet has not only accelerated repetition, but it has also made it more obvious. This doesn't seem to affect the discourse one bit. In the United States, the cancel culture discussion was strongly fueled by newsletters on the Substack platform. Yascha Mounk's Persuasion and Weiss's Common Sense (since retitled and expanded into The Free Press) seem to resonate with their readers, even though, or perhaps precisely because, the individual articles are very similar to one another.

Perhaps the repetitiveness of these newsletters is less noticeable to end users thanks to the email format. Given how often their anecdotes wind up in newspaper articles in languages other than English, it is possible that the repetition becomes less obvious once you leave the anglosphere. But in the end, and even where the repetition is not quite as obvious, hardly anyone begins reading these essays not knowing what their ultimate verdict will be. This is in its own way remarkable—after all, when the anecdotes do enter print media in the UK, France, Switzerland, Germany, Spain, Argentina, or Brazil, it is often in the form of the essay. The essay is supposed to be open-ended, with a little freedom to associate. When it comes to cancel culture essays, this is true, but only very selectively, and that selectivity itself is deeply telling.

Essayism

Cancel culture anecdotes are often imprecise. Faced with an anecdote like Jordan Peterson's, it's difficult to answer even the most basic of questions: When did the story happen? Who did what? What were the consequences? Either the text does not provide such details, or it is more effective if you ignore them. It's noticeable, of course, that these are some basic questions any journalist is supposed to ask, but cancel culture anecdotes do not appear as journalism very frequently. Rather, they are deployed according to a fictional or essayistic logic.

Outside of North America, cancel culture anecdotes, like the PC ones before them, appear mostly in daily newspapers, rather than in the blockbuster *Atlantic* cover stories Americans likely associate with them. Above all, they thrive in the culture pages. The stakes of this difference can be clarified through the case of German cancel culture discourse. The *Neue Zürcher Zeitung* (NZZ) mentioned the expression "cancel culture" in 116 articles before August 2022 (the number of articles on themes of censorship and political correctness was of course larger). Of those articles, almost half (58, to be exact) appeared in the culture pages of either the *NZZ* or its Sunday edition the *NZZ am Sonntag* (*NZZaS*), which is differently organized. Marc Neumann, who is stationed in Washington and appears to have been one of the first to import the term "cancel culture" into German-language discourse, wrote almost 30 stories with cancel culture themes (though not always using the word) in the 365 following days. All of them appeared in the culture pages.

Where else did "cancel culture" appear in the paper? I found 25 articles in the opinion section of the newspaper (another 6 times in the Sunday paper), 12 times in the international section (twice in the *NZZaS*), 7 times in the media section. By contrast, the word ended up on the newspapers' front page a paltry 3 times. In the German conservative daily *Die Welt* (excluding this paper's

Sunday edition), there appeared 174 articles with the word "cancel culture" during the same period—80 in the culture section and another 20 were in the literary section. In the politics section, the word is found in 28 articles, and in the essay section 26 times. A total of 7 editorials mentioned the word, as did 3 articles on the paper's front page. "Cancel culture" appears in proximity to art and essayism, and while article after article emphasize the political importance of dealing with it, it is largely absent from political reporting.

The primacy of the culture pages changes the genre in which cancel culture anecdotes operate once they begin circulating. The protagonist of your average cancel culture episode is the protagonist of a novel—alienated from his environment, the society that surrounds him, learning important and unwelcome life lessons, usually entirely reactive, and almost always a "he." The person stringing together this episode with two or three others is not a novelist, but rather an essayist (he, too, is normally a "he"). Cancel culture texts in general move away from their specific anecdotes and stake out broader, abstract claims in a manner that is eminently essayistic. Vibes are one part of this mixture, the free association by which these connections are usually made is another.

Since Montaigne, the essay has been a form that hopes to get at something objective by emphasizing the subjective, be it the somatic, the personal, the everyday. As Theodor W. Adorno once wrote, the essay is always partial: "Its concepts are neither constructed from a first principle nor do they round off to an ultimate truth." The essay's "interpretations," Adorno says, are "as a matter of principle over-interpretations." Adorno thought that the "over" in the essay's interpretation is precisely where the essay articulates its "spiritual autonomy."[52] In other words, a good essay puts things together in a way you might not have considered or allows you to see a specific cultural object in a particular way. A good essayist comes at received wisdom from unexpected, counterintuitive angles.

Most German newspapers have a feuilleton section, which, since the nineteenth century, has tended to combine journalism with a more openly rhetorical style. Until today, the comparisons in this section can be a little more daring, the metaphors more recherché, the syntheses more inspired. The facts still matter—after all, this is still journalism. But they are filtered through the subjectivity of a solitary critical mind. The feuilleton writer goes to the same operas as the others but sees something different. When this combustible mixture works, it can be exciting to read. When it goes wrong (German has the accusation of *Feuilletonismus*), it is contentless, shallow posing. Hermann Hesse described the "age of the feuilleton" in his novel *The Glass Bead Game*:

> In that feuilleton world they had constructed of paper, people postulated the total capitulation of Mind, the bankruptcy of ideas, and pretended to be looking on with cynical calm or bacchantic rapture as not only art, culture, morality, and honesty, but also Europe and "the world" proceeded to their doom.[53]

English has no comparable term. But every American under a certain age knows an analogous description: "Oh, you mean a hot take," my students say when I teach them Hesse's novel. The hot take is a position taken in conscious rejection of the societal consensus—and, if we're honest, probably only because that consensus exists in the first place. The point is not that this type of digital pose is simply identical to the kind of essayism we find in the culture pages. But the two clearly move in the same space. Writers for the culture pages are neither hot takers nor trolls, but their positionality is driven by the same "imp of the perverse": a desire to express, connect, and emphasize what no one else has bothered to express, connect, emphasize in public discourse, perhaps for the good reason that it is pure rubbish.

The transitions between the two are fluid: A bad culture writer can definitely be simply a troll with a newspaper salary. Thanks to the internet (and thanks to internet lingo), today's audience also has a precise description at their disposal, when this happens. There is an early novel by Patricia Highsmith called *The Blunderer*, which is about a (likely) murderer who may or may not have imitated a previous killing. As Highsmith writes about her own book, it's about two murders: one committed "by a more or less cool killer, the second by an amateur attempting to copy the first, because he thinks the first killer has gotten away with it."[54] The second killer's less-than-perfect crime threatens to expose the perfect crime of the first. The internet is committing the same crime that the feuilleton section (and similar fora in other countries) have been getting away with for decades, but more clumsily, more obviously, more carelessly. And precisely in doing so, it focuses attention on the problems of the former.

Whether it is in Germany, France, Brazil, Argentina, or Italy: in many cancel culture texts, this essayistic subjectivity can cover up the inadequacies of the evidence. As a form, the essay is allowed to rely on momentary impressions and make overly bold transitions. The essay celebrates the "spiritual autonomy" described by Adorno, the associative freedom of the author, but in doing so comes dangerously close to arbitrariness. But of course, at least in the newspaper essay, in an essay that is taken seriously and widely discussed or recommended, it is arbitrariness with a certain power behind it. Its subjectivity uses arbitrariness as a gesture of empowerment by those already in power. After all, the essay's arbitrariness can easily recapitulate bad reasoning and motivate bad reasoning among a broader public. Worse, it can then reflect that bad reasoning back to them as though it were in fact bold, free thinking. In other words, the risk with an essay is that it might sell you orthodoxy as heterodoxy.

In closing this chapter, I want to walk the reader through an essay that demonstrates this danger clearly. Written by political scientist and editor Josef Joffe, it appeared in the feuilleton of *Neue Zürcher Zeitung* in May 2021 with the title: "Rename, Banish, Cancel: Well-Meaning Revolutionaries Are at Work in Europe." The subhead read: "It's Easy to See Where This Is Going." So where is "this" going? You'll have to wait to find out, for we open the article with a passage from Dickens's *Tale of Two Cities* describing the famous scarf that Madame Defarge knits. This episode, we learn, is "the essence of all revolutions": They never stop, they must always escalate. This is followed by three paragraphs about Robespierre—the "logic of purification" among the Jacobins, the Cultural Revolution, the New Calendar. Then a paragraph that begins with the French Revolution, briefly touches on Orwell's Newspeak, and then an "adaptation" of a famous Lenin quote.

After two more paragraphs about the Chinese Cultural Revolution (we are now halfway into the essay), we arrive at the present moment. How does our present moment (with its "renaming, banishment, cancellation") relate to the expansive panorama of the past unfurled in the first half of the essay? This remains unclear, as the transition sounds like this: "Fortunately, US institutions are quite civil in comparison. If the people who are 'woke' (awakened, enlightened) impose right-thinkingness—they aim at social, not physical death." Between the *terreur*, Soviet communism, and the Chinese Cultural Revolution, the essay has thus far taken stock of historical errors with millions of victims. And here's what this monstrous tally reminds the author of this essay of: "Teachers, journalists, and authors are being accused of wrong thinking and are being canceled."[55]

As daring as this comparison is, the essay doubles down on it. The text compares "the physical [cruelty]—torture, terror, death" in "Paris and Beijing" to the "moral annihilation" through cancellation; the "show trials under Stalin, Hitler, and Mao" are juxtaposed with today's rash of "mental executions"; Robespierre's "welfare committee" is positioned as a spiritual ancestor to Black Lives Matter. Instead of supporting any of these comparisons, the author moves on to Freud's study of "Little Hans." And then—in the fourth column of a full-page article—we finally get to two examples: a pamphlet apparently issued by the state of Oregon on white supremacy in math curricula, and an episode (unrelated to specific critics) in which Jane Austen's House (a museum in Hampshire) appears to have pointed out Austen's connections to British colonialism.

The almost spectacular detours, the downright obscene disproportion, between maximalist claims and historical references on the one hand and ridiculously minor evidence on the other are by no means mistakes; they constitute the essay's stylistic principle. The text functions primarily through suggestion, but at the same time seems to be unaware of the central irony that it issues an ominous, urgent warning ("It's easy to see where this is going"), but in relation to a phenomenon that has been described in the same set of newspapers, using the same historical comparisons and the same language, since 1990. If you're mathematically inclined, that's thirty-four times longer than Robespierre's reign of terror and three-and-a-half times as long as the Chinese Cultural Revolution. What is supposedly being criticized—as best as I can tell—is cancel culture. It is never named precisely; rather it is suggested by way of its comparisons. The phenomenon supposedly under discussion shows up in seven paragraphs (out of a total of twenty) in the piece. Dickens, Freud, and Joseph Heller's *Catch-22* together account for the same number of paragraphs.

There is a performative subjectivism at work here, a wild ride through whatever books and historical events the author happens to care about. What it never gets around to is the incendiary and presumably important warning (if it were true) that Black Lives Matter protests will end in massive bloodshed. All of the stylistic devices that can make the essay as a form so exciting are here turned into an absurdity. The counterintuitive but suggestive comparisons? Here they are nothing more than unreflected snap judgments. And the subjectivity that governs everything is only an illusion. In truth, the text reflects a *sensus communis*. Its subjectivism does not suggest the destabilization of the collective but rather emphasizes its permanence. Verdicts like Joffe's have been rehashed in European newspapers for more than thirty years.

If readers get anything out of the impressionistic mishmash of this essay, it is this: The reassuring experience that what may seem at first glance like measly anecdotes, albeit possibly annoying ones, can legitimately be treated as massive threats to society. Readers who enjoy this sort of text get to bask in received wisdom and rote judgment, all the while being told that their bleating along with the tired anti-PC rhetoric of yesteryear actually makes them heterodox thinkers. This is probably why writers of these texts often claim that cancel culture has not yet fully arrived wherever the author is currently writing, but that its foreshocks can be felt. You get to feel like a lone prophet, a bold outlier, a member of that small minority who can read the signs—all while talking exactly like everybody else.

SEVEN

Cosmopolitan Provincialism

How Cancel Culture Gets Imported

The academic philistines are at it again—but now they are getting help. The University of California at Santa Barbara has rescinded the appointment of a CIA officer as a visiting lecturer after a violent protest by students and a political science department recommendation.

—LES CSORBA, *Campus Report* (December 1987)[1]

The Historical-Cultural Research Center at the University of Trier is ending the three-month guest professorship of the military historian Martin van Creveld, professor emeritus of history at the University of Jerusalem, after his first lecture, after the student council at the university described van Creveld's theses as "misogynistic, militaristic, latently anti-Israel, vulgar, scientific, and methodologically primitive."

—NETZWERK WISSENSCHAFTSFREIHEIT (2011 INCIDENT, documented in 2021)[2]

The cultural transfer—by which the idea of cancel culture has made its way from US college campuses and Twitter niches to newspapers from Sao Paolo to Berlin to Moscow—is a complicated one, because it really comprises several transfers. There is the word itself that travels the globe, and, as we have seen, attaches itself to a slightly different set of anxieties wherever it is used. Then there is the supposedly unified phenomenon that, according to those who warn about cancel culture in Sao Paolo, Berlin, or Moscow, is spilling over from the United States to Canada, the UK, Russia, Brazil, and France in what French newspapers often call a "woke wave."

What makes this second transfer complicated is that it is at once overly self-reflexive and not self-reflexive enough. On the one hand, you don't have to scratch very far beneath the surface to find that worries about the spillover of US woke culture are really worries about the dominance of US culture and media more generally. In 2020 French President Emmanuel Macron warned that "certain social science theories entirely imported from the United States" would promote "separatism" in France, if left unchecked.[3] In fact, in countries with a history of colonizing others, the way some media describe the American language of wokeness imposing itself on their country often sounds like a form of colonization. At least in their imaginations, cancel culture colonizes the erstwhile colonizers.

On the other hand, those same texts and pundits who warn loudly of, say, "gender theory" or "identity politics" being imported from the United States, and who accuse activists of being overly deferential to American influences, tend not to notice that they are recycling wholesale forty years of conservative US discourse, terminology, and, often enough, anecdotes. They are, in a way, never more American than when they're being anti-American. They are provincial in their supposed cosmopolitanism and are surprisingly networked and cosmopolitan when they are at their most provincial. This chapter traces this strange dynamic.

The idea that cancel culture is an American phenomenon that is now arriving in other nations is incorrect in that there is no one thing that gets exported as cancel culture. Instead cancel culture is, in each country or public, a particular hell of that public's making. But the idea is wrong for another, related reason: Notice that in the picture of cultural transfer proffered in European or South American cancel culture narratives, the particular national public is positioned as a more or less passive recipient.

Cancel culture stories were able to succeed in the United States because of certain long-established narrative and argumentative tradition—for instance, a particular way of paying attention to campuses or a particular style of telling anecdotes. On the one hand those anecdotes and modes of attention spill over to Europe, and they do so relatively directly. On the other hand, that doesn't mean that they arrive in Europe like pathogens introduced into a previously unexposed population. Cancel culture stories are able to succeed in Europe because various countries have preestablished modes of interpretation, which are often local and specific, while also understanding themselves as responding to international pressures. By 2019, when cancel culture entered their public discourse, countries like the UK,

Germany, and France had built up an intricate vocabulary and conceptual arsenal to stage the arrival as an invasion from the outside.

The United Kingdom

The British debate over cancel culture, much like the earlier one about political correctness, can look quite a bit like its US cognate. However, as John Lea pointed out in a 2009 book, worries about PC in the UK had subtle differences from those in the US academy. Both the animating anecdotes and the etiology suggested by the descriptor "political correctness" had less to do with the universities themselves than with the intersection between state regulation and the postsecondary education sector. Whereas the PC panic in the United States emanated from the avatars of the Reagan administration and drew its examples from private institutions, from the first the UK version seemed to focus on the role of government in people's lives.

Some of this had to do with the structure of UK higher education, where a centralized bureaucracy holds more power than, say, the National Endowment for the Humanities in the United States. But part of it was also because the UK had political correctness before there was political correctness: It just wasn't about the university. In the campaigns leading up to the 1983 and 1987 elections, major right-wing tabloids ran campaigns against the "loony left."[4] Their animus was mostly directed at local authorities, above all at councils in London and other urban areas. Whether it was the *Sun*, the *Daily Mail*, or the *Mail on Sunday*, the papers created both a terminology and a storehouse of anecdotes that "contained many of the ideas seen subsequently in the conservative anti-PC campaigns in the US."[5]

Many of these culture war issues had to do with homosexuality or supposedly anti-racist language policing. None of them, as far as I was able to tell, had to do with the universities. Ironically, given that the incipient PC panic was going to be all about threats to freedom of expression, the most lasting impact of the campaign was the law called Section 28, which forbade local authorities from "intentionally promot[ing] homosexuality or publish[ing] material with the intention of promoting homosexuality"—a provision that led to a massive wave of self-censorship among Britain's teachers and remained in effect until 2000.

Lea argues that the term "political correctness" quickly became a substitute for "loony leftism" in UK media. This is in spite of the fact that "loony leftism" was supposed to be a properly British phenomenon (though with foreign analogues), while "PC" was understood at least initially to be a US import, and specifically one concerned with higher education, as opposed to the secondary schools that had been central to the Thatcher government's battle against the local councils. The import of the new, university-focused PC-discourse was largely carried by two groups: right-wing journalists and left-wing academics. In fact, Lea points out that academic critiques from the Left in the UK, such as the work of Frank Furedi, "invoke much the same conceptual language of . . . conservative authors" from the United States.[6] Furedi's books in particular echo the neoconservative worry about an ascendant "therapeutic culture" (expressed by authors such as Charles Sykes and Thomas Sowell, who in turn drew on earlier critiques by Philip Rieff and Christopher Lasch)—a puzzling set of influences for an ostensibly left-wing critique.

In the UK, as in Germany and France, complaints about political correctness had a way of making self-styled leftists sound like right-wingers. Part of the reason was likely that the period in which the concept of political correctness first came to prominence in the UK coincided with a move to the center by the Labour Party. Not just among conservatives, but among leftists too, the vocabulary of PC came to be associated with New Labour.[7] As a result, there was a robust tradition in the UK of critiquing PC and identity politics from the Left in the 1980s and 90s—from Stuart Hall to Eric Hobsbawm.

But at least for some of the critics, there were likely deeper affinities at play, although they only gradually revealed themselves. In other words: Worrying about PC was a pretty easy way to begin one's gradual path from Left to Right. When bemoaning the new spirit of PC, left-wingers and right-wingers could mourn the loss of a "cultural whole": Right-wingers were nostalgic for a national unity conceived in identitarian, almost *Völkisch*, terms; left-wingers longed for the erstwhile monoliths of the working class and Communist International, or at least for left-wing movements that felt more integrative and broad-based. More to the point for our discussion, so long as you held forth about PC, which everyone unanimously hated, you didn't have to say explicitly, or even admit to yourself, which of the two you meant. As in other countries, then, complaints about PC likely functioned as a way for certain individuals to make reactionary points without fully owning up to a rightward drift in their own thinking.

When the Brexit referendum arrived, it was also grafted onto these long-established discursive patterns. On May 16, 2016, the *Daily Express*, the *Daily Mail,* and several other tabloids reported on an incident in Brighton and Hove. The local council had decided to take a garbage truck out of circulation, given that it had a Union Jack emblazoned on its side. The outgoing mayor, a Tory, branded the decision "political correctness gone mad."[8] The *Daily Star* called it "PC madness."[9] On June 23, on the eve of the vote that took the UK out of the European Union, the *Express*, which had pretty much made Brexit its mission, reported that "a shock poll has revealed 81 percent of voters felt bullied and unable to express their true feelings in the EU debate because of a culture of political correctness."[10] Bullying, self-censorship, stifled debate: These were the central buzzwords of the PC wars, but also the framing that cancel culture debates would largely take on.

But in the UK case, it was also a pure 80s revival: a classic "loony left" story, complete with a mustache-twirling local council, combined with a thoroughly post-PC concern with the silencing of dissent. The self-assurance with which the *Express* could fuse old and new might explain what was unique about the UK's relationship to political correctness and what came to shape its relationship to the neologism "cancel culture" once it arrived.

Firstly, in US media, the term "political correctness" constituted something like a marketing coup. The Right was able to get centrist publications like *Time*, *Newsweek*, or the *New York Times* to report their concerns and import its framing with a relatively straight face. In the UK, by contrast, the term found its native home in right-wing (in the case of the *Express*, Far Right) print media, which constitute, after all, the vast majority of the UK media ecosystem. "Political correctness" was thus the name these papers gave to objections to, and critiques of, their own policy preferences. The framing the *Express* chose on the day of the referendum suggests that the editors themselves didn't think Brexit would carry the day. In UK media, the strange combination of dissidence and identification with power structures (and the state) that characterizes descriptions of cancel culture elsewhere too is perhaps clearer than anywhere else. The *Express* was standing up for the heterodox expression of those scrappy few, the 51 percent of Britons who were about to take the other 49 percent on a wild ride.

Secondly, it is noticeable that the *Express*'s framing suggests that political correctness is about a reassertion of national control—over and against both the larger unit (the international order, the EU) *and* the smaller (the local council). In their general thrust, PC stories (like cancel culture stories after them) can sound libertarian—they are about set-upon individuals who just want to go about their everyday business without the loony left telling them where to put their Union Jacks or how to shape their bananas. But the villains in this story—as is so often the case in the UK—are the local government and the customs of urbanites.

This is clearly true for fears of cancel culture elsewhere too, but it was far clearer in the UK: These worries about the Left imposing their views are not about escaping dominance; they are about exercising it. The persistent fixation on the local councils as the antagonist suggests that this was never about taking back local control, but rather about centering control at the national level. Behind the pleas for individual freedom lie fantasies of national unity. These fantasies of national unity seemed to cut across the political spectrum. Worries about political correctness had connected a Far Left with the right wing—many of Brexit's left-wing supporters (Frank Furedi and his influential online journal *Spiked* among them) had started as left-wing critics of political correctness.

Cancel culture arrived after Brexit, but it appears to have become at least in part a crutch for managing the shambolic aftermath of the decision to leave. Just like PC during the Vote Leave campaign, cancel culture allowed people and media who had—lest we forget—gotten what they wanted to nevertheless feel vaguely aggrieved about what was happening. Just like political correctness, cancel culture in the UK context spoke to fantasies of national purity and national unity. And just like PC, cancel culture allowed the central government—especially under Rishi Sunak—to flex its muscle, all the while miming a laissez-faire posture. From the first, the fight against cancel culture in the UK had nothing to do with getting left-wingers out of everyone's business, but rather getting right-wingers into it.

Much more straightforwardly than in the United States, complaints about cancel culture at UK universities have led to greater oversight and even interference. In the United States, when Representative Elise Stefanik decided to haul three university presidents before Congress to testify with the obvious intent of forcing them to resign, critics, not just on the Left, described what she did as cancel culture. When activist Chris Rufo fulminates against woke ideologies that restrict free speech at American universities but suggests as the cure a state takeover of higher education, then this is interpreted as an inconsistency—and at times as cancel culture in its own right. In the UK, where the main discourse about political correctness, especially in the tabloid press, had been illiberal for decades, there was no such contradiction. Rather, using the banner of freedom of speech to curtail freedom of speech was instead very much in keeping with past practice.

Thus, conservative journalist Toby Young parlayed his bona fides as a Brexiteer, and his history of "politically incorrect comments,"[11] into a succession of official posts that all put him in charge of overseeing universities: In 2018 Theresa May appointed him to the board of directors for the newly created Office for Students (OfS), conceived as a regulator for universities. In 2020 Young co-founded the Free Speech Union to combat the threat of cancel culture. A 2023 analysis by Huw Davies and Sheena MacRae found that the Free Speech Union shared a significant number of members with *Spiked* and the anti-trans LGB Alliance.[12]

This is not a coincidence: While a lot of the classic cancel victims in US folklore were in fact (temporarily) brought down by #MeToo, in the UK "cancel culture" is essentially code for trans activists and campaigners for a racial reckoning, in particular with Britain's colonial past. In 2021, Gavin Williamson, then Boris Johnson's education secretary, accused UK universities of seeming "more interested in pursuing a divisive agenda involving cancelling national heroes, debating about statues, anonymous reporting schemes for so-called microaggressions and politicising their curricula."[13] It is worth noting that the anecdotes he alludes to had very little to do with the university—the Winston Churchill Memorial Trust (Churchill being the "national hero" he's referencing) is not affiliated with any UK university. And enslaver Edward Colston ("debating about statues") graced Colston Avenue in Bristol, not the campus of the university there. Controlling the universities in this language game is a stand-in for controlling . . . more than the universities. It is about expending government efforts to arrest or reverse recent societal developments (above all, the 2020 George Floyd protests)—without fully acknowledging what that would entail.

Williamson quickly introduced the Free Speech Bill that would combat the "chilling effect" of "cancel culture." As Williamson put it in a speech in the Commons, "if universities would not protect free speech, then the government would."[14] The threat he described was supposedly new (and anchored by a then freshly imported neologism), but every single shibboleth he repeated had been rehearsed for decades. Under the Sunak government, the fight against wokeness has become the fallback pitch—if government can't do anything else for you, the idea seems to be, at least it can protect you from the wokesters. Over the course of decades, this discourse has allowed gestures of strident illiberalism and quasi-authoritarianism to dress themselves in the vestiges and verbiage of radical liberalism. A similar process has played out in Germany, albeit in a highly compacted form.

Germany

Thilo Sarrazin was senator of finance in Berlin for the Social Democratic Party (SPD), and later worked at the German Bundesbank, but throughout the aughts made headlines for controversial positions that smacked less of social democracy and more of social Darwinism. In 2010, he wrote the book *Deutsch-land schafft sich ab* (*Germany Abolishes Itself*), which argued that the German welfare state was incentivizing the "wrong" citizens to procreate (in an interview he helpfully clarified he was referring to "little head-scarf girls") and that Muslim populations' unwillingness to "integrate" into German society created a demographic time bomb.[15] Doing the publicity rounds for the book, Sarrazin, if anything, doubled down, with claims that Islam disposed immigrant men to a life of crime and that demographic replacement would drop German IQs, as well as opining on the genetics of Jewish people.

The book made major waves in Germany, selling about 1.5 million copies and spending twenty-one weeks at the top of the sales charts. The reaction in newspapers and magazines was generally negative, but opinion surveys registered a great deal of popular support for Sarrazin's theses—especially among older, male, middle-class, and conservative readers (i.e., among the readers of those same newspapers and magazines). The editor in chief of the *Frankfurter Allgemeine Zeitung*, Frank Schirrmacher, described Sarrazin as the "ghost-writer of a frightened society."[16] Schirrmacher didn't mean anything like a "silent majority," but rather made the point that Sarrazin's entire mode of argumentation (drawing on genetics, generations, evolution) was something that postwar German society had understandably repressed after 1945. Thanks to Sarrazin, it was back and unlikely to be fully banished again.

What Schirrmacher didn't say was that conservative print media would have to adjust to this categorial shift. They would have to find ways of talking in these registers, all the while pretending they were doing no such thing. The stage was thus set for a meta-debate, one in which one side didn't have to say that they believed in x (fill in the objectionable trope here), just that they believed that writing about x was unfairly, dangerously, dictatorially restricted. The result would be a renewed interest on the part of print media in the supposed silence of the supposed silent majority. The model for how to do this came from the most likely of sources—Sarrazin himself.

In 2014, Sarrazin wrote a follow-up to his bestseller, *Der neue Tugendterror* (*The New Moral Terror*), a mix of media criticism and autobiography, in which he used the reception of his 2010 book to thematize "the limits of free speech" in Germany. "Where it excessively restricts the legitimacy of different values and questions, political correctness slides into narrowness of opinion, even opinion terror."[17] Exhibit A was what he now called his own "case," or what we would today call his "cancellation." Chapter 2 of *The New Moral Terror* was titled "How I Clashed with the Rule of Opinion: A Case Study."

It's of course a little strange to chart the utterly anomalous reception of *Germany Abolishes Itself* as an indicator of anything; and it's a bit strange to complain about the suppression of ideas that sold more copies than any other nonfiction book in German postwar history. We can recognize in this shift something that would later come to characterize cancellation narratives: It was unclear what distinguished Sarrazin's injury from having simply been criticized for views he had ventured. But there was a vocabulary available to articulate what made his case special, different, an indicator of "recent" societal and discursive shifts—even if it was, somewhat ironically, an older vocabulary.

In 1990s Germany, the term "political correctness" had been discussed far and wide in media across the political spectrum—first to describe what was allegedly happening in the United States, later as something that was in the process of spilling over to Germany. By the 2010s, however, the term's use had begun to splinter: It was still routinely invoked by culture writers, but its invocation was, well, routine. Those books that still positioned PC as an existential threat to Germany, the West, and freedom tended to come from Far Right publishers and politicians— even though they occasionally succeeded in getting mainstream media to care. Not much of Sarrazin's argument was new; when it came to "political correctness," his book largely rehashed an argument made by Alexander Gauland—who would later become chair of the Far Right Alternative for Germany (AfD)—that had appeared in the centrist daily *Tagesspiegel* in 2012.[18] But whether Sarrazin used the words himself or others used them in reacting to his book, his intervention repopularized a long lexicon of terms and phrases that had either fallen out of use or become a preserve of Far Right publishing: the "dictatorship of opinion," the "cartel of opinion," the "terror of virtue," the "good people" (*Gutmenschen*).

Each of these had even earlier ancestry. Sarrazin's use had a funny way of both activating that ancestry and making it forgotten. The very title of Sarrazin's book—*The New Moral Terror*—after all, implied an older one. And occasionally reiterating what is at heart the same discourse seems to be part of PC's enduring appeal, not just in Germany. Still, when warnings about cancel culture first arrived in Germany, they not only drew on the anecdotes and anxieties of the US discourse, but also on the historical comparisons and buzzwords of the Sarrazin debate. This is true for France as well: The central concept was preserved in its anglophone original for a reason: to signal otherness and suggest cultural colonization by American wokesters. But that central concept was then embedded in a rotating roster of associated terms that no one ever really bothered to distinguish from one another, instead swapping them out for one another once they had given the first term enough of a workout.

Ulf Poschardt, editor of Germany's conservative *Die Welt,* takes aim, week after week, at a leftie, eco-conscious (more recently "woke") milieu, which, he says, is trying to "infantilize," "silence," "reeducate," or even "exterminate" all heterodox thought.[19] The details of his description never really change, but the descriptors rotate with great frequency. At some point, the targets of his ire were *Gutmenschen* ("good people"), then they were the "opinion and moral elites," the "*juste milieu,*" the "authoritarian moralists," the "humorless bourgeoisie," then they were the "ivory tower." The writers at his newspaper add further descriptors: "Left-green," "Woko Haram," "wokistan." Who exactly is meant by these labels is never entirely clear, partly because the metaphors, implicit comparisons, and historical resonances shift with each new or recycled term. Some sound funnier than they sound threatening, some historical comparisons are clearly hyperbolic, and some others appear to be offered seriously. All of them are at least somewhat ironic, but the polemic behind them seems deadly serious. When "cancel culture" entered the German lexicon, it was and wasn't new: The term itself had a feeling of newness and was dutifully trotted out and discussed in article after article. But whenever it came to explaining and describing this supposedly new (and foreign) phenomenon, the old terms were suddenly back to lend their support.

There is another feature shared by the reception histories of the term in specific countries: Cancel culture narratives connect with populations that have recent, albeit possibly misleading, memories of some societal concern about which they felt they could not speak freely. When I toured Germany with the German edition of this book in the summer of 2023, one surprisingly frequent topic of censorship and cancel culture that I was asked about was the COVID-19 pandemic. People felt that in media and in the broader culture there had been a prohibition against expressing dissatisfaction with lockdowns or concerns about vaccines.

Looking over actual media from 2020 to 2022, this turns out to be a false impression—if anything, German media had bent over backwards to platform views that, even at the time, one could have known were not really worth taking seriously. But anyone who lived through the pandemic years will recall the feelings of friction as responses in the face of a global health catastrophe slowly and subtly diverged, and how those divergences became both highly politicized and highly personal. Most of us will recall thinking close friends or family were not careful enough or were overly careful. We rolled our eyes at them using cloth masks or not using them, wiping down their groceries or not wiping them down. And most of us will recall stewing silently and pointedly *not saying anything* while friends, neighbors, and—purely hypothetically—in-laws did what appeared to be, either in its carelessness or overcaution, perfectly deranged. As a result, people felt that they had self-censored, more importantly had been deprived of a voice. Complaining about "cancel culture" was the vocabulary that allowed them to articulate this frustration.

Sarrazin's tale of censorship did something similar. After all, as a statement of fact, the idea that his views had been suppressed was contradicted by his books' massive impact and sales success between 2010 and 2014. But Sarrazin's diagnosis still caught on, because of a much more impactful later event: the so-called refugee crisis of 2015. Everyday Germans may not have found the former bank director's complaints about having been silenced persuasive. But at least some—especially older, white, and middle-class Germans—will likely have used Sarrazin's vocabulary to explain their feelings to themselves in 2015.

In 2014, Sarrazin complained that his warnings about invading Muslim hordes had been suppressed by a moralizing media consensus. In 2015, nearly a million refugees, many of them from Muslim nations, had arrived in Germany, and, for a while at least, the social consensus was characterized by considerable warmth towards the new population. Media and everyday observers registered the new *Willkommenskultur* ("welcome culture") with some surprise. But there were of course those who felt differently and who—like anti-vaxxers in 2020—had to grapple with being in a small minority while understanding themselves instinctually as the silent majority. Whatever else a term like "cancel culture" is, it reframes a shifting social consensus that the speaker doesn't share, turning the consensus into something uncanny, sinister, and even conspiratorial.

With "the terrorism of virtue," "dominance of opinion," "rituals of denunciation," or "rules of speech and thought," Sarrazin's vocabulary allowed that minority of Germans who didn't feel the way most of their compatriots did about the refugees to give expression to their discomfort—and to imply that the majority in truth shared their discomfort but were afraid to speak openly about it. This strikingly resembles an experience clearly encapsulated in worries about cancel culture: the idea that most people won't say what they're really thinking (because they are cowed by left-wing censors or by Greta Thunberg), though—if they could—they'd say exactly what I'm thinking.

Sarrazin's book also set the tone when it came to the implicit timeline around the supposed gradual narrowing of discursive possibilities. By including the word "new" in his book title, Sarrazin wanted to emphasize that the outbreak of the PC groupthink he was describing was a relatively recent phenomenon. But the rest of the title—"moral terror"—undercut the newness. For readers in 2014, the term would have activated a long range of associations. For one thing, most reviewers understood the "terror" in the title not to refer to terrorism, but to the *terreur* of Robespierre. But in fact the term had been part of complaints about political correctness since the 90s. Dieter Zimmer had written in 1993 that "whoever diverges in any way from the PC camp, even only on a single point, is immediately interned in the camp for enemies."[20] Note the slide in the meaning of the word "camp": In the first part of the sentence, the author appears to be thinking of an army's camp, where the PC brigades hang out; by the end of it, we appear to be in an internment camp.

The word "terror" had a strange dual function: It allowed writers to move effortlessly from an experience of being of a different opinion than most of the people around them, to something that smacked of totalitarianism. And it seemed to relativize actual totalitarianism, to demote it to a mere metaphor. The novelist Martin Walser had begun invoking "moral terrorism" in the early 90s to describe how "the discourse" "labels what is sayable and declares the rest taboo."[21] The phrase was frequently invoked by the Austrian Far Right politician Jörg Haider throughout the 1990s.[22] Two authors associated with Germany's New Right, Ulrich Schacht and Heimo Schwilk, wrote in 1994 about the "moral terrorism of the PC *Blockwarte*" of their day, alluding to the infamous low-level Nazi functionaries who surveilled their immediate neighborhood.[23] Sarrazin's vocabulary was thus not new, although it was all about newness. It reactivated older diagnoses, articulated longstanding grievances, revivified existing argumentative pathways. But it did so as it pretended to describe a very recent, likely accelerating development.

One thing this continuity of language may hide rather than make visible is that while complaints of a "dictatorship of opinion" could sound eerily similar between texts from 1994 and 2014, the opinions one supposedly was "no longer" allowed to express had shifted. Earlier references to *Tugendterror* had been all about Germany's (or Austria's) relationship to the Nazi past. Walser had used the term to fulminate against "the moral cudgel" that supposedly was Auschwitz. Haider used the word to explain why he was the victim when his musings on the advantages of Nazi rule generated understandable media opprobrium.[24] The "newness" of the "moral terror" Sarrazin described constituted less a revised diagnosis of the object (the "moral terror"); rather, it comprised a permission to redeploy a vocabulary that was very openly steeped in the Neue Rechte (New Right) of the 1990s, in historical revisionism, and in what in German are called *Schlussstrichdebatten*, debates about putting an end to the German processes of self-interrogation and self-castigation.

Except the discourse was now recycled with a new target: Gone were references to Auschwitz, gone were calls to being proud of Germany again. Instead, the things that one was allegedly not allowed to talk about were Islam, multiculturalism, refugees, and to a lesser extent LGBT people. Essays and speeches by Martin Walser and Botho Strauss ("today, the well-intentioned is more vicious than outright nonsense"[25]) attacked what they regarded as a facile left-wing moralism as an explicit call for a conservative alternative. When their key terms were recycled by Sarrazin, however, their vocabulary, which in the 1990s had been distinctly conservative, was understood as liberal.

In his article about *l'affaire* Sarrazin, Frank Schirrmacher made a suggestive point that wasn't widely noticed at the time: Many in the German feuilleton thought of Sarrazin as a *Bildungsbürger*, that is to say a bourgeois who defended class distinctions alongside a canon of German culture that justified those distinctions. This was certainly how most Germans read Sarrazin. But Schirrmacher pointed out that this was, of course, not what Sarrazin was doing: He was interested in genetics, inheritance, literal biological patrimony. So while Sarrazin presented himself as defending German culture against immigrant newcomers, he "in truth no longer believes in its binding power"; his "flight into biologism," Schirrmacher wrote, was "what invariably happens when societies . . . mistrust their own values."[26] And this was what Sarrazin's reception was ultimately about: a segment of the population furious in its defense of values it wasn't sure it entirely believed in anymore.

France

In both the case of political correctness and cancel culture, American signifiers rather than actual conditions seem to have been imported to Germany. Nevertheless, the feeling of being caught up in developments from abroad is an important emotional factor that probably makes the import effective in the first place. A similar process of identification and disidentification can be seen in France: As the political scientist Alex Mahoudeau shows in his book *La panique woke*, the term "le wokisme" emerged as an all-purpose formula on the other side of the Rhine at exactly the same time as cancel culture was establishing itself in Germany. But it did so in a network of semi-related concepts: "indigénisme," "islamogauchisme," "communautarisme," "neo-féminisme intersectional," "politiquement correct," or "cancel culture."[27]

For all the differences of vocabulary, the French diagnoses and German ones were remarkably similar. And just like in Germany, the pattern proved remarkably invariant over time. Here is a description of "thought taboos" from a German-language 1997 essay on the "terror of virtue":

> Only brutal openness, only unvarnished discourse and the resulting decisive action, could now point the way out of the crisis—but free speech is encircled by taboos. In a quasi-religious manner, barriers to thinking are systematically erected in order to obscure the view of reality and possible solutions.[28]

Here is a description from France, almost twenty-five years later—from an essay by the political scientist Josepha Laroche, entitled "La Censure lexicale de la bien-pensance" (Lexical Censorship of Right-Thinking):

> In the France of 2019, certain essential topics for the future of our country—for instance, the migration question or the salafization of society—cannot be calmly addressed to give rise to real, argued, documented, and impartial exchanges. Instead, the "good camp" fights tirelessly to silence all opposition to its doctrine.[29]

In France, like in Germany, the late 2010s saw a reactivation of older discourses about what Laroche calls "ideological intimidation strategies" but with new premises and a partly updated vocabulary. An article like Laroche's (which appeared in the *Revue des Deux Mondes*) can sound very familiar to American ears: Ideological intimidation "forbids any distance from the 'empire of political correctness'"; "whoever does not submit to its Newspeak [*novlangue*] sees their position criminalized in the name of morality."[30] The examples—public figures accused of Islamophobia, the disinvitation of a French rapper, scandals caused by the novelist Michel Houellebecq—resemble the kinds of stories that would pepper this sort of article in the United States.

In Germany, 2015 proved the moment when an older, identifiably niche and identifiably right-wing vocabulary was repurposed to fit a new situation and a new user base. Suddenly people, who would have recoiled from murmurs about a "moral terror," a "moral cudgel," or "a spiral of silence" when they were identifiably part of a revisionist vocabulary about Nazism and German national identity, could wield the same terminology about other topics and count on far broader acceptance. But the "refugee crisis" of 2015 furnished a very specific experience for socially conservative Germans: For a moment at least, a consensus that had seemed ironclad (that Germany was *not* an "immigration country" and that any admission of immigrants had to come with the exacting of a pound of flesh, lest the Far Right act up) seemed to come unstuck. Public opinion appeared to move decisively in a different direction and away from their positions. The experience must have been deeply uncanny for many public commentators, and that uncanniness was best expressed through the vocabulary they inherited from the New Right.

It is striking that a very similar process had played out in France just two years earlier, but in arena of family and sexual identity. François Hollande had campaigned for the French presidency in 2012 partly on a promise to extend marriage rights to same-sex couples. Hollande won on May 6 of that year, and by November 2012 Justice Minister Christiane Taubira had introduced to the National Assembly a law amending the Napoleonic Code to define marriage as a contract "between two persons of different or of the same sex." In October of 2012, the opposition to the project founded La Manif pour tous (LMPT), "the protest for all." Large protests across France followed in November and again in January and March of 2013. A media campaign, including books and articles, likewise warned against gay marriage and gay adoption.

The gay marriage fight was defined by several of the crossovers that would define the reception of Sarrazin's book in Germany a year later. There were genuinely unusual crossovers—the fight against Loi Taubira united Catholic reactionaries and the feminist thinker Sylviane Agacinski, wife of former socialist Prime Minister Lionel Jospin. But la manif and its organizers also stoked the confusion by deploying a dizzying menagerie of free-floating signifiers: the French Marianne (symbolizing Liberty, Equality, Fraternity) walked alongside Gavroche from Les Misérables; a group of Antigones; bare-chested "Hommen" (modeled after the bare-breasted activists of Femen); racist caricatures next to repurposed anti-racist slogans from the 1980s. The citational mania, to say nothing of a puzzling tendency toward male nudity, suggested nothing so much as a gay pride march.[31] The gay marriage debate could thus combine racist and anti-racist signifiers, feminist and anti-feminist rhetoric, defenses of laïcité and religiously motivated attacks on the same.

Above all, the gay marriage debate in France became a debate about the debate one supposedly wasn't allowed to have. Of course, millions protested in the streets, and the conservative press and politicians across the political spectrum spoke out against the law. But they did so in a tone of stifled heterodoxy. As in the case of Germany two years later, the criticisms of the new law kept framing a shift in public opinion as essentially a suppression of one point of view. Frigide Barjot (real name Virginie Tellenne), one of the main organizers of la manif, wrote in her pamphlet "against gay 'marriage'" that "public opinion reflects above all what people hear in the media, especially when they only open their columns to Act Up activists (200,000 euros subvention, 137 adherents)."[32]

The majority of French citizens who were in favor of gay marriage? They were actually dupes of a tiny *minority* of queer "militants." The slow but persistent change in public opinion around the issue? A sign of brainwashing and thus a sign of democratic illegitimacy rather than legitimation. The rhetoric of "compassion, tolerance, progress, future"? A way of weaponizing the "fear of general reprobation."[33]

What *la manif* reactivated was less the American-style model of the silent majority, but rather a fear that seems far more common in European reflections on identity politics (or, as the French sometimes put it, *communautarisme*) and cancel culture. This is the fear that political correctness *creates* (and does not merely reflect) a divided society. The law at issue (*mariage pour tous*) and its public rebuke (*manif pour tous*) each staked a claim to universality. The dialogue that Barjot claimed wasn't happening really was about who constituted "everybody," who was there "for everybody," and who (by implication) was dividing "everybody."

The debate about the supposed non-debate drew on earlier antecedents. In 2013, a long special section of *Valeurs actuelles*, one of the main publications of the French Far Right, was titled "La tyrannie des bien-pensants," "the tyranny of the right-thinking." The term *bien- pensance* has long been used in a pejorative and ironic way (it crops up in Proust and in translations of Orwell), usually to describe a kind of easy and fearful bourgeois conformism. In the twenty-first century the phrase "tyranny of the right-thinking" was most associated with the supposed orthodoxies of political correctness. A book edited by journalist Jean-Marc Chardon in 2002 had collected dozens of articles exemplifying debates the French were allegedly not having, not daring to have, not allowed to have. A similar sense—that a debate that was very much occurring was in fact not occurring, not allowed to occur—prevailed around *la manif*. The opponents of gay marriage, *Valeurs actuelles* explained, had been "manhandled by the government throughout this debate. Christiane Taubira, the magazine wrote, "doesn't seek to debate, she seeks to reduce the opposition to silence."[34]

When the vocabulary of political correctness (or *le politiquement correct*) arrived in France in the early 1990s, it melded with a preexisting discourse. In the wake of the 200-year anniversary of the French Revolution, there was a renewed interest in a French national identity, and—more to the point—a drive to articulate what was not part of that identity. This was the period when France first debated banning Islamic headscarves, when there were first attempts to tamp down engagement with France's colonial past, when Jean-Marie Le Pen's Far Right National Front Party consolidated its mid-1980s electoral gains and

156 The Cancel Culture Panic

translated them into media presence. This was the beginning of a process that the political scientist Frédérique Matonti has described as a reactionary turn in French politics.[35]

It was also a moment that saw three things intertwine in French public discourses. Firstly, concerns about a "fracturing" of social cohesion in the United States (which authors linked to identity politics, above all the Nation of Islam, and political correctness). Secondly, a fear that a similar process of fracturing and erasure was seizing hold of France, such that difficult truths could no longer be expressed. And thirdly, a renewed wave of Islamist terrorism. In the 90s, these three were often fused through the word "fatwa," which managed to be metaphorical and literal, linking supposed prohibitions on speech to very real terrorist violence. In the 2020s, this same nexus is expressed through the term "islamogauchisme," which suggests that "postcolonial" elites are aiding and abetting Islamists through their political correctness.

The French discourse around *le politiquement correct*, and later cancel culture and wokism, had a paradoxical relationship to colonial structures. It was fairly open about the fact that one of the things it no longer wanted to apologize for was French colonialism and imperialism. "You are supposed to hate the French for being French, on account of this people having always been racist and xenophobic,"[36] Georges Dillinger complained in an essay about PC in 1996. But at the same time, the discourse positioned political correctness, cancel culture, and wokism as themselves forms of cultural colonialism and imperialism. The title of Mathieu Bock-Côté's book *L'Empire du politiquement correct* (2019) makes this explicit, as do Laroche's constant references to Orwell: They regard political correctness as a form of anglophone colonialism, even imperialism. From the beginning in the 1990s, then, French adaptions of the political correctness panic were intended to defend the republic from three foreign enemies: migrant outsiders, global US dominance, and a conformist elite that enabled them both.

Given that the historically significant year 1989 was the starting gun for the discourse, there are good grounds for the suspicion that this was all a form of French majoritarian identity politics. At the same time, it is important to note that this is not how the discourse presented itself at the time: It was an early stirring of what Joshua Paul has called "anti-identity identity politics"[37]— meaning group claims that refuse to understand themselves as group claims, yes, that present themselves as the negation or transcendence of such claims. The defenses of the 1990s were not of French ethnic identity, but of an idea, a system—*laïcité*, constitutionality, the legacy of the Enlightenment. The main objective of criticizing *le politiquement correct* in France was not to safeguard some kind of French identity; it was to preserve French political cohesion. In practice, though, the two could be hard to tell apart. People wanted to assert the primacy of certain principles, but almost invariably they slipped into talking about race.

It was this emphasis on social cohesion that gave the French critique of *le politiquement correct* in the 90s something we have observed before: the characteristic chimeric quality of PC discourse. In the United States leftists could agree with Christian conservatives on the evils of PC, and indeed leftists could sound conservative and Christian conservatives could sound leftist when it came to political correctness. In France, too, highly divergent political groups began worrying, and for strangely complementary reasons, about the fraying of societal bonds under the assault of political correctness. Georges Dillinger (a pseudonym for Georges Busson) writing in the journal *Revue des Deux Mondes* in 1996, posited that "political correctness" abetted "the destructive hatred for the 'social model'"—meaning the defining identity around which society is modeled. He helpfully clarified: "in France the French, in the US the 'WASP.'"[38]

But Dillinger linked the weakening of this supposedly monolithic French identity to other broad societal trends. A later book by the same author on the topic bears the subtitle *From a Charred Christianity to an Unbridled Individualism*.[39] Busson/Dillinger was an Algerian *pied-noir*, a former colonial Frenchman who had resettled in France after Algeria won independence. When he criticized historical erasures, he seemed to mostly think of French Algeria and the French colonial empire.[40] But for him, the term "political correctness" meant more: The reevaluation of France's colonial empire in fact entailed a much greater silencing of "traditional" categories. In his essay in the *Revue des Deux Mondes*, Dillinger laments "the multiplying interdictions on vocabulary," but he doesn't seem to be thinking about words like "handicapped" or "pet": Rather, he describes how "words like 'moral' or 'virtue' must be avoided for fear of ridicule; homeland [*patrie*], discipline, moral order have become cursed concepts."[41]

The *Revue des Deux Mondes* is a right-of-center publication, but it is nominally laicist or secular. But when it came to *le politiquement correct*, the magazine happily published essays that sounded like a Catholic reactionary's fever dream. These kinds of confusions abounded throughout the 90s. The journalist and essayist Jean-Marie Domenach, for instance, former editor of *Esprit* and exponent of the Catholic Left, thematized political correctness in *The Twilight of French Culture*, albeit with a merciful question mark in the title (*Le*

Crépuscule de la culture française?). French culture, we learn in his book, is under attack from "an ideology of the *bien-pensants.*"[42]

All of this returned in 2012 and 2013 with *la manif* and the renewed concern that the *bien-pensants* were dividing the French nation. They were importing American thinking about gender (*theorie du genre*) and race ("identity politics") and forcing it on an unwilling populace, overcoming its healthy, natural skepticism with moral browbeating. *La manif* and its intellectual flanks had really made a dual case of how this process worked. First, there were those who could not help themselves (minority voices who in a way couldn't help but assert themselves hysterically, even if their narcissism ruptured the social fabric), and who almost compulsively poisoned the discourse. Identity politics, Laurent Dubreuil wrote in 2019, "is conditioned by a wound that seems incurable but finds temporary relief [only] when it censors or denounces."[43] The relentlessness of the acolytes of identity politics in these types of narratives finds its complement in the lethargy of those well-meaning (*bien-pensant*) hypocrites who let it happen, out of a fear of being perceived as politically incorrect.

French public discourse had long been preoccupied with the idea that the unifying power of French culture was slackening, that particularism was rupturing the social fabric. This may well be the reason why the term "cancel culture" did not become as dominant in French media as it did, for instance, in German newspapers. That honor belongs to *woke* and *le wokisme*, use of which has become absolutely epidemic in France. While there has been a consistent trickle of major French books about cancel culture, the books about *wokisme* constitute a veritable flood: The last two years alone have seen the publication of Philippe Forest's *Déconstruire, reconstruire: La querelle du woke* (2023), Anne De Guigné's *Le Capitalisme woke* (2022), Pierre Valentin's *Comprendre la révolution woke* (2023), Nora Bussigny's *Les Nouveaux Inquisiteurs: L'enquête d'une infiltrée en terres wokes* (2023), Nathalie Heinich's *Le Wokisme serait-il un totalitarisme?* (2023), Samuel Fitoussi's *Woke fiction—Comment l'idéologie change nos films et nos series* (2023), Jean-François Braunstein's *La religion woke* (2022), Audrey Millet's *Woke washing: Capitalisme, consumérisme, opportunism* (2023), Pierre Merle's *L'emprise woke* (2023), and at least a dozen others.

Just glancing over the list of books gives you a sense of the narrative that has made *le wokisme* so potent a concept in France. The subtitle (when translated) of Sylvie Perez's book *En finir avec le wokisme* describes woke as *An Anglo-Saxon Counteroffensive*. Bérénice Lévet's book carries the subtitle *French Spirit Against Wokism*. Mathieu Bock-Côté's *La Revolution racialiste* has the subtitle *And Other Ideological Viruses*. Journalist Anne Toulouse's 2022 book

Wokisme asks in its subtitle *Will France Be Contaminated?* The French edition of Gad Saad's 2020 book *The Parasitic Mind* is titled *The New Virus of Thought: Wokism, Cancel Culture, and Racialism*. Together, these books make clear that the cancel culture story in France—much more overtly and emphatically than the story of political correctness—is a tale of colonization, of invasion, of infection, of contamination. Just as in the panic about gender theory that accompanied *la manif*, wokism and cancel culture are about US political ideas insinuating themselves into an unwilling French public, destroying French culture, and threatening French political cohesion.

But of course, this desire for cultural cohesion is not agnostic with regards to content. Culture has to be there for everybody. But as with *la manif*, the question is who gets to be everybody. France's wokism pessimists often make it sound like the particularist identities that threaten to stymie the unifying power of culture can come from just about anywhere. But, then again, they are warning about "wokism"—a term that began its global circulation in the wake of the Black Lives Matter protests. As the right-wing philosopher Bérénice Levet put it in a 2022 radio interview: "Wokist ideology locks the individual into the narrow circle of his identities."[44] Which certainly makes it sound like certain narrow circles are a bigger problems than others. A white supremacist, a French cultural chauvinist, could also be said to be "locked into the narrow circle of his identities"—but surely we wouldn't call that wokism. No, for Levet there clearly are identities that destroy the social fabric, and there are others—her own, for one—that do not. Identity is other people. She is the universal.

This framing positions French culture as wokism's/cancel culture's primary victim. Sure, this is still about words one is supposedly no longer allowed to say; sure, it is still about historical figures one is now supposedly no longer allowed to celebrate. But behind it all lies the supposed destruction of culture as a binding, unifying force. This is why cancel culture had a much more difficult time in French discourse: Culture wasn't the *agent* of the wokism debate; culture was the *victim*. "Isn't the expression cancel culture oxymoronic?" *Le Figaro* asked the medievalist Hubert Heckmann, author of the book *Cancel!* in an August 2022 interview.[45] "Culture," in other words, is the opposite of "cancellation." "Cancellation" destroys culture and therefore can't have or express one.

More importantly, the endless parade of books and articles in France continues and totalizes the confusion exploited by the semiotics of *la manif*. Its vocabulary is anti-colonial, though it refuses to feel bad about colonialism; the books appear obsessed with social cohesion, but also regard an emerging multicultural consensus as illegitimate and ultimately as no consensus at all. They invoke the specter of totalitarianism to impugn fairly anodyne activism, while unleashing an apocalyptically violent, and at times downright fascist, vocabulary of viruses, contamination, and impurity. The books combine revisionist and deeply conservative talking points with leftist signifiers and slogans. Last and possibly least, these books seem to exploit an instinctive revulsion on the part of many French readers to a profusion of anglophone terms in French public discourse—by unleashing a massive torrent of anglophone neologisms on an unsuspecting public.

EIGHT

Cancel Culture Adaptation

> Beyond Latin America, not just authoritarianism and imperialist wars threaten freedom and culture, but also the academic deformation of cancel culture, that kind of dictatorship of single thought that prevents the free exchange of ideas in the university, the media, and social networks in the name of political correctness and identity fanaticism.
>
> —MARIO VARGAS LLOSA (2023)[1]

People the world over have learned to worry about cancel culture. But in each place, people worry about it in their own way. The warning over a rising tide of illiberal left-wing cancel culture has proved so enduring and so eminently portable because it functions as a meme. Some aspects of it are ported over more or less directly from the United States. But they meld with local ingredients. Even in countries where the public seems convinced that both the phenomenon and the descriptor "cancel culture" are one-to-one imports from the United States, there are preexisting language games that the new conceptual arsenal slots into.

It's not that each national public and national media appear to see something altogether different in cancel culture. There are clear patterns. The German, Swiss, French, and British public seem fixated on US universities, whereas in Russia and Turkey the focus is on popular culture and social media. Of the 1,042 Portuguese language articles (most of them Brazilian) that contain the phase *cultura do cancelamento* on LexisNexis, only 144 (13 percent) contain the word "university." By comparison, of the roughly 7,500 German-language texts over the same timeframe in the same database, 1,650 (or 22 percent) do.

In some media systems, the term "political correctness" was well established when "cancel culture" was added to the vocabulary in 2019. In others it had either never succeeded or had waned in use. France and Germany had a long history of deploying the term, including to describe developments at home. Other national publics usually utilized it to relay events and development in the United States. The Chinese Wikipedia entry for "cancel culture" cites only one person not associated either with the United States or the UK (Pope Francis) and no non-US cases. The Spanish-language entry mentions one—a comedian fired by Greenpeace in Spain—and an open letter expressing support for the "Harper's Letter" on free expression signed by several Latin American authors. The French edition has an entire paragraph on France, but it contains no examples. Portuguese Wikipedia has no non-US examples.

Since the term "cancel culture" was usually self-consciously imported—meaning it was used as and clearly designated as an imported term—it is perhaps not surprising that in many countries the term became an opportunity to articulate one's relationship to the United States, to US culture, and to US cultural dominance. "Cancel culture" comes into many of these public debates as part of what Daniel Bernabé complains is "a whole torrent of Anglicisms": "Pink washing, male tears, TERF, not all men, cisgender, manspreading," an "endless glossary" that has a funny way of being too universal and not universal enough. For Bernabé, the fact that these are all English-language terms signifies two things at once. They "denote where the theories that make up the new activisms come from"—namely the United States. But they also indicate "how the postmodern forgets its specificity about the territory to export concepts like any other merchandise."[2] Bernabé raises—from a decidedly left-wing perspective—something that also drives more conservative critics of cancel culture to distraction: It's too American but doesn't have the good sense to stay American.

But this, too, turns out to be far from universal. Turkish media clearly marked the term as American, but in Turkish cancel culture texts, there is little anti-American animus attached to that fact. In their telling, Turkey is not the innocent victim of a foreign cancel culture, but instead had cancel culture well before Americans managed to find a name for it. When a group of US intellectuals published an open letter about the dangers of cancel culture in *Harper's*, the move received much global attention—most of it with an implicit warning about the creeping advance of "American conditions." But in the Catalan edition of *El Pais*, longtime editor Lluís Bassets Sánchez wrote that the letter could "be read in a Catalan key with respect to the last ten years of [our] political life." "When it comes to cancel culture," he wrote, "we have been the pioneers."[3] The majority of Western publics, media, and authors see in cancel culture tales a sign that the United States has exported one of its unique pathologies; others suggest that these stories from the United States are a distant echo of their country's own.

While the United States is usually positioned as the originator of cancel culture, and while much of the media discourse around it draws on American motifs, this doesn't mean that the discursive transfer only happens bidirectionally between the US exporter and whichever country we're looking at. Turkish media pay attention to Russian uses of the term, and some German newspaper writers seem to respond to a preexisting Turkish media discourse around "lynching" when discussing cancel culture. Swedish media appear to look to German discourses when describing what is supposedly happening in the US. German writers look to France and Swiss writers look to Germany when trying to describe what might happen in their own country if cancel culture were left unchecked. But in the end, it isn't a truly international discourse: It is only a creaky interlocking of vaguely similar language games convinced that, and drawing power and plausibility from the conviction that, they are all speaking of the same thing.

Canceled Culture, Canceled State: Russia

In October 2021 Vladimir Putin gave a speech as part of the Valdai Discussion Club in Sochi, which was already very much about the rhetorical ramp-up before Russia's large-scale invasion of Ukraine the next year. In the speech, he attacked the культура отмены (culture of cancellation). This culture, he explained, was a dangerous Western import, meant to gag and enslave Russia. In February 2022, while bombs were already falling on Kyiv, Putin compared the West's reaction to Russia to the fate of Harry Potter author J. K. Rowling. "They're now engaging in the cancel culture, even removing Tchaikovsky, Shostakovich, and Rachmaninov from posters. Russian writers and books are now canceled."[4] The West had, Putin went on at a televised meeting with various cultural figures, "recently . . . canceled the children's writer Joanne Rowling because she—the author of books that have sold hundreds of millions of copies worldwide—fell out of favor with fans of so-called gender freedoms."[5]

The uses to which Putin and his regime put the term "cancel culture" aren't particularly shocking: They fit rather neatly into narratives of Russian victimhood and Western cultural aggression that Putin's regime has leaned on with great regularity. "Cancel culture" is one more code word for the supposedly corrosive (and anti-Russian) influence of Western thought. As so often in Russian propaganda, the very fact of disagreement in the West is taken as a token of Western weakness. Cancel culture is another way to accentuate the uncanny, uncomfortable aspects of a democratic public sphere. Perhaps it is not shocking, then, that Putin would find his way to this term. But what might be more worth asking is: How did Putin hear about the travails of J. K. Rowling?

"Cancel culture" first appeared in anglophone *Russia Today* segments and articles via a minor Twitter personality from the United States, who otherwise fulminated against SJWs (social justice warriors) and #GamerGate *bêtes noires* Anita Sarkeesian and Zoë Quinn. While western European media resolutely connect cancel culture to the university, to high culture, and to public debate, the Russian reception (especially when it is aimed back at the West, as *Russia Today* is) sticks to the internet and pop culture. *Russia Today*'s international edition has mentioned "cancel culture" over 1,300 times since 2019—usually by amplifying US voices that warn about it. Presumably Putin doesn't consume his own English-language propaganda. But while Putin of course relies on speechwriters for many remarks, his choice of J. K. Rowling as an example of a canceled person seems instructive. To some extent he appears to have followed his own propaganda machine in understanding cancel culture as an internet-based pop culture phenomenon. As journalist Roman Badanin points out, Putin is (most likely) a grandfather. While he was probably fed the "cancel culture" talking points by "court sociologists," Rowling may have made it onto his radar primarily because he was a reader of her works.[6]

When cancel culture did make its way into more established media channels—and began to touch on art and culture, which are so central to western European cancel culture debates—it did so in the uniquely distended sense in which Putin used it in 2022. The specific artists and artworks allegedly suppressed and censored were Russian—operas by Tchaikovsky, concerts by Anna Netrebko. And the ultimate canceled object was Russian culture and, to some extent, the Russian Federation itself. VCIOM (ВЦИОМ—Russian Public Opinion Research Center) is a Kremlin-affiliated demographic institute that conducts regular surveys in the Russian Federation. Since the 2022 crackdowns, it is among the few institutes that still does so. VCIOM has been asking Russians about cancel culture since 2021.

The results of these surveys are moderately interesting, but direct comparisons to similar surveys in the West are made difficult by VCIOM's rather unique framing. The "cancel culture" VCIOM is concerned with the institute describes as follows:

> Western countries are canceling Russian culture: Tchaikovsky and Shostakovich are being removed from the programs, Russians are being dismissed

from theaters, and concerts are being canceled. Anything can be put under ban—Russian art and even Russian classical literature.[7]

On the one hand, this seems a rather opportunistic attempt to graft a preexisting propaganda narrative onto whatever conceptual flotsam comes one's way. This is precisely what the Kremlin has decried as "Russophobia" at every turn for years now; as Eliot Borenstein has argued, it is "one of the few stable pillars in the ever-shifting ideology that might be called 'Putinism.'"[8] On the other hand, VCIOM's framing blurts out what cancel culture narratives in other countries come close to suggesting without ever quite getting there.

For one thing, this framing treats cancel culture as identical with the structures of government and the state. In the United States, there are of course voices that identify the ideology of wokeness with the structure of the administrative state. But they are clear (and Far Right) outliers in US discourses. Most critics of wokeness or cancel culture seem instead to think that they need to protect state institutions from wokeness. Christopher Rufo may claim that, in the wake of the civil rights movement, American institutions were "captured" by "a new ideological regime" of Marxist critical theorists, which "gnawed, chewed, smashed, and disintegrated the entire system of values that came before it," a transformation "so gradual and bureaucratic, it largely escaped the notice of the American public."[9] But that only highlights that most versions of anti-woke and anti-cancel culture narratives do not take this step. VCIOM and Rufo, on the other hand, seem to largely agree on this framing. In VCIOM's question "Cancel culture" appears as a "cancel-culture policy." It is an agenda; it represents a state-run policy program. And the classics it defends no longer matter as classics; they merely matter as representative for the real injured party in the scenario—the abstract entity "Russia."

Elsewhere in the survey, too, the exact numbers gathered by VCIOM aren't nearly as informative as the institute's framing of its questions. The fact that slightly more women than men say they're "worried about the attempts by Western countries to exclude Russian culture from the public sphere" is a lot less interesting than the fact that such attempts "by Western countries" are simply assumed in the questions. Only one statistic is perhaps surprising, and it concerns what Russians interviewed by VCIOM thought ought to be done about the "cancellation" of Russian culture. When asked how they thought "Russia should protect its rights in culture," 30 percent of respondents suggested "engaging mass media," 20 percent said engaging "Western opinion leaders," 16 percent said "creating associations aiming to protect Russian culture," 14 percent said "raising awareness," 12 percent suggested going to the courts, and 9 percent advocated for petitions.[10]

VCIOM's framing of cancel culture may strike Western readers as a distorted version of US debates, but in this one respect Russian fears seem to mirror American ones: Cancel culture is an existential threat, but the best way to combat it is to raise awareness and yell about it in mass media. At a time when the Kremlin and its affiliated media issued apocalyptic threats and claimed that NATO was a party to the war in Ukraine, the Russians interviewed by VCIOM seem to have intuited that yelling about cancel culture is attention warfare. Its currency, its injury, its remedy, its *lingua franca* are eyeballs, clicks, minutes of airtime, units of discursive oxygen.

Mobs Online and Off: Turkey

Turkish media tend not to use the anglophone "cancel culture" but rather speak of a "lynching culture" (*linç kültürü*). On the one hand, this term is often deployed as straightforward translation of "cancel culture" (the other, rarer one being *İptal kültürü*). Turkish Wikipedia glosses "lynching culture" as a translation of an anglophone concept. Vladimir Putin's reference to an "infamous" or "so-called cancel culture" in 2022 became in Turkish *meşhur linç kültürü*—the famous lynching culture.[11] And many of the motifs of Western discourses recur in Turkish ones: social media, celebrities, social ostracism.

At other times, Turkish authors seek to distinguish one from the other. They are not entirely wrong to do so, as the use of *linç* to mean something very much like "canceling" predates wider adoption of the term "cancel culture" in the United States. Something similar is true of the usage of the term *linç kültürü*, which, while less common, appeared long before "cancel culture" became a common term in English. It designates, as Pierre Hecker writes, "a state of public outrage and mobilization that seeks to restore the dignity of the nation."[12] Where western European invocations of "cancel culture" emphasize the word's North American provenance (and the Russian invocation emphasizes the Western provenance) as a sign that a set of social and discursive practices that are designated by this neologism are "now" making their way to France, Germany, the Netherlands, and so forth, the Turkish reception is largely free of this fear of social contagion. To hear Turkish politicians tell it, no one is forcing cancel culture on Turkey. Rather, Turkey had cancel culture before the West.

What makes *linç kültürü* a strange beast compared to its anglophone cognate is that, as the journalist Tanıl Bora has pointed out, there is a tradition of lynching as a political tool on the Turkish Far Right, and a concomitant acknowledgment of its uses by Far Right parties. Whether it is against Kurdish or Armenian activists and journalists, against sexual minorities or other suspected outsiders, there is a tradition of political speech leading to violence, and a fairly direct relationship between what Bora calls "symbolic lynching" and actual lynching; in Turkey, historically "this transition is not very difficult anyway."[13] There is an entire vocabulary excusing mob violence as *millî refleks* (national reflex), *millî irade* (national will), and *millî öfkesi* (national anger). There exists on the Turkish Right a rhetoric around spontaneous violent expression and around actual violence, which is implicitly affirmative when it comes to certain kinds of vigilantism.

So *linç kültürü* isn't necessarily a metaphor—except, of course, when it is. The word *linç* can be found applied to J. K. Rowling and Dave Chappelle—or to a violent attack on two trans sex workers in Ankara's Iskitler district by a group of thirty people. The term "lynching" in Turkish has come to refer to literal violence (or calls for violence that are likely to be heeded), but it can just as easily be about metaphoric opprobrium, for instance in gossip magazines or later in online spaces. And this latter discourse can sound an awful lot like US or French complaints about cancel culture.

Consider a 2017 article about "celebrities who were lynched" (*linç edilen ünlüler*) from *Yeni Şafak*, a daily very much in line with President Erdogan's AKP Party. The "famous names who were lynched by their followers" referred to celebrities who had attended an event with President Erdogan. If you were to substitute "canceled" for "lynched," this could be a story in a US newspaper. In fact, it recalls the first occurrence of the term "canceled" in the *New York Times*: Rapper Kanye West complaining "'I'm canceled. I'm canceled because I didn't cancel Trump.'"[14] This right down to the fact that "lynching" here means nothing more than that social media users were not nice to a celebrity, and right down to the fact that nothing actually happened. The celebrities, despite the "lynching," *Yeni Şafak* told its readers, "still did not hesitate to share those moments."[15]

Here we have *Yeni Şafak* employing a shell game familiar to readers in other countries: Celebrities embraced a specific political cause; they received blowback online; it didn't change anything for them, but the newspaper frames the backlash as dangerous and the celebrities' going about their business as bravery. At the same time, perhaps more overtly than in the United States, in France and Germany (and perhaps similarly to Russia and Brazil) the "cancelable" action taken by the celebrities consists in an identification with the structures of the state. The real victims of this metaphorical cancel culture are Erdogan and the AKP. As in Putin's rhetoric, where "behind" any individual cancellation ultimately looms an attempt to cancel Russia as such, this use of "lynching culture" seems to position the government as the ultimate victim of cancel culture. There have been articles that seem to understand one form of lynching to consist of unfairly linking opposition politicians to President Erdogan—for instance, when Muharrem İnce, founder of the Homeland Party, was called an "AKP member, a man of the palace" online.[16] Even here, then, the ultimate canceled object is, at least implicitly, AKP rule.

Power Relations, Historical Revisionism, and Cancel Culture Narratives

This idea—that identification with massive state power can actually make one a victim—occurs again and again in international cancel culture discourse. The very first article about the phenomenon in the Brazilian newspaper *Folha de Sao Paulo* brought up gymnast Diego Hypolito as a victim of "cancellation." Hypolito, "months after coming out as gay," was "canceled by people linked to the Left and the LGBT community." His crime? "Appearing in a photograph alongside Jair Bolsonaro."[17] On the Argentinian Far Right, as part of a broader revisionism about the Argentine military dictatorship, the "cancel culture" label has been applied retroactively in order to reverse historical culpability.

Similarly, in Argentina there has been an attempt to shift focus away from the *Proceso* junta (1976–1983) and its "Dirty War" and towards left-wing terrorism opposed to the regime. Javier Milei, elected president in the 2023 election under the Libertad Avanza banner, but above all his-then running mate (and today's vice president) Victoria Villarruel were keen to switch focus from the atrocities committed by the junta (and the need to work through them) and towards those committed against it—invoking cancel culture as an argument. As Argentina's most influential conservative daily *La Nación*, wrote in 2021, "everything is forgiven to the Left; [for the] Right, not even one wrong word. The victims of the guerrilla terrorism of the 70s are still hidden." Then it added: "We had [in the 1970s] an early preview of what we know today as cancel culture."[18]

Cancel culture narratives frequently skew our impressions of societal power relations—those who would seem to hold little power in society appear as the prosecutors, the tormentors; those who would seem to have all of the power are the victims. Populist regimes that thrive on both fantasies of omnipotence and fantasies of powerlessness tend to emphasize this aspect of the narrative. They are also drawn to the discourse's inevitable slide between metaphoric violence and real violence. "Cancel culture," when it is described in Turkish media, is often treated as synonymous with "online shitstorm"—meaning it becomes a description of unruly speech in the few venues in Turkey not dominated by Erdogan and his allies. Erdogan himself made this explicit in the final stretch of the Turkish presidential campaign in May 2023: "Lynching culture is ingrained in the soul of [opposition party] CHP."[19] Erdogan and his allies bemoan metaphoric violence while implicitly condoning literal violence.

This is just as true of someone like Donald Trump, of course, who can bemoan (symbolic) mob violence against his person or his supporters while stoking actual mob violence by his followers. At the same time, this opportunistic adoption of the US cancel culture discourse does point to real fault lines in Turkish public discourse that don't have obvious US analogues. Ahmet Hakan, editor of *Hürriyet*, who was himself injured during a mob attack in front of his house in 2015, has insisted that "cancel culture" and "lynching culture" are not the same.[20] But of course making this distinction is not easy when online speech spills directly into political violence. A 2023 column by the investigative journalist Nedim Şener in *Hürriyet* is illustrative of this trend: Cancel culture for Şener seems to be largely identical with a decline of decorum brought about by social media, anonymity, and troll accounts—although his point is how easily online abuse can translate into offline violence. Şener singles out politicians from the Kemalist İyi Parti but points out that İyi head Meral Akşener has likewise endured online "lynching culture."[21]

In this respect, what is happening in Turkey resembles what is happening France: In a society in which speech has recently been followed by politicized violence, the relationship to online opprobrium can become deeply ambivalent. Where does mean-spirited backlash end and where does dangerous incitement begin? Looking again at Turkey points to another commonality: Once the warning about cancel culture gets dissociated from historical patterns of violence and attaches to whatever those with the biggest microphones worry about, then real violence risks being abused as a reservoir for metaphoric comparisons, and those most likely to suffer politicized violence risk being presented instead as its implicit authors.

CONCLUSION

Liberalism and Illiberalism

> Harvard must create an academic environment with real academic freedom and free speech, where self-censoring, speech codes, and cancel culture are forever banished from campus.
>
> —BILL ACKMAN, post on X (Twitter) (January 2, 2024)[1]

Talking about cancel culture or wokeness always means not talking about other things. This fact—that it occupies space in the attention economy that we all sense *could* (and perhaps *ought*) to be taken up by something else—lends the discourse its often-unserious tone. Like whataboutism, it can feel reflexive, slapdash, or, at its worst, like trolling. But the same fact might also point to a very serious threat this discourse poses.

It's not surprising that conservative voices enjoy fulminating about radicals on university campuses. What can be amazing is the single-mindedness with which they do so. On February 24, 2022, Vladimir Putin's army had just invaded neighboring Ukraine; meanwhile the Conservative Political Action Conference (CPAC) was taking place in Orlando, Florida—the big show for the right wing of the Republican Party since 1974. Putin's invasion should have been a natural topic for the speakers: The Cold War seemed to be back, and America's enemies were massing at the borders of the free world—specifically, an old enemy that conservatives had traditionally used to put pressure on the Democratic Party and to stoke fear. And yet, the name Putin was largely missing from the conference. Those speakers who, like Florida Governor Ron DeSantis, were eager to position themselves as presidential contenders for the 2024 election seemed to recognize only two enemies capable of striking fear into the heart of red-blooded Americans: wokeness and cancel culture. As DeSantis warned:

> The woke is the new religion of the left. And this is what they have in mind. That's why they want CRT, because they want to divide the country. That's why they removed statues of Thomas Jefferson and Abraham Lincoln and Teddy Roosevelt, take George Washington's name off schools, because they want to erase that history, they want to delegitimize our founding institutions, and they want to replace that with their left-wing ideology as the foundational principles of our modern-day society.
>
> Wokism is a form of cultural Marxism. It is not just about raising taxes, or bad economic policy. It's about tearing at the fabric of our society and trying to replace it with something that will be much, much more sinister.[2]

For DeSantis, the Cold War and its logic were still highly relevant—not in relation to Russia, power blocs, or arms races, mind you, but rather when it came to woke students and campus activities. The word "Russia" never came up, which also meant that February 24 was not, at least in Orlando, a turning point. The fears of the Cold War were present, but they were almost in reenactment costumes. The discourse around cancel culture and wokeness is panicked, hysterical, rushing from one freak-out to the next. And yet it has a strangely calming effect on those for whom it works. It's the freak-out you've gotten used to. DeSantis mimed the hits for a conservative movement at peace and at one with itself. This movement no longer had to adapt to external impulses, but rather could live reasonably well with whatever projections it had created of its opponents over the decades.

The scene in Orlando may be far from the editorial offices of *Le Figaro* or the *Neue Zürcher Zeitung*, but this strange stasis-in-excitation pervades much of the European coverage of cancel culture as well. Although the writings are clearly preoccupied with the novelty, the suddenness, the foreboding with which cancel culture looms, at times you can sense a certain comfort of the familiar between the lines. They are back, the terms and anecdotes of yesterday: the *bien-pensants* and the *Gutmenschen*, the spirals of silence and silent majorities; the jealousies that suddenly became big politics; the sputtering careers revived by threadbare victim narratives. They constitute the rules to a game you know. You may insist what is happening is unprecedented, but the very roteness of your response suggests that what is actually happening is a well-honed reflex kicking into gear. The fear of cancel culture, which is so easily recognizable as a cover version of political correctness, took the sting out of the fear of what was genuinely new.

And so behind the fundamentally nugatory freak-out about cancel culture there is, in the end, a genuine fear—about change in society and who gets to talk; about who gets listened to and who gets to be an expert, including an expert on their own experience. And behind the unchanging vocabulary and repetitive anecdote-mongering may well be a genuine shift. This shift has to do with how the kinds of people who consume cancel culture stories—mostly in ambitious dailies in Europe, or in opinion magazines in the United States— relate to liberal democracy as such. And this is far less a story about conservatism, but rather one about liberalism.

With Defenders Like These, Who Needs Illiberals?

As readers will have noticed, discourse around cancel culture and political correctness are often located at a point of undecidability. Their critics regarded them as straightforwardly conservative discourse, but most of the people engaged in them were insistent that they were either themselves speaking from a liberal position or were, in this regard, making a liberal point. This is the shift between Ronald Reagan's and Bill Bennett's attacks on the American university as bastions of un-American activities to Dinesh D'Souza's worry that political correctness represented "illiberal education" and threatened America's inherent liberalism.

The affective dimension of the cancel culture discourse clearly understands itself as liberal, even libertarian. The cancel culture doomsters want freedom from interference; they see powerful quasi-governmental forces meddling in the individual's business. They regard themselves as fighters for either negative freedom (defending the ability to speak without improper imposition) or for positive freedom (defending the freedoms of discourse that make it possible for individuals to speak up in the first place). It won't come as a surprise to a reader of the previous eight chapters that I don't fully support this self-conception on the part of anti-woke crusaders. However, I would urge that this self-conception remains interesting. If for no other reason that it clearly entwines itself with motifs and ideas we recognize as liberal.

Finally, the discourse around cancel culture as a supposed threat to liberalism is largely promoted by writers for and readers of major news publications from *Le Figaro* to the *Wall Street Journal* to the *Atlantic*. Readers and writers of such periodicals must have noticed that what they took to be courageous calls for a defense of liberal values in recent years have increasingly become an opening gambit whose endgame usually consists of more-or-less straightforwardly illiberal restrictions on woke speech and institutions. There is a cognitive dissonance to be resolved here as well: How do these valiant fighters for freedom from the discourse police deal with the very obvious fact that, more often than not, their campaigns open the door to a far more real and ruthless discourse police from the other side of the political spectrum?

As the concept of cancel culture began to establish itself in discursive communities the world over, those who had made it their political linchpin frequently showed openly authoritarian tendencies. DeSantis is, as of this writing, no longer known for principled opposition to cancel culture and wokeness; instead, he is associated with legislation like the Stop WOKE Act, which banned specific books and information from Florida classrooms. He is not known as a champion of academic freedom, but rather as one who pushed to establish state control over Florida's public universities, a move clearly copied from Viktor Orbán and his treatment of Central European University. He is not known for protecting books from being banned and for helping individuals express themselves freely; in the name of combating cancel culture, he has exceeded that culture's imagined excesses.

As Tressie McMillan Cottom has pointed out, this is where the fixation on elite private universities as stand-ins for "the" university becomes quite dangerous. "Because most students attend public universities," she writes, "state-level threats to higher education are especially troubling."[3] Many other governors have followed DeSantis's example—usually in the name of battling critical race theory, the woke campus, or cancel culture. But thanks to the panics around CRT, wokism, or cancel culture, we seem too fixated on Harvard, Stanford, or— in a pinch—Berkeley, to really care. Commentators sometimes call this "cancel culture from the Right."[4] This is a misnomer, since cancel culture was always supposed to function independently of (or even contrary to) established power structures. We have a term for the cancel culture that emanates from a governor's mansion: It's government censorship.

This pattern has held in many, if not all, countries in which there have been robust discussions about cancel culture: Eventually the defense of freedom begins to look an awful lot like its restriction. Italy's Fratelli d'Italia have proposed legislation to protect Italy's historic patrimony and cultural identity from the sinister forces allegedly bent on destroying it.[5] France's minister of culture in early 2023 expressed the wish "that this year will allow us to act . . . against identity assignments and the culture of *annulation*, in other words 'cancel culture.'"[6]

During the leadership contest that would lead to Liz Truss's elevation to UK prime minister in the summer of 2022, Truss's rival Rishi Sunak leaned heavily on culture war tropes, including cancel culture and wokeness. "Left-wing agitators," he told a party gathering in West Sussex, were trying to "take a bulldozer to our history, our traditions, and our fundamental values." He decried "pulling down statues of historic figures, replacing the school curriculum with anti-British propaganda," and "rewriting the English language so we can't even use words like 'man,' 'woman,' or 'mother' without being told we're offending someone."[7] However, his defense of free speech—when it came to specific proposals pitched to the Tory members—seemed to largely involve *restrictions* on speech: blocking schools from offering gender-neutral spaces, codifying what could and could not be covered in sex education.

In 2023, finally, Parliament passed (and the king signed) the Higher Education (Freedom of Speech) Act. The act itself doesn't mention cancel culture, but everyone involved in the drafting, sponsorship of, and advocacy for the bill had made their name in the fight against cancel culture and wokeness. From columnist Toby Young (who had founded the Free Speech Union in February of 2020 specifically to combat cancel culture) to Gavin Williamson (who as education secretary sought to punish universities for "deplatforming" usually conservative speakers), it is quite clear what threat the act was intended to counter: left-wing students protesting conservative speakers.

The act's provisions aim mostly to make supposed acts of cancellation costly: Speakers can now seek compensation for deplatforming, and the Office for Students (OfS) can now levy fines on institutions that it deems to have uninvited speakers. In the end, then, the act most likely will extend protections for some kinds of speech while dramatically chilling some other kinds. It's not difficult to see how the Sunak government got there—after all, they were not protecting freedom of speech as a principle but rather as part of a war on woke. Their complaints were never content-independent, nor—as many academic critics of the Higher Education (Freedom of Speech) Act have since pointed out—could they really be. There is simply speech that a university might reasonably want to deplatform (the act's critics mentioned Holocaust denialism as an example); the question is where one draws the line. But in its universalist, technocratic language, the act actually ensures that campus speech coming from specific ideological and identity positions will be far riskier going forward. And when Harvard donor Bill Ackman wrote on X (Twitter) that his goal was that "self-censoring, speech codes, and cancel culture are forever banished from campus," what he ended up actually asking for were resignations, inquiries, and firings.[8]

As I have shown in previous chapters, this kind of oscillation between universalism (all speech needs to be protected) and a not-so-covert parochialism (in order to protect freedom of speech, certain kinds of speech I don't like should be discouraged) is the central confusion of the cancel culture panic. Is canceling something we all risk doing when we log onto Twitter or Facebook and choose to get worked up about some outrage or another? Or is it something only university students do, only woksters, only trans people, activists, leftists, and so on? The Higher Education (Freedom of Speech) Act shows what happens when this central confusion begins to inform law.

Whether or not this act, and others like it, will have teeth is another matter entirely. But it's worth noting that legislation like this exposes a necessary contradiction in the panic about cancel culture: It demands certain freedoms but can only think to achieve them by doing away with other freedoms. This contradiction has been part of this particular discourse since the 1980s, at least in its US version. After all, when US conservatives first began to use campus politics to win elections in the 1960s—paradigmatically in Reagan's attacks on UC Berkeley—they combined two lines of tradition. After the Supreme Court's decision in *Brown v. Board of Education* there were "traditionalists" (read: segregationists) who wanted to dismantle public education rather than see it integrated (advocating for school vouchers, for instance). They soon found fellow travelers in libertarians like Milton Friedman and Friedrich Hayek, who were (at least officially) uninterested in integration issues but who advocated for school vouchers since they saw them as weakening the state's monopoly on education.[9]

For much of the 1960s and 70s, then, the attack on higher education was an overtly reactionary one, albeit one subtended by an undercurrent of libertarianism, meaning essentially that it was radically liberal. In the 1980s, this shifted: The main targets of campus critiques were now Harvard, Stanford, Yale—that is to say, private institutions. The arguments advanced now became neoliberal or libertarian, but they were not particularly subtly overlaid with moral opprobrium of a decidedly reactionary and revanchist extraction.

The pitch was fundamentally technocratic but also always moralistic. This meant that it was supposedly about rules that could be applied across the political spectrum and applied automatically. But by discounting the real historically grown inequalities that speech is always also about, it actually had a clearly reactionary bent. Chief Justice John Roberts's famous objection to affirmative action—"the way to stop discrimination on the basis of race is to stop discriminating on the basis of race"—perhaps best encapsulates this mode of argumentation: It pretends at an obviousness that exists only if one discounts much of history; its simplicity is meant to sound principled, but it reeks of trolling; and its near-tautological character is meant to suggest that it comprises no political choice but rather the absence of choice.

While the cancel culture panic is reactionary in its basic affects and (often unstated) aims, it also expresses a crisis within liberalism. Writers warning about the new left-wing McCarthyism and the new fundamentalism clearly want to think of themselves as preserving a marketplace of ideas over and against overregulation. This is what Jordan Peterson's fight against Bill C-16 in Canada was about, and it's what US conservatives argue against when they attack DEI initiatives, which they cast as distorting a natural (meritocratic) system of selection, hiring, and promotion. But, in the end, when it comes to making demands, the demands boil down to . . . the government regulating the marketplace of ideas. This glaring contradiction has to be abjured, and has to be abjured repeatedly. This is what happens in cancel culture discourse. Cancel culture discourse constitutes one long attempt to convince the audience that this contradiction is no contradiction at all.

Hierarchies, Expertise, Institutions: Our Heterodox Critics Are Orthodox People

Consider the way cancel culture stories think about hierarchies; consider the way they think about which hierarchies deserve disrupting and which do not; and consider how they think about universality. Whatever we mean by "liberalism," it is characterized by formal equality, freedom from excessive state interference, and an opposition to traditional strictures on human freedom. Whether one is talking to a Democratic senator in the United States or a person with "classical liberal" in their Twitter bio in France or Germany, how exactly these various points are emphasized and set in relation to one another can differ a great deal.

The philosopher Elif Özmen has identified the allergy to "natural" hierarchies as the central liberal principle.[10] Whether we credit this or not, it is noticeable that stories about cancellation combine the rhetoric of laissez-faire neutrality (everyone should get to say their piece) with an almost Burkean insistence on hierarchies that are either traditional or natural. Dig a little below the surface, and such stories are voicing concerns about people who ought to be listened to no longer being heard, the important texts being excised from the curriculum, those who shouldn't have to worry about expressing their opinions suddenly having to think twice. Certain people, texts, questions *deserve* our attention; other people, texts, and questions are illegitimate and their claims on our attention pathological.

Plenty of interpreters of libertarianism, most recently Jason Stanley, have pointed to the way libertarians seem to be hypersensitive to certain hierarchies and forms of dependence and just as readily justify others as "natural" as an intrinsic contradiction of certain kinds of absolute liberalism.[11] We needn't even go that far. What one observes in the cancel culture discourse is simply that the same people who cheer on "disruption" when it happens in certain cultural fields also want to hold on to arenas in which that disruption is illegitimate. Many of the same papers that warn of students or the internet illegitimately usurping power from professors and university administrators react with little-disguised glee when yet another Silicon Valley start-up "disrupts" a previously well-regulated industry. Their moral furor at attempts to change the power dynamics of one sector is matched only by their moral furor at *not* attempting to change the power dynamics in another.

The reason of course is that some hierarchies are seen as natural or legitimate, others as either contingent or as actually counter to nature. This is why cancel culture stories—while they warn of social control, authoritarianism, and state terror—always wind up calling for the state to regulate what people (*other* people) do and say. State intervention is legitimate if it sustains the "natural order" of things. Ron DeSantis calls himself a "small government" conservative or a "constitutional" conservative, but he seems intent on shrinking government down to a size where it can fit into your HR meeting, your locker room, or your gender studies seminar. DeSantis has repeated this self-portrait in his 2012 and his 2023 books. The cancel culture discourse, in its sheer endlessness and mindless repetition, allows politicians and media to pretend at consistency and steady handedness, when in fact their positions are fairly clearly torn between genuinely liberal impulses and equally openly illiberal ones. Cancel culture warnings constitute one immense offer of self-deception.

But technocracy itself has an ambivalent relationship to cancel culture stories: In part what we're seeing in the cancel culture discourse is technocracy coming face-to-face with what it has wrought. Cancel culture is all about how easy it is to fire people. Its anecdotes tend to take place within fields like academia and journalism—rather than, say, big law firms—fields, in other words, in which the neoliberal turn has eroded job security and increased precarity. Of course cancel culture stories do not ask about or emphasize that precarity, but rather thematize the supposed cultural shift. They are little morality plays that pointedly eschew considerations of political economy.

Many writers, editors and journalists have for years warned that market forces have created a toxic attention economy in young adult literature: A shrinking number of publishers nudge their (often young, often minoritized) authors, editors, and assorted creatives to be hyper-present on online platforms, while also becoming extremely sensitive to the reactions of those same online spaces. At the same time, the people creating the works around which the online fandom has congregated are increasingly free agents, only one canceled contract away from not being authors, illustrators, or editors at all. The reason why authors in YA indeed deal with something that indeed resembles descriptions of cancel culture is thus not that the young readership has opinions online—who doesn't? It is that the economic forces around YA publishing translates this readership's favor or disfavor with unusual directness into professional consequences. But that's not what we complain about when we complain about cancel culture.

When it comes to the campus, something very similar is true: Cancel culture discourse partakes of the neoliberalization of the university but refuses to get upset about that neoliberalization. It reflects the increased claim students feel they have on an education that can cost them hundreds of thousands of dollars. But, ask yourself what solutions the usual cancel culture invective proposes for the problems it diagnoses, and you'll once again find mostly funding cuts. This discourse fulminates against the results of market forces dominating fields that had once been at least partially insulated from them, but its prescription simply involves the greater unshackling of market forces.

This suggests that in this discourse, liberalism—in however refracted a manner—comes face-to-face with its own inconsistencies. And the fury and obsessiveness with which it dwells on these stories may be a way of swatting away that contradiction. I have emphasized throughout this book the way universalism and particularism switch places in cancel culture discourse: The discussion largely oscillates between a purely formalist approach—pretending that it cares for the ability to express an opinion, abstracted from any specific content—and a not-so-implicit focus on a very specific set of opinions. Critics often regard this as an inconsistency, but here too it can seem that in fact the inconsistency is the principle. The discourse circulates endlessly between a universalist pose and a set of rhetorical tropes that belie that pose. And that may be what makes this discourse—in spite of all its apocalyptic sound and fury—ultimately so reassuring to many of its consumers. It rehearses how particular kinds of particularism stand in unproblematically for the universal—or used to. How "white American" simply used to be called "American," how "male" used to be just "person," how "German" and "French" used to mean "non-immigrant German and French people."

Marine Le Pen in France frequently relies on the trope that the French are uniquely capable of universalism—thanks to their long tradition of *laïcité*, the legacy of the French Revolution, and of the Enlightenment.[12] She simply tells her voters that they are more capable of universalism than others (meaning, usually, Muslims, immigrants, non-whites). Particularism is, to purloin Sartre's famous line, other people. The sociologist Joshua Paul has pointed out that there exists an "anti-identity identity politics," which stakes particularist claims by identifying them with the universal; this kind of identity politics "assumes a universal identity and rejects the recognition of particularity according to social cleavages."[13] Paul particularly identifies this with the hashtag #AllLivesMatter, which in 2020 circulated as a response to Black Lives Matter. But in a certain way, this subject position characterizes much of our current discourse: one that indignantly rejects any particular self-description and that always describes its own interests as those of "society."

Finally, complaints about cancel culture coincide with the rise of another cultural phenomenon that's difficult to name and more difficult to pin down. The best description I can think of is the petulant rage of those with societal power at the suggestions that they may have societal power. This figure certainly found its epitome during the Trump years with a president claiming to be a victim of the government he was heading, with a Supreme Court looking to pathologize any expression of anger over the massive changes it had wrought in the lives of millions of Americans, with the pouting posture adopted by police departments across the United States over any attempts to check their lethality. But it is of course much older. The ability to understand oneself as a victim while one is actually visiting untold misery on the less fortunate has been key to backlash politics in the United States at least since the 1980s. Power's denial of its own effects didn't start with Reagan, and who knows if it peaked with Trump. But the panic over political correctness was one of the central ways in which this reactionary reflex among (some) conservatives was made plausible to a broader swath of the electorate and the public.

At least initially, this was a gesture of retrenchment rather than counterrevolution. The ideal world that those panicked about political correctness seemed to envision was characterized by an almost preternatural stasis. The way attention, sympathy, interest, expertise, and privilege were distributed was simply to be frozen in the state they were in a few years ago. And it showed: Critiques of political correctness were a way to address problems in a way that ensured that they would never be truly addressed. Warnings about cancel culture (like the PC warnings before them) never say exactly what should happen to ward off the terrors they habitually invoke. In doing so, they allow conservatives (whether neo- or paleoconservatives) to sound liberal and, conversely, liberals (neo- or paleo-) to sound like conservatives. This stasis was a pillar of the global order in the Western democracies since 1989. The fight against cancel culture has at times been presented as a defense of liberalism. In reality, it is part of the backlash that threatens liberal democracy in the first place.

Identity Politics

Those who most stoke cancel culture narratives may be trying to work out certain contradictions in their own political self-conception. But the discourse wouldn't have had the success that it has had across many different countries if it didn't meet people where they were.

Speaking about "cancel culture" allows authors, politicians, members of the media to pathologize certain affects, particularly if they emerge from specific groups: women, people of color, trans people. But it also allows them to downplay the affects that govern their own interventions. This is neatly incapsulated in the language game around identity politics that has followed worries about cancel culture as its shadow twin in much of the Western world: Almost all of the authors whose work I have addressed—whether they write in English, German, French or Spanish—also write about identity politics. And when they do, these critics can sound, frankly, somewhat hysterical.

There are very interesting analyses and critiques of identity politics—from Judith Butler's *Gender Trouble* to Olúfẹ́mi O. Táíwò's *Elite Capture*. But these are about the internal contradictions of Left organizing and the ways tactics can buy into existing power structures. No one would really mistake them for the kind of concern trolling from self-professed liberals—which basically regards "identity" itself as a problem, as an effect of "narcissism," a "therapeutic" impulse, or a politics of "grievance." Such is the nature of the liberal scolds' language game that—no matter the overheated pitch of their rhetoric—in their own self-conception they cannot possibly be the hysterical ones.

Rather, they see themselves (and their audience gets to see itself) as the rational, enlightened descendants of Voltaire. Irrationality and counter-enlightenment are to be found on the opposite side. Writing about Greg Lukianoff and Jonathan Haidt's 2017 book *The Coddling of the American Mind*, the communication scholar Moira Weigel described a "contemporary liberal style of thinking" that prefers to focus on identity politics: "The point of the style is to signal the distance between the authors and the partisans of identity who are too emotional to think clearly."[14] The characterization of identity politics—that it is incapable of irony and humor, immediately "triggered," and "coddled," that it is all about feeling insulted, hurt, and offended—may strike readers as fundamentally unkind. But perhaps more telling is the characterization that emerges as the opposite of this caricature: the liberal critic who is above all calm, rational, dispassionate.

These gestures of "reasonableness," which implicitly explain any objection or critique of their own position as sensitivity, hurt, or neurosis, have had immense success across the globe. It is a position that the dramatist Bernd Stegemann has utilized in annual bestsellers in Germany; it is the one occupied by Caroline Fourest in France; and Jordan Peterson, who in his famous video utters age-old conservative nostrums and constantly talks about his own "fear" but nevertheless clearly sees himself as a spokesperson for the levelheaded, reasonable majority. Here is how Peterson describes the people who worry about political correctness: "They're not . . . you wouldn't call them conservative. You certainly wouldn't describe them as right-wing. They are human beings. . . . Their concerns are not driven by their political ideologies, it's that simple."[15] The ideologues were *other* people; their agendas came from *outside*, especially from the United States. Peterson—just like the heroes of the campus novel—only reacted to the madness that was dropped on his doorstep.

This is the pitch of the cancel culture panic: We are the calm ones, the untriggered ones, no matter how unhinged we may act and sound. And what's more, we are the only ones who argue honestly and rationally. This last point in particular seems to explain the success of cancel culture worries among people who regard themselves as liberal.

In Chapter 7, we met Ulf Poschardt, editor of Germany's right-wing daily *Die Welt*. In almost all of Poschardt's columns, he attacks "rigid" "Calvinist" "moralists," usually, it seems, his neighbors in a trendy upper-middle-class Berlin neighborhood, whether those moralists care about race, gender, the climate, or electric cars. And in almost every column we meet a very specifically imagined ideal type of "liberal" as a counter. Everything the "wokesters" do wrong, this liberal does right. He (and the pronoun is both owed to German grammar and very much a choice) is the "responsible citizen." His actions express a personal kind of "sovereignty." He "has courage where others shy away." He embodies the Enlightenment. He embodies reason. He "doesn't require moralism, because he values his integrity as the foundation of a happy life and enjoyment."[16] In a "state-worshipping, moralizing, freedom-skeptical country" like Germany, he is almost inevitably a loner.[17] He likes to drive fast cars. But he is also "harassed with threats of moral ostracism."[18] More importantly, he is not a solipsist: It's the new McCarthyites of the Left who pursue their "feudal inclination" of "absolutizing their own sensitivities."[19] The liberal, by contrast, sees the big picture, the general interests, the whole of society.

With impressive openheartedness, Poschardt paints a portrait of the artist as a manly liberal. Just as openly the image of vigorous liberalism changes at every turn into one of harassed masculinity, challenged by "a good-natured generation of meaning-seekers, moralists and team players."[20] This liberalism presents its self-confidence, its autonomy, and its courage so forcefully that you can't help but doubt how much conviction there really is behind it. You can see in this figure a residue of all the crises that it confidently pretends to shunt aside. Above all, however, you can see a very decisive self-contradiction. On the one hand, Poschardt's invocation of the sovereign, mature, ideal liberal clings tightly to traditional categories (in particular to very specific ideas of autonomy, of individuality, of masculinity, of rationality), which he sees as destabilized by modern society. On the other hand, however, he is generally hostile to the traditional and established—his ideal type breaks with old moral pieties and frees himself from traditional entanglements. He's a bit anarchic, a punk in a sports car.

This is not actually a contradiction. Cancel culture as an idea seems to appeal to writers and editorial boards, not out of some fear of the new or concern over the loss of old discursive dominance. Rather it reflects a worldview generally affirmative of disruption, but anxious that disruption proceed according to the old rules. The well-deserved shake-up that comes for everything should exclude certain privileges—probably because they are perceived as "natural" or, however you couch it, as God-given.

Many of the newspapers in the German-speaking world that most obsessively cover the disruptions wrought by cancel culture are otherwise stalwarts of deregulation, otherwise celebrate the tech industry's shake-up of tradition. Cancel culture stories allow these newspapers to make a distinction between two forms of disruption: the legitimate anti-elitism of the Right and the illegitimate, elitist challenge of the identity politics Left. In fighting back against a question they see as imported from the United States—how to adjust our values to living in a multicultural society—they repress, or defer answering, another one imported from the United States: what sort of liberalism they want to represent.

Cancel Culture and the Illiberal International

Vladimir Putin has drawn on cancel culture rhetoric. Former Brazilian President Jair Bolsonaro seems to have largely left Twitter for Gettr, a social media platform launched by senior Trump advisor Jason Miller after January 6, whose initial pitch was that it "champions free speech [and] rejects cancel culture."[21] Italian Prime Minister Giorgia Meloni's 2021 book *Io sono Giorgia* warned that "political correctness is a shock wave, a cancel culture that tries to upset and remove everything beautiful, honorable, human that our civilization has developed."[22] Turkish President Recep Tayyip Erdogan is fond of accusing his opposition of being in league with something like "cancel culture." The French Right, from Marine Le Pen to Éric Zemmour, exploited a rhetoric around "wokism," "communitarianism," and "cancel culture" during the 2022 elections.

Right-wing Silicon Valley billionaires from Peter Thiel to Elon Musk have made cancel culture a priority, and mostly seem to boost Far Right candidates and parties in claiming to combat it. Germany's Far Right Alternative für Deutschland is fond of the term. Of course, as we have noted, the Far Right did not originate the term "cancel culture"; and in many Western countries it has not even been the main purveyor of cancel culture discourse. But much of the terminology and many metaphors we encounter in writings about cancel culture had prehistories on the Far Right. Whatever else it is, cancel culture discourse sweeps a lexicon that previously lived in marginal right-wing spaces into something like the mainstream.

Whether one calls it fascism, authoritarianism, or just populism, the years since 1989 have seen something new emerge within conservatism—or perhaps better stated, have seen something reemerge that in the post-45 consensus of governing conservative parties had been sidelined or only half acknowledged. There are multiple reasons proposed for this: Without anti-communism to rally around, conservatism's corrosive edge turned towards democratic institutionalism instead; the commitment to liberal democracy that came easily during the Cold War, and that—in the hands of someone like Buckley—very clearly included grudging and tactical toleration of pluralism, may have outlived its usefulness; within the EU, the status of the nation-state has transformed since 1989, putting pressure on the understanding of politics that implicitly subtended postwar center-right Christian democratic parties from Germany's Christian Democratic Union (CDU) to Greece's Nea Demokratia.[23]

We may suspect—like Corey Robin—that the divide between the old center-right model and the new right-wing populism was never as robust as the conservative mainstream wants us to believe.[24] We may think that many conservatives were fooling themselves all along. But it is important that generations of politicians, public figures, media figures, and ordinary voters did experience this development as an evolution. At times they participated in the shift freely and affirmatively, at other times reluctantly or unconsciously. But a big part of that transition was that they couldn't distribute their affects and allegiances consistently, that they had to pick and choose where to apply their principles. They had to demand respect for political offices and institutions that their avatars were busy demeaning. They fetishized "law and order" while increasingly recoiling at any attempt to apply said law and order to people who looked, felt, or thought like them. They insisted on faith in the same institutions that they claimed had degenerated almost beyond recognition.

Figures like the Le Pens, the Trumps, Jörg Haider, Silvio Berlusconi, Boris Johnson, and Jair Bolsonaro are just the more spectacular names among a broader shift among the intelligentsia, politics, and voters. In this shift, more and more voters, politicians, and journalists seem to be inhabiting two mutually contradictory worlds at the same time. They retain a certain conservative institutionalism, while they simultaneously participate in the populist/authoritarian degradation of institutions. They gleefully contribute to the hollowing out of the very institutions whose aura they then petulantly invoke.

Is it a coincidence that the complaint about cancel culture has become a central concept of this formation? I don't think so. Like all moral panics, the fear of cancel culture articulates an ultimately affirmative relationship to existing structures of power and privilege. The cancel culture panic thrives on the assumption that those who hold power—from elected officials to editors to professors to mainstream writers—deserve that power to some extent. And it provides an all-encompassing explanation as to why those who question the privilege and power of those with privilege and power are not actually worth listening to. They are, after all, "Twitter mobs" who practice "wokeness" as an "ersatz religion." They subscribe to the "cult of gender," are responsible for a "new McCarthyism," and are humorless, graceless, and ultimately faceless.

The fear of cancel culture expresses—in a way—a deep trust in established institutions and elites. This professor was an expert in US race relations and now stands accused of racism! This industrialist donated entire buildings to his community, and now they're trying to take his name off it, just because he owned slaves! Think of all the books, films, and songs we're not getting due to our overly censorious culture—books, films, and songs that, in a legitimate and just world, would exist and dominate our airwaves. Cancel culture discourse wants to believe in our hierarchies with an almost childlike intensity.

Then again, it does not. The university portrayed in the cancel culture anecdote only teaches nonsense, big business slowly drifts into insignificance because of "woke capture," the military is weak and unready due to DEI, experts and technocrats have become beholden to politically correct groupthink and esoteric ideologies. Cancel culture narratives are both implicitly elitist and anti-elitist. They are pseudo-populist (they appeal, after all, to our gut instinct as to what's right and wrong, what should be taught and what shouldn't), but they are also anti-populist, in that they don't dislike hierarchies *as such*—they just think different people ought to be on top. Cancel culture as a worry allows people to participate in two language games at once—two language games, I suspect, in which they still to some extent feel at home. And—more importantly—it allows them to momentarily deny that these two language games are in serious, even existential, contradiction. In complaining about Oberlin College or transgender activism, you get to fancy yourself an institutionalist conservative and a populist firebrand at the same time.

This is the central feeling of the cancel culture discourse: It scornfully celebrates the hollowing out of the very institutions whose aura and established hierarchies it wants to protect. It is a confusing but also a confused discourse: In it, the desire to destroy coincides with an obsession with preservation. You'd like to prohibit gender studies at all universities, but God forbid anyone criticizes a young adult book that you sort of liked in 1967. It is from these kinds of contradictions that the discourse about cancel culture derives its broad range and its astonishing reach. Because it expresses a reality of life—a spirit that still sees itself as liberal or conservative—but has long been (and has long repressed awareness that it is) something completely different, something far darker.

Acknowledgments

The Cancel Culture Panic started out as a translation of my book *Cancel Culture Transfer*, which was published by Suhrkamp Verlag in 2022. But so much had happened around cancel culture that I decided to revise, expand, rearrange, and rework pretty much the entire book. This, then, is a book I essentially wrote twice. Thus, the list of people who have shaped my thinking, who have tested and contested my ideas, and who have helped my research is absolutely enormous.

I firstly want to thank my colleagues at the Michelle R. Clayman Institute for Gender Research—above all Alison Crossley, Bethany Nichols, and Theresa Rosinger-Zifko. Theresa helped me fact-check and finalize the German edition. Eren Yurek and Quinn Dombrowski tracked down even the most recherché books and assisted me in wrangling very different kinds of texts in various languages into usable corpora. Sawyer Williams and Lauren Koong aided me in double-checking the translations and fact-checked the new portions. Caro de Sa, Tania Flores, and Meryem Deniz sifted through the large corpora from various countries.

My Stanford colleagues—above all, Josh Landy, Lea Pao, Ray Briggs, Angèle Christin, Yuliya Ilchuk, and Cécile Alduy—read drafts or helped me refine my ideas. Moira Donegan's guidance was instrumental in shaping this version of the book. At Suhrkamp, Christian Heilbronn and Heinrich Geiselberger were instrumental both in shaping the German edition of this book and in encouraging me to think big when it came to an English edition. At Stanford University Press, Kate Wahl and Caroline McKusick helped make the English edition a reality. Above all, however, this book couldn't exist in this version without Erica Wetter's enthusiastic feedback and guidance and Jennifer Gordon's brilliant edits and fact checking.

Many others have labored in the mines of cancel culture anecdotes and the roles they play for reactionary centrism, liberalism, and right-wing populism, and I have benefited from their research, their work, and their support. A huge thanks to Michael Hobbes, who was always ready to exchange debunkings when a new anecdote came across the transom, to Matt Sitman, who helped me understand the inner workings of the right-wing noise machine and how one succeeds in it. Thomas Zimmer's insights into the American right wing and how its ideas ricochet across the globe were immensely important for this book.

I relied on help from the Princeton University Library, Special Collections at Dartmouth College and at Cornell University, the Bancroft Library at Berkeley, the Presidential Libraries of Ronald Reagan, George H. W. Bush, and Bill Clinton to track down various documents and chase down leads. Even when they didn't pan out, folks there were uniformly lovely and enthusiastic, always eager to delve into the weirder aspects of their institution's history.

Samuel Huneke read various drafts of the book and explored the discursive explosion of anti-wokeness with me. Oliver Nachtwey and Carolin Amlinger helped me refine my ideas and also enriched my work with their incredible empirical studies. Moira Weigel's research and insights into the language games around anti-CRT and anti-DEI movements, and her attention to what modes of reading and theorizing subtend these, were immensely influential on my own thinking. Bruno Perreau's work on the French Right and gender panic has remained deeply influential for me, and though he has moved on to less depressing topics, he allowed me to pull him back into the morass. Vanessa Vu's insights into the German publishing landscape were incredibly important, as were those of about a dozen others who didn't want their names to appear in these acknowledgments.

I also owe a debt of gratitude to Marc Neumann, himself the author of many a cancel culture article, who was kind enough to contact me after the German edition came out. In our ensuing discussions, we did not exactly see eye-to-eye, but his insights and support have hopefully ensured that I wasn't too unfair to the purveyors of the kinds of texts I criticize here. Relatedly, I want to thank those colleagues, editors, and authors—I won't name them here—who have decidedly different opinions on the topic I explore in this book. I think they are wrong on this subject, but discussions with them, reading their texts, and getting to watch them take shape have helped me make sure that while this book is a polemic, it hopefully engages deeply with the rhetorical and discursive moves it criticizes.

I dedicate this book to my family: my parents, who went from sort of finding cancel culture stories credible to hunting down ridiculous new items for me to collect in my overflowing archive; my husband, whose own finely tuned bullshit detector was often a vital first step in determining which one of the near-infinite number of rabbit holes to venture down; and my daughter, who I hope will one day be able to exist in white-dominated spaces without a fancy fake discourse to imply that maybe she doesn't deserve to be there.

Notes

Preface

1. "A Letter on Justice and Open Debate," *Harper's* (October 2020): https://harpers.org/a-letter-on-justice-and-open-debate/

2. Editorial Board, "America Has a Free Speech Problem," *New York Times* (March 18, 2022): https://www.nytimes.com/2022/03/18/opinion/cancel-culture-free-speech-poll.html

3. Anne Applebaum, "The New Puritans," *The Atlantic* (August 31, 2021): https://www.theatlantic.com/magazine/archive/2021/10/new-puritans-mob-justice-canceled/619818/

4. Post on Twitter (X) by Elon Musk (May 19, 2020): https://twitter.com/elonmusk/status/1262783922708058113

5. "Remarks by President Trump at South Dakota's 2020 Mount Rushmore Fireworks Celebration," *Trump White House Archives* (July 4, 2020): https://trumpwhitehouse.archives.gov/briefings-statements/remarks-president-trump-south-dakotas-2020-mount-rushmore-fireworks-celebration-keystone-south-dakota/

6. Philip Pullella, "Pope Warns About Dangers of 'Cancel Culture,'" *Reuters* (January 10, 2022): https://www.reuters.com/article/idUSKBN2JK171/

Introduction

1. Stanley Cohen, *Folk Devils and Moral Panics: The Creation of the Mods and Rockers* (New York: Routledge Classics, 2002).

2. Quoted in AFP, "Blanquer s'inquiète des pratiques de l'Unef, 'qui ressemblent au fascisme,'" *Le Point* (March 19, 2021): https://www.lepoint.fr/societe/blanquer-s-inquiete

-des-pratiques-de-l-unef-qui-ressemblent-au-fascisme-19-03-2021-2418519_23.php. Unless indicated otherwise, I am responsible for all translations in this book.

3. William F. Buckley, Jr., "Our Mission Statement," *National Review* (November 19, 1955): https://www.nationalreview.com/1955/11/our-mission-statement-william-f -buckley-jr/

4. Buckley, "Our Mission Statement."

5. On David Shor, see Yascha Mounk, *The Identity Trap: A Story of Ideas and Power in Our Time* (New York: Penguin, 2023), 116; on Erika López Prater, see Greg Lukianoff and Rikki Schlott, *The Canceling of the American Mind: Cancel Culture Undermines Trust and Threatens Us All—But There Is a Solution* (New York: Simon & Schuster, 2023), 13.

6. Rebecca Lewis and Angèle Christin, "Platform Drama: 'Cancel Culture,' Celebrity, and the Struggle for Accountability on YouTube," *New Media & Society* 24, no. 7 (2022): 1632–1656.

7. On the Hindley case, see Benjamin Ginsberg, *The Fall of the Faculty: The Rise of the All Administrative University and Why It Matters* (New York: Oxford University Press, 2011), 98; Greg Lukianoff, *Unlearning Liberty: Campus Censorship and the End of American Debate* (New York: Encounter Books, 2012), 203.

8. Alan Charles Kors and Harvey A. Silverglate, *The Shadow University: The Betrayal of Liberty on America's Campuses* (New York: The Free Press, 1999), 332.

9. Cohen, *Folk Devils and Moral Panics*.

10. Cohen, *Folk Devils and Moral Panics*, 50.

11. Cohen, *Folk Devils and Moral Panics*, 87.

12. Cohen, *Folk Devils and Moral Panics*, vii.

13. Cohen, *Folk Devils and Moral Panics*, 1.

14. Cohen, *Folk Devils and Moral Panics*, vii–viii; italics in the original.

15. Cohen, *Folk Devils and Moral Panics*, 2.

16. Cohen, *Folk Devils and Moral Panics*, xxxvii.

17. Cohen, *Folk Devils and Moral Panics*, xxxvii.

18. Erich Goode and Nachman Ben-Yehuda, *Moral Panics: The Social Construction of Deviance,* 2nd ed. (London: Wiley, 2010), 41.

19. John Taylor, "Are You Politically Correct?" *New York* (January 21, 1991).

Chapter 1

1. Erich Goode and Nachman Ben-Yehuda, *Moral Panics: The Social Construction of Deviance*, 2nd ed. (London: Wiley, 2010), 40.

2. This understanding seems to underlie Anne Applebaum's essay, "The New Puritans," for example, when she expresses concern that the "new mob justice" threatens democracy. Anne Applebaum, "The New Puritans," *The Atlantic* (August 31, 2021): https://www .theatlantic.com/magazine/archive/2021/10/new-puritans-mob-justice-canceled/619818/

3. See, e.g., Jonathan Rauch, "The Cancel Culture Checklist," *Persuasion* (August 6, 2020): https://www.persuasion.community/p/the-cancel-culture-checklist-c63

4. Omri Boehm, "Sie Wollen ihn Stürzen Sehen," *Zeit Online* (December 2, 2020): https://www.zeit.de/2020/49/immanuel-kant-rassismus-philosophie-aufklaerung -identitaetspolitik-cancel-culture

5. Alan Dershowitz, *Cancel Culture: The Latest Assault on Free Speech and Due Process* (New York: Hot Books, 2020).

6. Marc Fabian Erdl, *Die Legende von der Politischen Korrektheit: Zur Erfolgsgeschichte eines Importierten Mythos*. (Bielefeld: Transcript, 2004), 66.

7. Michael Hobbes, "Don't Fall for the 'Cancel Culture' Scam," *HuffPost* (June 10, 2020): https://www.huffpost.com/entry/cancel-culture-harpers-jk-rowling-scam_n_5f0887b4c5b67a80bc06c95e

8. The NAS list can be found here: https://www.nas.org/storage/app/media/New%20Documents/academic-cancellations-updated-march-2-2020.pdf

9. Author's interview with Michael Hobbes, July 23, 2022.

10. Steven Pinker and Bertha Madras, "New Faculty-Led Organization at Harvard Will Defend Academic Freedom," *Boston Globe* (April 12, 2023): https://www.bostonglobe.com/2023/04/12/opinion/harvard-council-academic-freedom/

11. Pinker and Madras, "New Faculty-Led Organization at Harvard."

12. Ellen Schrecker, *No Ivory Tower: McCarthyism and the Universities* (New York: Oxford University Press, 1986), 44, 280.

13. The figures from the Department of Education's National Center for Education Statistics can be found here: https://nces.ed.gov/programs/coe/pdf/2023/CSC_508c.pdf

14. The network's list can be accessed at https://www.netzwerk-wissenschaftsfreiheit.de/dokumentation/

15. Mark Bridge, "Bruce Gilley's Biography of Imperialist Sir Alan Burns Cancelled After Petition," *Times* (London) (October 9, 2020): https://www.thetimes.co.uk/article/bruce-gilleys-biography-of-imperialist-sir-alan-burns-cancelled-after-petition-9qv536tjz

16. Jochen Bittner, "Denkverbote helfen nicht gegen rechts," *Die Zeit* (November 19, 2020).

17. Thomas Ribi, "Jeder Darf meine Meinung Haben," *Neue Zürcher Zeitung* (April 12, 2021): https://www.nzz.ch/nzz-live-veranstaltungen/jeder-darf-meine-meinung-haben-ld.1610493

18. Pano Kanelos, "We Can't Wait for Universities to Fix Themselves. So We're Starting a New One," *The Free Press* (November 8, 2021): https://www.thefp.com/p/we-cant-wait-for-universities-to

19. Piero Vietti, "I dissidenti della cancel culture fondano ad Austin una università 'ferocemente libera,'" *Tempi*, (November 9, 2021): https://www.tempi.it/universita-austin-weiss-boghossian/

20. Pablo Pardo, "Intelectuales y académicos crean una universidad contra 'la tiranía de la corrección política,'" *El Mundo* (November 11, 2021): https://www.elmundo.es/cultura/2021/11/11/618c2409fc6c83e0188b45af.html

21. Claire Conruyt, "États-Unis: Des profs lancent une université afin de lutter contre l'idéologie woke dans l'enseignement supérieur," *Le Figaro Étudiant* (November 10, 2021): https://etudiant.lefigaro.fr/article/etats-unis-des-profs-lancent-une-universite-afin-de-lutter-contre-l-ideologie-woke-dans-l-enseignement-superieur_2d08df78-4170-11ec-bcd5-4e44c42d570c/

22. Mel Stiksma, "Understanding the Campus Expression Climate: Fall 2020," 2021, 2; the report can be found here: https://heterodoxacademy.org/wp-content/uploads/2021/03/CES-Report-2020.pdf

23. The phrasing of the questions, crosstabs, and raw data can be found here: https://heterodoxacademy.org/reports/2020-campus-expression-survey-report-2-2/

24. Eric Kaufmann, "Academic Freedom in Crisis: Punishment, Political Discrimination, and Self-Censorship," Center for the Study of Partisanship and Ideology (March 1, 2021). The survey is no longer online, but can be found through the Internet Archive's Wayback Machine: https://web.archive.org/web/20210309210629/https://cspicenter.org/wp-content/uploads/2021/03/AcademicFreedom.pdf

25. Editorial Board, "America Has a Free Speech Problem," New York Times (March 18, 2022): https://www.nytimes.com/2022/03/18/opinion/cancel-culture-free-speech-poll.html

26. For the poll question wording, see https://scri.siena.edu/wp-content/uploads/2022/03/FS0222-Crosstabs.pdf

27. Nicholas Grossman, "Free Speech Might Hurt Your Feelings," Arc Digital (March 27, 2022): https://www.arcdigital.media/p/free-speech-might-hurt-your-feelings

28. Kenji Yoshino, Covering: The New Assault on Our Civil Rights (New York: Random House, 2006), 22.

29. Institut für Demoskopie Allensbach, "Die Mehrheit fühlt sich gegängelt" (June 2020): https://www.ifd-allensbach.de/fileadmin/kurzberichte_dokumentationen/FAZ_Juni2021_Meinungsfreiheit.pdf

30. Richard Bernstein, "The Rising Hegemony of the Politically Correct," New York Times (October 28, 1990): https://www.nytimes.com/1990/10/28/weekinreview/ideas-trends-the-rising-hegemony-of-the-politically-correct.html

31. Jerry Adler et al., "Taking Offense: Is This the New Enlightenment on Campus or the New McCarthyism?" Newsweek (December 24, 1990): 48–55.

32. John Taylor, "Are You Politically Correct?" New York (January 21, 1991).

33. Matthias Matussek, "Kunst als Schauprozeß," Der Spiegel (April 11, 1993): https://www.spiegel.de/kultur/kunst-als-schauprozess-a-50d91233-0002-0001-0000-000013680102

34. Jan Fleischhauer, "Aufruhr auf dem Campus," Der Spiegel (August 4, 2002): https://www.spiegel.de/wirtschaft/aufruhr-auf-dem-campus-a-763faoab-0002-0001-0000-000023740193

35. "Die Mehrheit fühlt sich gegängelt," Institut für Demoskopie Allensbach (June 2021): https://www.ifd-allensbach.de/fileadmin/kurzberichte_dokumentationen/FAZ_Juni2021_Meinungsfreiheit.pdf

36. Edward Schlosser, "I'm a Liberal Professor, and My Liberal Students Terrify Me," Vox (June 3, 2015): https://www.vox.com/2015/6/3/8706323/college-professor-afraid; Peter Boghossian, "My University Sacrificed Ideas for Ideology. So Today I Quit." The Free Press (September 8, 2021): https://www.thefp.com/p/my-university-sacrificed-ideas-for

37. "Kretschmer kritisiert 'Kultur des Abkanzelns,'" Zeit Online (June 21, 2023): https://www.zeit.de/news/2023-06/21/kretschmer-kritisiert-kultur-des-abkanzelns

38. The term "so called," marking both the newness of the word and its foreign extraction, is a common feature attached to "cancel culture" in several languages—Пресловутая in Russian, or *chamada* in Brazilian Portuguese.

39. Emily A. Vogels, Monica Naderson, Margaret Porteus, Chris Baronavski, Sara Atske, Colleen McClain, Brooke Auxier, Andrew Perrin, and Meera Ramshankar, "Americans and 'Cancel Culture': Where Some See Calls for Accountability, Others See Censorship, Punishment," *Pew Research Center* (May 19, 2021): https://www.pewresearch .org/internet/2021/05/19/americans-and-cancel-culture-where-some-see-calls -for-accountability-others-see-censorship-punishment/

40. The survey can be found at: https://www.ifop.com/wp-content/uploads/ 2021/03/117936-R%C3%A9sultats.pdf

41. Editorial Board, "America Has a Free Speech Problem."

42. Jeffrey M. Berry, James M. Glaser, and Deborah J. Schildkraut, "Race and Gender on Fox and MSNBC," *The Forum* 18, no. 3 (2020): 297–317.

43. Editorial Board, "America Has a Free Speech Problem."

Chapter 2

1. Earl Ryan, "Liberation from Logic: Feminism in the Academy," *Campus* (Spring 1991): 2.

2. Edward Schlosser, "I'm a Liberal Professor, and My Liberal Students Terrify Me," *Vox* (June 3, 2015): https://www.vox.com/2015/6/3/8706323/college-professor-afraid

3. John K. Wilson, *The Myth of Political Correctness. The Conservative Attack on Higher Education* (Durham: Duke University Press, 1995), 8.

4. Wilson, *The Myth of Political Correctness*, 5.

5. Dinesh D'Souza, "Introduction," in *Illiberal Education: The Politics of Race and Sex on Campus* (New York: Vintage, 1992), xiv; quoted in Wilson, *The Myth of Political Correctness*, 5.

6. Quoted in Wilson, *The Myth of Political Correctness*, 13.

7. William J. Clinton, "Remarks at a Fundraiser for Senator Daniel Patrick Moynihan in New York City," *Presidency: UCSB* (December 13, 1993): https://www.presidency .ucsb.edu/documents/remarks-fundraiser-for-senator-daniel-patrick-moynihan-new -york-city

8. George H. W. Bush, "Remarks at the University of Michigan Commencement Ceremony in Ann Arbor," *Bush41library* (May 4, 1991): https://bush41library.tamu.edu/ archives/public-papers/2949

9. Bush, "Remarks at the University of Michigan."

10. Jerry Adler et al., "Thought Police: Taking Offense," *Newsweek* (December 24, 1990).

11. Richard Bernstein, "The Rising Hegemony of the Politically Correct," *New York Times* (October 28, 1990) https://www.nytimes.com/1990/10/28/weekinreview/ ideas-trends-the-rising-hegemony-of-the-politically-correct.html

12. John Taylor, "Are You Politically Correct?" *New York* (January 21, 1991): 34.

13. Joachim Gauck, *Toleranz: Einfach schwer* (Freiburg: Herder, 2019), 147.

14. Michael Wurmitzer, "Cancel-Culture gegen Künstler und Werke: Debatten einfach ausradieren," *Der Standard* (June 28, 2020): https://www.derstandard.de/story/2000118351994/cancel-culture-gegen-kuenstler-und-werke-debatten-einfach-ausradieren

15. Claudia Ihlefeld, "Cancel Culture oder die Grenzen des Zumutbaren," *Heilbronner Stimme* (November 8, 2021): https://www.stimme.de/schwerpunkte/wochenthemen/cancelculture/cancel-culture-oder-die-grenzen-des-zumutbaren-art-4552744

16. Marc Neumann, "Beleidige alle schnell Beleidigten: Wie ein mutiger amerikanischer Komiker erfolgreich gegen den Strom schwimmt," *Neue Zürcher Zeitung* (September 20, 2019): https://www.nzz.ch/feuilleton/dave-chappelle-auf-netflix-beleidige-alle-schnell-beleidigten-ld.1509465

17. Zsuzsa Breier, "Cancel Culture: Wo wieder Mauern aufgebaut werden," *Neue Zürcher Zeitung* (August 30, 2021). https://www.nzz.ch/feuilleton/cancel-culture-wo-wieder-mauern-aufgebaut-werden-ld.1641911

18. Adrian Lobe, "Strg+Alt+Entf," *Die Welt* (July 10, 2020): https://www.welt.de/kultur/plus211310909/Die-Geburt-der-Cancel-Culture-aus-dem-Geist-des-Valley.html

19. Marc Neumann, "Beleidige alle schnell Beleidigten: Wie ein mutiger amerikanischer Komiker erfolgreich gegen den Strom schwimmt," *Neue Zürcher Zeitung* (September 20, 2019): https://www.nzz.ch/feuilleton/dave-chappelle-auf-netflix-beleidige-alle-schnell-beleidigten-ld.1509465

20. Meredith D. Clark, "Drag Them: A Brief Etymology of So-Called 'Cancel Culture,'" *Communication and the Public* 5, no. 3–4 (2020): https://journals.sagepub.com/doi/10.1177/2057047320961562

21. Author's interview with Liat Kaplan (September 14, 2022).

22. Stanley Cohen, *Folk Devils and Moral Panics: The Creation of the Mods and Rockers* (New York: Routledge Classics, 2002).

23. Neumann, "Beleidige alle schnell Beleidigten."

24. The text was reprinted as Jochen Bittner, "Nicht einknicken! Dein Mitbürger, der Unterdrücker," in *Zerreißproben. Leitmedien, Liberalismus und Liberalität*, eds. Stephan Russ-Mohl und Christian Pieter Hoffmann (Köln: Halem, 2021), 135; see also: https://www.zeit.de/2021/11/identitaetspolitik-rassismus-soziale-gerechtigkeit-intersektionalitaet

25. Yannick Chatelain, "Cancel Culture ou Cyber-haine déguisée?" *Forbes* (August 14, 2022): https://www.forbes.fr/politique/cancel-culture-ou-cyber-haine-deguisee-cancel-culture-la-liberte-de-conscience-en-danger/

26. The Colbert Report, "Who's Attacking Me Now?" *YouTube* (April 1, 2014): https://www.youtube.com/watch?v=MBPgXjkfBXM

27. Meredith Clark, "Black Twitter: Building Connection Through Cultural Conversation," in *Hashtag Publics: The Power and Politics of Discursive Networks*, ed. Nathan Rambukkana (Bern: Peter Lang, 2015), 205–218.

28. Melissa Brown, "Virtual Sojourners: The Duality of Visibility and Erasure for Black Women and LGBTQ People in the Digital Age," in *Networked Feminisms: Activist Assemblies and Digital Practices*, ed. Shana MacDonald, Brianna I. Wiens,

Michelle MacArthur, and Milena Radzikowska (Lanham: Rowman & Littlefield, 2021), 49–65.

29. Roderick Graham and Shawn Smith, "The Content of Our #Characters: Black Twitter as Counterpublic," *Sociology of Race and Ethnicity* 2, no. 4 (2016): 433–449.

30. Clark, "Drag Them," 90.

31. Post on Twitter (X) by Colleen (December 27, 2016): https://x.com/colleenenen/status/813773366750547971?s=46

32. Raven Maragh-Lloyd, "Black Twitter as Semi-Enclave," in *Race and Media: Critical Approaches,* ed. Lori Kido Lopez, (New York: New York University Press, 2020), 165.

33. For a psychoanalytic interpretation of this gaze, see Hortense Spillers, "Mama's Baby, Papa's Maybe: An American Grammar Book," *Diacritics* 17, no. 2 (1987): 64–81.

34. Petter Bae Brandtzaeg and Marika Lüder, "Time Collapse in Social Media: Extending the Context Collapse," *Social Media + Society* (January–March 2019): 1–10.

35. Post on Twitter (X) by Hannaeh Belser (October 28, 2016): https://x.com/hannaehwrites/status/792025338616418304?s=46

36. Quoted in Jonah E. Bromwich, "Everyone Is Canceled," *New York Times* (June 28, 2018): https://www.nytimes.com/2018/06/28/style/is-it-canceled.html

37. Bromwich, "Everyone Is Canceled."

38. Bromwich, "Everyone Is Canceled."

39. Editorial Board, "America Has a Free Speech Problem," *New York Times* (March 18, 2022): https://www.nytimes.com/2022/03/18/opinion/cancel-culture-free-speech -poll.html

40. Richard Godwin, "So Gen Z, Tell Us What You Really Want," *Times* (London) (April 4, 2019): https://advance.lexis.com/api/document?collection=news&id =urn:contentItem:5VT7-VH51-JCBW-N1WC-00000-00&context=1516831

41. Étienne Sorin, "Seule l'Europe dit 'I love you' à Woody Allen," *Le Figaro* (June 13, 2019): https://advance.lexis.com/api/document?collection=news&id=urn:contentItem :5W9V-T201-JCJ6-Y1DP-00000-00&context=1516831

42. "Give Me Your Tired, Your Poor, Your Huddled Masses Marginalised on the Twitter Feed," *Australian* (September 27, 2019): https://advance.lexis.com/api/ document?collection=news&id=urn:contentItem:5X4M-XGV1-JD3N-50KP-00000 -00&context=1516831

43. Oliver Polak, "Stand Up Männchen," *Die Welt* (July 25, 2019): https://advance .lexis.com/api/document?collection=news&id=urn:contentItem:5WN4-JCP1-DY2B -S3S6-00000-00&context=1516831

44. Maximiliano Torres, "'Le llueve' a Woody Allen," *Milenio* (December 1, 2019): https://advance.lexis.com/api/document?collection=news&id=urn:contentItem :5XMW-K331-JBJN-M1NN-00000-00&context=1516831

45. Andrés Barba, "Cultura de la cancelacion," *El Pais* (December 6, 2019): 13: https:// advance.lexis.com/api/document?collection=news&id=urn:contentItem:5XNR -7V81-JCN5-52SY-00000-00&context=1516831

46. Bruno Molinero, "Boicotes virtuais se descolam de atos concretos e alimentam a intolerância," *Folha de Sao Paulo* (December 30, 2019): https://www1.folha.uol.com .br/ilustrada/2019/12/boicotes-virtuais-se-descolam-de-atos-concretos-e-alimentam -a-intolerancia.shtml

47. Peggy Noonan, "Get Ready for the Struggle Session," *Wall Street Journal* (March 7, 2019): https://www.wsj.com/articles/get-ready-for-the-struggle-session-11552003346

48. Ingraham Angle, "Cancel Culture Takes Aim at the Oil and Gas Industry," *Fox News* (September 6, 2019): https://www.foxnews.com/video/6084207258001

49. Ribi, "Jeder Darf meine Meinung Haben."

50. Carolina Schwarz, "Was kommt nach dem Vorwurf," *taz* (September 26, 2019): https://taz.de/Placido-Domingo-sagt-Met-Auftritt-ab/!5626451/

51. Susan Vahabzadeh, "Wer einem nicht passt, muss verschwinden," *Süddeutsche Zeitung* (October 28, 2019): https://www.sueddeutsche.de/kultur/cancel-culture -meinungsaeusserung-rechtsstaat-1.4657929

52. Vahabzadeh, "Wer einem nicht passt, muss verschwinden."

Chapter 3

1. Thomas Short, "'Diversity' and 'Breaking the Disciplines': Two New Assaults on the Curriculum," *Academic Questions* 1, no. 3 (Summer 1988): 15.

2. Toby Young, "I Am Living Proof That 'Two-Tier' Exams Work," *Spectator* (June 30, 2012): https://www.spectator.co.uk/article/i-am-living-proof-that-two-tier-exams-work/

3. Harald Martenstein, "Cancel-Culture," *Zeit Magazin* (March 10, 2021): https:// www.zeit.de/zeit-magazin/2021/11/cancel-culture-william-shakespeare -kruemelmonster-diskriminierung

4. A complicating factor in the data from the National Center for Education Statistics is that the census also includes institutions that are not accredited. The NCES recorded 5,999 Title IV institutions in the 2019–2020 academic year, but of these, only 66 percent were degree-granting postsecondary institutions. The most recent figures can be found here: https://nces.ed.gov/fastfacts/display.asp?id=1122; historic figures can be found here: https://nces.ed.gov/programs/digest/d15/tables/dt15_105.50.asp

5. This data can be found here: https://mlaresearch.mla.hcommons.org/2017/06/26/ the-decline-in-humanities-majors/

6. Adam Begley, "The Decline of the Campus Novel," *Lingua Franca* 7, no. 7 (1997): 39–46, quote at 40.

7. Begley, "The Decline of the Campus Novel," 40.

8. Jeffrey J. Williams, "The Rise of the Academic Novel," *American Literary History* 24, no. 3 (2012): 561–589.

9. Robert F. Scott, "It's a Small World, After All: Assessing the Contemporary Campus Novel," *Journal of the Midwest Modern Language Association* 37, no. 1 (2004): 81–87, quote at 83.

10. Quoted in Scott Sherman, "David Horowitz's Long March," *The Nation* (June 15, 2000): https://www.thenation.com/article/archive/david-horowitzs-long -march/

11. Megan Brenan, "Americans' Confidence in Higher Education Down Sharply," *Gallup* (July 11, 2023): https://news.gallup.com/poll/508352/americans-confidence-higher-education-down-sharply.aspx

12. William F. Buckley, Jr., *God and Man at Yale* (Chicago: Regnery, 1951), 190.

13. Buckley, *God and Man at Yale*, xv.

14. Buckley, *God and Man at Yale*, 150.

15. Buckley, *God and Man at Yale*, 148.

16. Buckley, *God and Man at Yale*, xvi.

17. Buckley, *God and Man at Yale*, 18.

18. Buckley, *God and Man at Yale*, 28.

19. Buckley, *God and Man at Yale*, xv–xvi.

20. Buckley, *God and Man at Yale*, 45–46.

21. Allan Bloom, *The Closing of the American Mind: How Higher Education Has Failed Democracy and Impoverished the Souls of Today's Students* (New York: Simon & Schuster, 1987).

22. John Taylor, "Are You Politically Correct?" *New York* (January 21, 1991): 34.

23. Roger Kimball, *Tenured Radicals: How Politics Has Corrupted Our Higher Education* (New York: Harper & Row, 1990), xvii.

24. Roger Kimball, "Reflections on *Tenured Radicals* (2008)," in *Tenured Radicals: How Politics Has Corrupted Our Higher Education* (Chicago: Dee, 2008), xxxviii.

25. Post on Twitter (X) by Jeremy Wayne Tate (April 19, 2022): https://x.com/jeremytate41/status/1516473174346670083

26. Bloom, *The Closing of the American Mind*, 65.

27. Ezra Bowen, "Education: The Canons Under Fire," *Time* (April 11, 1988), quoted in John K. Wilson, *The Myth of Political Correctness. The Conservative Attack on Higher Education* (Durham: Duke University Press, 1995), 65.

28. Les Csorba, ed., *Academic License: The War on Academic Freedom* (Evanston: UCA Books 1988), vii.

29. Earl Ryan, "Liberation from Logic: Feminism in the Academy," *Campus* 2, no. 3 (Spring 1991): 2.

30. Catharine R. Stimpson, "The Female Sociograph: The Theater of Virginia Woolf Letters," in *Where the Meanings Are*, ed. Catharine R. Stimpson (London: Routledge, 2014), 130.

31. Short, "'Diversity' and 'Breaking the Disciplines,'" 15.

32. Young, "I Am Living Proof That 'Two-Tier' Exams Work."

33. Quoted in Marc Fabian Erdl, *Die Legende von der Politischen Korrektheit: Zur Erfolgsgeschichte eines Importierten Mythos* (Bielefeld: Transcript, 2004), 99.

34. Erdl, *Die Legende von der Politischen Korrektheit*, 100.

35. Harald Martenstein, "Cancel Culture," *Zeit Magazin* (March 10, 2021): https://www.zeit.de/zeit-magazin/2021/11/cancel-culture-william-shakespeare-kruemelmonster-diskriminierung

36. Quoted in Gerard J. De Groot, "Ronald Reagan and Student Unrest in California, 1966–1970," *Pacific Historical Review* 65, no. 1 (1996): 107–129, quote at 107.

37. Ronald Reagan, "Excerpts from a Speech by Ronald Reagan, Cow Palace," *Reagan Presidential Archive* (May 12, 1966). Video of Reagan's "Morality Gap" speech can be found here: https://diva.sfsu. edu/collections/sfbatv/bundles/229317; transcription is mine.

38. Reagan, "Excerpts from a Speech by Ronald Reagan, Cow Palace." The text preserved in the Reagan Presidential Archive diverges from what is accessible on video.

39. California Legislature, "Thirteenth Report Supplement of the Senate Factfinding Subcommittee on Un-American Activities," *Journal of the Senate, Legislature of the State of California* 1 (1966): 134.

40. Garry Wills, *Reagan's America: Innocents at Home* (Garden City: Doubleday, 1987), 123.

41. John Patrick Diggins, *Ronald Reagan: Fate, Freedom, and the Making of History* (New York: Norton, 2007), 70.

42. Quoted in De Groot, "Ronald Reagan and Student Unrest in California, 1966–1970," 108.

43. Lisa McGirr, *Suburban Warriors: The Origins of the New American Right* (Princeton and Oxford: Princeton University Press, 2001), 238.

44. De Groot, "Ronald Reagan and Student Unrest in California, 1966–1970," 107.

45. Post on X (Twitter) by Bill Ackman (January 2, 2024): https://twitter.com/BillAckman/status/1742441534627184760

Chapter 4

1. Douglas Fowler, "The Humanities in the Missionary Position," *Heterodoxy* 1, no. 5 (October 1992): 16.

2. Lynne Cheney, "Telling the Truth: A Report on the State of the Humanities in Higher Education," *National Endowment for the Humanities* (September 1992): https://files.eric.ed.gov/fulltext/ED350936.pdf

3. George H. Nash, *The Conservative Intellectual Movement in America Since 1945* (New York: Basic Books, 1976).

4. Midge Decter, *Liberal Parents, Radical Children* (New York: Coward, McCann & Geoghegan, 1975), 19; italics in the original.

5. Decter, *Liberal Parents, Radical Children*, 17.

6. Barbara Ehrenreich, *Fear of Falling: The Inner Life of the Middle Class* (New York: Pantheon, 1989), 59.

7. Ehrenreich, *Fear of Falling*, 154.

8. John Ganz, "Finding Neverland: The American Right's Doomed Quest to Rid Itself of Trumpism," *New Republic* (February 17, 2020): https://newrepublic.com/article/156368/finding-neverland-conservative-quest-rid-trumpism

9. Allan Bloom, *The Closing of the American Mind: How Higher Education Has Failed Democracy and Impoverished the Souls of Today's Students* (New York: Simon & Schuster, 1987), 243.

10. Allan Bloom interview with Alexander Heffner on *The Open Mind*, on PBS, 1987.

11. Edward Jayne, "Academic Jeremiad: The Neoconservative View of American Higher Education," *Change* (May–June 1991).

12. Jayne, "Academic Jeremiad," 32.

13. Charles J. Sykes, *ProfScam: Professors and the Demise of Higher Education* (Washington, DC: Regnery, 1988), 252.

14. Dinesh D'Souza, *Illiberal Education: The Politics of Race and Sex on Campus* (New York: Vintage, 1992), 229.

15. Jayne, "Academic Jeremiad," 41.

16. "Der Rückzug des amerikanischen Geistes—Ein Bestseller von Allan Bloom," *Neue Zürcher Zeitung* (August 6, 1987): 19.

17. Daniel Hofmann, "PC, Political Correctness—Notizen zu einem amerikanischen Phänomen," *Neue Zürcher Zeitung* (October 24–25, 1992): 65.

18. Caroline Fourest, *Génération offensée: De la police de la culture à la police de la pensée* (Paris: Grasset, 2020), 126.

19. Bloom, *The Closing of the American Mind*, 91.

20. Richard Bernstein, "The Rising Hegemony of the Politically Correct," *New York Times* (October 28, 1990): https://www.nytimes.com/1990/10/28/weekinreview/ideas-trends-the-rising-hegemony-of-the-politically-correct.html

21. Richard Bernstein, "Black and White on Campus: Learning Tolerance, Not Love, and Separately," *New York Times* (May 26, 1988): https://www.nytimes.com/1988/05/26/us/black-and-white-on-campus-learning-tolerance-not-love-and-separately.html

22. Dinesh D'Souza, "The New Segregation on Campus," *American Scholar* 60, no. 1 (1991): 17–30.

23. David O. Sacks and Peter A. Thiel, "The Diversity Myth: 'Multiculturalism' and the Politics of Intolerance at Stanford" (Oakland: Independent Institute, 1995): 131.

24. "Racist E-Mail at Boston College Has Had an Effect on the White Male Students," *All Things Considered* (January 18, 1999).

25. Greg Lukianoff and Jonathan Haidt, *The Coddling of the American Mind: How Good Intentions and Bad Ideas Are Setting Up a Generation for Failure* (New York: Penguin, 2018), 8.

26. Julie J. Park, *Race on Campus: Debunking Myths with Data* (Cambridge, MA: Harvard Education Press, 2018), 22.

27. See "Study Suggests 'Self-Segregation' Is a Myth," *Chronicle of Higher Education* (April 13, 1994).

28. Fourest, *Génération offense*, 126.

29. See, for instance, Valerie A. Lewis, "Social Energy and Racial Segregation in the University Context," *Social Science Quarterly* 93, no. 1 (2012): 270–290.

30. Christian Makarian, "USA: la vague 'Woke' ou la regression démocratique," *Le Télégramme* (January 31, 2021): https://www.letelegramme.fr/monde/etats-unis-la-vague-woke-ou-la-regression-democratique-3752642.php

Chapter 5

1. The Editors, "Reductio ad Absurdum," *Heterodoxy* 1, no. 5 (October 1992): 3.

2. Dinesh D'Souza, *Illiberal Education: The Politics of Race and Sex on Campus* (New York: Vintage, 1992), 194.

3. D'Souza, *Illiberal Education,* 194–196.

4. John Taylor, "Are You Politically Correct?" *New York* (January 21, 1991): 32.

5. C. Vann Woodward, "Freedom & the Universities," *New York Review of Books* (July 18, 1991): https://www.nybooks.com/articles/1991/07/18/freedom-the-universities/

6. Maarten Huygen, "De adeldom van de onderdrukten; Minderheden bedreigen de academische vrijheid aan Amerikaanse universiteiten," *Handelsblad* (April 27, 1991): https://www.nrc.nl/nieuws/1991/04/27/de-adeldom-van-de-onderdrukten-minderheden-bedreigen-6965244-a540459

7. Daniel Hofmann, "PC, Political Correctness—Notizen zu einem amerikanischen Phänomen," *Neue Zürcher Zeitung* (October 24–25, 1992): 65.

8. Nicolas Weill, "Les new black intellectuals de Harvard," *Le Monde* (April 25, 1997).

9. Jan Fleischhauer, "Aufruhr auf dem Campus," *Der Spiegel* (August 4, 2002): https://www.spiegel.de/wirtschaft/aufruhr-auf-dem-campus-a-763fa0ab-0002-0001-0000-000023740193

10. D'Souza, *Illiberal Education*, 194.

11. Jon Wiener, *Historians in Trouble: Plagiarism, Fraud, and Politics in the Ivory Tower* (New York: New Press 2005), 60.

12. Wendi Grantham, "Course Displayed Racial Insensitivity," *Harvard Crimson* (February 17, 1988): https://www.thecrimson.com/article/1988/2/17/course-displayed-racial-insensitivity-pon-february/

13. Quoted in Wiener, *Historians in Trouble*, 60.

14. Susan B. Glasser, "Thernstrom Waits for Charges," *Harvard Crimson* (March 5, 1988): https://www.thecrimson.com/article/1988/3/5/thernstrom-waits-for-charges-pa-professor/; quoted in Wiener, *Historians in Trouble*, 60.

15. Adam Shatz, "The Thernstroms in Black and White," *American Prospect* (December 10, 2001): https://prospect.org/features/thernstroms-black-white/

16. Stephan Thernstrom and Abigail Thernstrom, *America in Black and White: One Nation, Indivisible* (New York: Simon & Schuster, 2009), 494–495.

17. Sam Roberts, "Abigail Thernstrom, Scholarly Foe of Affirmative Action, Dies at 83," *New York Times* (April 20, 2020): https://www.nytimes.com/2020/04/20/us/abigail-thernstrom-dead.html

18. Todd Gitlin, "An Intolerance of the New Intolerance," *Los Angeles Times* (April 14, 1991): https://www.latimes.com/archives/la-xpm-1991-04-14-bk-99-story.html

19. Saul Bellow, *Mr. Sammler's Planet* (Harmondsworth: Penguin, 1970), 95–96.

20. Elaine Showalter, *Faculty Towers: The Academic Novel and Its Discontents* (Philadelphia: University of Pennsylvania Press, 2005), 100.

21. Stephen A. Holmes, "Affirmative Action's Unlikely Foes," *New York Times* (January 10, 1998): https://www.nytimes.com/1998/01/10/us/affirmative-action-s-unlikely-foes.html

22. Holmes, "Affirmative Action's Unlikely Foes."

23. See Holmes, "Affirmative Action's Unlikely Foes"; Shatz, "The Thernstroms in Black and White"; Roberts, "Abigail Thernstrom, Scholarly Foe of Affirmative Action, Dies at 83."

24. *North v. Board of Trustees of the University of Illinois*, 137 Ill. 296 (1891).

25. *North v. Board of Trustees of the University of Illinois*, 137 Ill. 296 (1891).

26. Whitman College Code, quoted in G. Thomas Edwards, "Student Activism at Pomona, Willamette, and Whitman, 1965–1971" (Walla Walla, WA, and Washington, DC: Whitman College and Northwest Archives, 2008), 15–16: http://www.campusactivism .org/server-new/uploads/student_activism_historypomona_willamette_whitman.pdf

27. Cited in D'Souza, *Illiberal Education,* 196.

28. Quoted in Wiener, *Historians in Trouble,* 63.

29. D'Souza, *Illiberal Education,* 196.

30. D'Souza, *Illiberal Education,* 196.

31. D'Souza, *Illiberal Education,* 196.

32. Glasser, "Thernstrom Waits for Charges."

33. Jonathan Rauch, *Kindly Inquisitors: The New Attacks on Free Thought* (Chicago: University of Chicago Press, 1993), 132.

34. Nancy Gibbs, "Bigots in the Ivory Tower," *Time* (May 7, 1990): https://content .time.com/time/subscriber/article/0,33009,970015,00.html; quoted in John K. Wilson, *The Myth of Political Correctness: The Conservative Attack on Higher Education* (Durham: Duke University Press, 1995), 100.

35. Lynne Cheney, "Telling the Truth: A Report on the State of the Humanities in Higher Education," *National Endowment for the Humanities* (September 1992): 5: https://files.eric.ed.gov/fulltext/ED350936.pdf

36. Wilson, *The Myth of Political Correctness,* 92.

37. David O. Sacks and Peter A. Thiel, "The Diversity Myth: 'Multiculturalism' and the Politics of Intolerance at Stanford" (Oakland: Independent Institute, 1995).

38. Jessica Murphy, "Toronto Professor Jordan Peterson Takes on Gender-Neutral Pronouns," *BBC News* (November 4, 2016): https://www.bbc.com/news/world-us -canada-37875695

39. Editorial Board, "The Stanford Guide to Acceptable Words," *Wall Street Journal* (December 19, 2022): https://www.wsj.com/articles/the-stanford-guide-to-acceptable -words-elimination-of-harmful-language-initiative-11671489552

40. Wilson, *The Myth of Political Correctness.*

41. Roger Kimball, *Tenured Radicals: How Politics Has Corrupted Our Higher Education* (New York: Harper & Row, 1990), 9.

42. https://www.smith.edu/your-campus/offices-services/office-student-affairs

43. Annie Karni, "Questioning University Presidents on Antisemitism, Stefanik Goes Viral," *New York Times,* (December 7, 2023): https://www.nytimes.com/2023/12/07/ us/politics/elise-stefanik-antisemitism-congress.html

44. This is my transcription of Congressman Kiley's remarks at the House Committee on Education and the Workforce, December 5, 2023. The video, with Kiley's remarks starting at 2:51:30, can be found here: https://www.youtube.com/watch?v =LoPUWpdsoxY

45. Joachim Gauck, *Toleranz: Einfach schwer* (Freiburg: Herder, 2019), 147.

46. Claudia Franziska Brühwiller, "Wer erlöst Amerika vom Wahn der Reinheit?" *Neue Zürcher Zeitung* (April 3, 2021): https://www.nzz.ch/meinung/usa-wer-erloest-amerika-vom-wahn-der-reinheit-ld.1788916

47. Quoted in Alexandre Devecchio, "Laurent Bouvet: Tom Wolfe et Philip Roth, ou le refus du *political correctness*," *Le Figaro* (May 25, 2018): https://www.lefigaro.fr/vox/culture/2018/05/25/31006-20180525ARTFIG00139-laurent-bouvet-tom-wolfe-et-philip-roth-ou-le-refus-du-political-correctness.php

48. See "A Letter on Justice and Open Debate," *Harper's* (July 7, 2020): https://harpers.org/a-letter-on-justice-and-open-debate/

49. Andrés Gómez, "Las guerras culturales y la era de la intolerancia," *La Tercera* (July 28, 2020): https://www.latercera.com/culto/2020/07/28/las-guerras-culturales-y-la-era-de-la-intolerancia/

50. Philip Roth, *The Human Stain* (New York: Houghton Mifflin, 2000), 2.

51. Philip Roth, "An Open Letter to Wikipedia," *New Yorker* (September 6, 2012): https://www.newyorker.com/books/page-turner/an-open-letter-to-wikipedia

52. Quoted in Blake Bailey, *Philip Roth: The Biography* (New York: Norton, 2021), 652.

53. Quoted in Derek Parker Royal, "Plotting the Frames of Subjectivity: Identity, Death, and Narrative in Philip Roth's *The Human Stain*," *Contemporary Literature* 47, no. 1 (2006): 114.

54. Showalter, *Faculty Towers*, 104.

Chapter 6

1. John Taylor, "Are You Politically Correct?" *New York* (January 21, 1991): 37.

2. Anthony Browne, *The Retreat of Reason: Political Correctness and the Corruption of Debate in Modern Britain* (London: Civitas, 2006), 49.

3. Dana Kennedy, "St. John's Professor Allegedly Fired for Reading Racial Slur from Mark Twain's Book," *New York Post* (May 15, 2021): https://nypost.com/2021/05/15/professor-allegedly-fired-for-reading-racial-slur-from-mark-twain-book/

4. Vimal Patel, "Colleges Are Losing Control of Their Story. The Banh-Mi Affair at Oberlin Shows How," *Chronicle of Higher Education* (October 31, 2019): https://www.chronicle.com/article/colleges-are-losing-control-of-their-story-the-banh-mi-affair-at-oberlin-shows-how/

5. Karl Marx, *Selected Writings* (New York: Hackett, 1994), 245.

6. David Brooks, "The Jordan Peterson Moment," *New York Times* (January 25, 2018): https://www.nytimes.com/2018/01/25/opinion/jordan-peterson-moment.html

7. Marc Neumann, "Der seltsame Fall des Herrn Peterson," *Neue Zürcher Zeitung* (February 13, 2020): 37.

8. Jordan B. Peterson, "Professor Against Political Correctness: Part 1," *YouTube* (September 27, 2016): https://www.youtube.com/watch?v=fvPgjg201wo; I would like to thank Jennifer Portillo for her heroic work transcribing this video for me. Michael Hobbes kindly shared several iterations of this particular meme with me that I had not found.

9. Jordan B. Peterson, "Canadian Gender-Neutral Pronoun Bill Is a Warning for Americans," *The Hill* (October 18, 2016): https://thehill.com/blogs/pundits-blog/civil-rights/301661-this-canadian-prof-defied-sjw-on-gender-pronouns-and-has-a/

10. Conor Friedersdorf, "Why Can't People Hear What Jordan Peterson Is Saying?" *The Atlantic* (January 22, 2018): https://www.theatlantic.com/politics/archive/2018/01/putting-monsterpaint-onjordan-peterson/550859/

11. Margaret Wente, "How Awful Is Jordan Peterson, Anyway?" *Globe and Mail* (February 5, 2018): https://www.theglobeandmail.com/opinion/how-awful-is-jordan-peterson-anyway/article37864567/

12. Douglas Murray, "Martyr for Free Speech," *Daily Mail* (February 15, 2020): https://www.dailymail.co.uk/news/article-8008279/Jordan-Peterson-vilified-crusade-against-political-correctness-seriously-ill.html

13. Peterson, "Professor Against Political Correctness: Part 1."

14. Suzanne Ghais, *Extreme Facilitation: Guiding Groups Through Controversy and Complexity* (San Francisco: Jossey-Bass, 2005), 13.

15. Author's communication with Suzanne Ghais (August 1, 2022).

16. John McCrarey, "Concerning Diversity Training" (March 21, 2010): https://mccrarey.com/concerning-diversity-training

17. Tweet by Lorna Page (November 4, 2010): @drlornapage; tweet by Lauren Elyse (February 10, 2015): @JustLaurenB.

18. Phil La Duke, "In the World of Safety, Political Correctness Endangers Lives" (August 25, 2017): https://philladuke.wordpress.com/2017/08/25/in-the-world-of-safety-political-correctness-endangers-lives/

19. Ray L. Burdeos, *Flips in Philadelphia in the Fifties* (Bloomington: AuthorHouse, 2006); Eliseo Art Arambulo Silva, *Filipinos in Greater Philadelphia* (Charleston: Arcadia, 2012), 71.

20. John Lea, *Political Correctness and Higher Education: British and American Perspectives* (London: Routledge, 2009), 2.

21. James Curran, Ivor Gaber, and Julian Petley, *Culture Wars: The Media and the British Left* (London: Routledge, 2018).

22. Brown, *The Retreat of Reason*, 1.

23. A LexisNexis search for *Huckleberry Finn* and "n****r" (spelled out) between January 1, 2010, and December 31, 2012, and sifting out irrelevant or repeat entries, produced sixty-five hits, almost all of which, it should be noted, dutifully repeated the offending word, which I will not do here.

24. Marco Frei, "Als Carmen noch eine Zigeunerin sein durfte," *Neue Zürcher Zeitung am Sonntag* (October 3, 2023): https://www.nzz.ch/feuilleton/als-carmen-noch-eine-zigeunerin-sein-durfte-ld.1758731

25. Sven F. Goergens, "Mit verräterischer Zunge," *Focus* (February 3, 2003): https://m.focus.de/panorama/boulevard/mit-verraeterischer-zunge-gesellschaft_id_1974436.html

26. Elisabeth Noelle-Neumann, "Politische Korrektheit—was ist das?" *Frankfurter Allgemeine Zeitung* (October 16, 1996): 5.

27. Vera Graaf, "Schöne neue Wörter," *Die Zeit* (June 12, 1992): https://www.zeit.de/1992/25/schoene-neue-woerter

28. Francis Fukuyama, *Identity: The Demand for Dignity and the Politics of Resentment* (New York: Farrar, Straus and Giroux, 2018), 118.

29. Graaf, "Schöne neue Wörter."

30. John K. Wilson, *The Myth of Political Correctness: The Conservative Attack on Higher Education* (Durham: Duke University Press, 1995), xiii.

31. Umberto Eco, "Ur-Fascism," *New York Review of Books* (June 22, 1995): https://www.nybooks.com/articles/1995/06/22/ur-fascism/

32. "Free Speech at Harvard?" *Campus Report* 2, no. 10 (November 1987): 1.

33. Stephen Goode, "The Right's Response to Radicalism," *Insight* (December 12, 1988): 47

34. Goode, "The Right's Response to Radicalism," 47.

35. Readers wanting to know more should consult Jane Mayer, *Dark Money: The Hidden History of the Billionaires Behind the Rise of the Radical Right* (New York: Knopf, 2017), 128.

36. Lee Edwards, *Educating for Liberty: The First Half-Century of the Intercollegiate Studies Institute* (Chicago: Regnery, 2003), 10.

37. John J. Miller, *A Gift of Freedom: How the John M. Olin Foundation Changed America* (San Francisco: Encounter Books, 2005), 140.

38. "Squeaky Chalk," *Campus Report* 2, no. 10 (November 1987): 2.

39. Bill Hutchinson, "Right Wing Watchdog Seeks Class Monitors," *Phoenix* (September 12, 1985).

40. Fox Butterfield, "The Right Breeds a College Press Network," *New York Times* (October 24, 1990): https://www.nytimes.com/1990/10/24/us/education-the-right-breeds-a-college-press-network.html

41. Sacks and Thiel's report on Stanford was published as a book in 1998: David O. Sacks and Peter A. Thiel, *The Diversity Myth: Multiculturalism and Political Intolerance on Campus* (Oakland: Independent Institute, 1998).

42. ISI Campus Representative Application Form, undated and unpaginated.

43. "At Dartmouth, More Campus Hooliganism," *Campus Report* (1987).

44. Bari Weiss, "Resignation Letter," available at: https://www.bariweiss.com/resignation-letter

45. Izadi and Jeremy Barr, "Bari Weiss Resigns from New York Times, Says 'Twitter Has Become Its Ultimate Editor,'" *Washington Post* (July 14, 2020): https://www.washingtonpost.com/media/2020/07/14/bari-weiss-resigns-new-york-times/

46. Jane Gallop, *Feminist Accused of Sexual Harassment* (Durham: Duke University Press, 1997); Jane Gallop, *Anecdotal Theory* (Durham: Duke University Press, 2002).

47. Scott Kerr, "Hand to Hand Combat," in *The Heterodoxy Handbook: How to Survive the PC Campus,* edited by David Horowitz und Peter Collier (Washington, DC: Regnery 1993), 150.

48. Bari Weiss, "A Witch Trial at the Legal Aid Society, *The Free Press* (July 12, 2021): https://www.thefp.com/p/a-witch-trial-at-the-legal-aid-society

49. The print title ("Eine lesbische Professorin ist die Hassfigur der Transsexuellen") became "Kathleen Stock—wie eine lesbische Professorin im Kulturkampf um Transsexuelle zur Hassfigur wurde" in the online version: Niklaus Nuspliger, "Kathleen Stock—wie eine lesbische Professorin im Kulturkampf um Transsexuelle zur Hassfigur wurde," *Neue Zürcher Zeitung* (April 22, 2022): https://www.nzz.ch/international/kathleen-stock-eine-professorin-im-kulturkampf-um-transsexuelle-ld.1671185

50. Kennedy, "St. John's Professor Allegedly Fired for Reading Racial Slur from Mark Twain's Book."

51. Philip Roth, "An Open Letter to Wikipedia," *New Yorker* (September 6, 2012): https://www.newyorker.com/books/page-turner/an-open-letter-to-wikipedia

52. Theodor W. Adorno, "Der Essay als Form," in *Gesammelte Schriften* (Frankfurt am Main: Suhrkamp, 2003), vol. 11, 10.

53. Hermann Hesse, *The Glass Bead Game: (Magister Ludi) A Novel*, trans. Richard Winston and Clara Winston (New York: Bantam, 1970), 15.

54. Patricia Highsmith, *Plotting and Writing Suspense Fiction* (New York: St. Martin's Press, 2001), 4.

55. Josef Joffe, "Irgendwann kollabiert das Absurde unters einem eigenen Gewicht," *Neue Zürcher Zeitung* (May 8, 2021).

Chapter 7

1. Les Csorba, "Campus Thought Control," *Campus Report* (December 1, 1987).

2. This 2011 incident was documented by the Netzwerk Wissenschaftsfreiheit (Academic Freedom Network) in 2021.

3. Macron's speech can be found here: https://www.elysee.fr/emmanuel-macron/2020/10/02/fight-against-separatism-the-republic-in-action-speech-by-emmanuel-macron-president-of-the-republic-on-the-fight-against-separatism.en

4. John Lea, *Political Correctness and Higher Education: British and American Perspectives* (London: Routledge, 2009), 158.

5. Lea, *Political Correctness and Higher Education*, 158.

6. Lea, *Political Correctness and Higher Education*, 180.

7. James Curran, Ivor Gaber, and Julian Petley, *Culture Wars: The Media and the British Left* (London: Routledge, 2018). See also Mark Fisher, *Capitalist Realism: Is There No Alternative?* (London: Zero Books, 2009); Toby Young, "I Am Living Proof That 'Two-Tier' Exams Work," *Spectator* (June 30, 2012): https://www.spectator.co.uk/article/i-am-living-proof-that-two-tier-exams-work/

8. Katie Mansfield, "'Political Correctness Gone Mad!' Brexit Bin Lorry Taken Out of Service on Election Day," *Express Online* (May 16, 2016): https://www.express.co.uk/news/uk/670396/Brexit-bin-lorry-taken-out-of-service-on-election-day-over-fears-too-political

9. Jack Bellamy, "That's Rubbish! Brexit Axe for Union Jack Truck! PC Madness!" *Daily Star* (May 17, 2016): 17.

10. David Maddox, "Shameful EU Bullies Have Stifled Healthy Debate," *Express* (June 23, 2016): 2.

11. "Toby Young Regrets 'Politically Incorrect' Comments," *BBC* (January 3, 2018): https://www.bbc.com/news/uk-politics-42552884

12. Huw C. Davies and Sheena E. MacRae, "An Anatomy of the British War on Woke," *Race and Class* 65, no. 2 (2023): 3–54.

13. Quoted in Richard Adams, "Universities in England Favour Cancel Culture over Quality, says Williamson," *Guardian* (September 9, 2021): https://www.theguardian.com/education/2021/sep/09/universities-in-england-favour-cancel-culture-over-quality-says-williamson

14. See: https://twitter.com/GavinWilliamson/status/1414645688294690826

15. Thilo Sarrazin, *Deutschland schafft sich ab* (Munich: DVA, 2010). The quote from the interview can be found here: https://www.faz.net/aktuell/politik/was-thilo-sarrazin-sagt-staendig-neue-kleine-kopftuchmaedchen-1869063.html

16. Frank Schirrmacher, "Ein fataler Irrweg," *Frankfurter Allgemeine Zeitung* (August, 30, 2010): https://www.faz.net/aktuell/feuilleton/sarrazin/die-debatte/sarrazins-konsequenz-ein-fataler-irrweg-11022033.html

17. Thila Sarrazin, *Der Neue Tugendterror: Über die Grenzen der Meinungsfreiheit in Deutschland* (Munich: DVA, 2014), 42.

18. Alexander Gauland, "Das politisch korrekte Deutschland," *Der Tagesspiegel* (December 10, 2012): https://www.tagesspiegel.de/meinung/das-politisch-korrekte-deutschland-6382147.html

19. Poschardt writes of "sin-free elites," "opinion and moral elites," who consider themselves to be "morally pure" and believe that they have the right to determine "what is right and wrong." This "secular Calvinist congregation," which is characterized by a "rigid Calvinism and authoritarian moralism," is a "cluster of green politics, subsidy-oriented NGOs, and a media-cultural complex." It pushes its agenda by means of "moral ostracism," with "moral blackmail," paving the way for a "postmodern illiberalism." "The predestined lead the way, the others cannot follow." They are "disenfranchising" the citizenry "in times of climate change and political correctness," sacrifice maturity to "moralistic rites." These "lying moral apostles and consensus opportunists" divide society and destroy "our shared language, our shared worldview, our shared idea of reality." Even though this "segregation according to moral criteria" seems like it would involve a lot of shouting, there is in fact no longer any real debate. "A drumbeat of moral cudgels drowns out all debate," and what should be robust "debates . . . are now just moral rites." Quotes from: Ulf Poschardt, "Das alte Gift Calvins," *Die Welt* (January 26, 2019); Ulf Poschardt, "Die gefährliche Verachtung der Marktwirtschaft," *Die Welt* (June 28, 2019); Ulf Poschardt, "Wir sind dabei, für immer abgehängt zu warden," *Die Welt* (February 14, 2019); Ulf Poschardt, "Von Umerziehungsgelüsten zu Auslöschungsfantasien," *Die Welt* (March 28, 2019); Ulf Poschardt, "Wo bleibendie Öko-Avengers?" *DieWelt* (June 21, 2019); Ulf Poschardt, "Das Recht, radikal zu sein,"

Die Welt (February 17, 2019); Ulf Poschardt, "Die große Entmündigung nimmt den Bürger als Geisel," *Die Welt* (March 10, 2019); Ulf Poschardt, "Das humorlose Bürgertum will auch noch die Ungläubigen bekehren," *Die Welt* (March 17, 2019); Ulf Poschardt, "Beschenkt und Gerührt," *Die Welt* (February 24, 2019); Ulf Poschardt, "Wir leben in einer Übergangszeit: Interview mit Michael Bordt," *Die Welt* (December 28, 2019).

20. Dieter Zimmer, "PC, oder: Da hört die Gemütlichkeit auf," *Die Zeit* (October 22, 1993).

21. Martin Walser, "Über freie und unfreie Rede," *Der Spiegel* (November 6, 1994): https://www.spiegel.de/politik/ueber-freie-und-unfreie-rede-a-b4e89236-0002-0001 -0000-000013684613

22. Klaus Ottomeyer, *Die Haider-Show: Zur Psychopolitik der FPÖ* (Klagenfurt: Drava, 2000), 74.

23. Heimo Schwilk, "Tugendterror: Die Tyrannei der Gutmenschen," in *Für eine Berliner Republik*, edited by Ulrich Schacht and Heimo Schwilk (München: Langen Muller, 1997), 61–64, quote at 64.

24. See also Friedemann Schmidt, *Die Neue Rechte und die Berliner Republik: Parallel laufende Wege im Normalisierungsdiskurs* (Wiesbaden: Westdeutscher Verlag, 2001), 181.

25. Botho Strauss, "Anschwellender Bocksgesang," *Der Spiegel* (February 7, 1993).

26. Schirrmacher, "Ein fataler Irrweg."

27. Alex Mahoudeau, *La panique woke: Anatomie d'une offensive réactionnaire* (Paris: Édition textuel, 2022), 13.

28. Schwilk, "Tugendterror: Die Tyrannei der Gutmenschen."

29. Josepha Laroche, "La Censure lexicale de la bien-pensance: Un vecteur de mise à mort sociale," *Revue des Deux Mondes* (June 24, 2019): https://www.revuedesdeuxmondes .fr/la-censure-lexicale-de-la-bien-pensance-un-vecteur-de-mise-a-mort-sociale/

30. Laroche, "La Censure lexicale de la bien-pensance."

31. Part of this discussion appeared previously in the *Los Angeles Review of Books*: https://lareviewofbooks.org/article/homophobes-without-homophobia/

32. Frigide Barjot, *Touche pas à mon sexe!* (Paris: Mordicus, 2012), 14.

33. Barjot, *Touche pas à mon sexe!* 15.

34. "La tyrannie des bien-pensants," *Valeurs actuelles* (November 14, 2013): 17

35. Frédérique Matonti, *Comment sommes-nous devenus réacs?* (Paris: Fayard, 2021).

36. Georges Dillinger, "Le politiquement correct: un individualisme déchaîné," *Revue des Deux Mondes* (September 1996): 64.

37. Joshua Paul, "'Not Black and White, but Black and Red': Anti-Identity Identity Politics and #AllLivesMatter," *Ethnicities* 19, no. 1 (2019): 3–19.

38. Dillinger, "Le politiquement correct: un individualism déchaîné," 55–67.

39. Georges Dillinger, *Le Politiquement Correct: D'un Christianisme Calciné à Un Individualisme Déchaîné* (Paris: Fisical, 1998).

40. Georges Laffly, "France-Algérie: La double méprise," *Le Spectacle du monde* (November 1995): 34–36.

41. Dillinger, "Le politiquement correct: un individualism déchaîné," 55–67.

42. Jean-Marie Domenach, *Le Crépuscule de la culture française?* (Paris: Plon, 1995).

43. Laurent Dubreuil, *La dictature des identités* (Paris: Gallimard, 2019), 66.

44. Bérénice Levet interview with Europe1 (May 23, 2022). The specific clip can be found at: https://www.youtube.com/watch?v=MyMa_4ZDv2M&pp =ygUYQsOpcsOpbmljZSBMZXZldCB3b2tpc21l

45. Quoted in Eugénie Boilait, "La 'cancel culture' fabrique-t-elle une génération d'ignorants?" *Le Figaro* (August 31, 2022).

Chapter 8

1. Quoted in Rebecca Pérez Vega, "Ve una 'dictadura'en la cancelación," *Reforma* (May 26, 2023): 14.

2. Daniel Bernabé, *La trampa de la diversidad* (Madrid: Akal, 2018): 163.

3. Lluís Bassets Sánchez, "El silencio de los intelectuales," *El Pais*, (July 20, 2020): 2. https://elpais.com/espana/catalunya/2020-07-19/el-silencio-de-los-intelectuales.html

4. Putin's remarks are quoted here: Pyotr Sauer, "Putin Says West Treating Russian Culture Like 'Cancelled' JK Rowling," *Guardian* (March 25, 2022): https://www .theguardian.com/world/2022/mar/25/putin-says-west-treating-russian-culture -like-cancelled-jk-rowling

5. Sauer, "Putin Says West Treating Russian Culture Like 'Cancelled' JK Rowling."

6. Author's communication with Roman Badanin (September 7, 2023).

7. "Cancellation of Russia and Ways to Fight It," Russia Public Opinion Research Center (June 6, 2022).

8. Eliot Borenstein, "Everybody Hates Russia: On the Uses of Conspiracy Theory Under Putin," *Social Research* 89, no. 3 (2022): 811.

9. Christopher Rufo, *America's Cultural Revolution: How the Radical Left Conquered Everything* (New York: Broadside, 2023), 4.

10. "Cancellation of Russia and Ways to Fight It."

11. "Savaşın ortasında ilginç polemik! Putin'e tepkisi sert oldu," *Hürriyet* (March 26, 2022): https://www.hurriyet.com.tr/dunya/savasin-ortasinda-ilginc-polemik-putine -tepkisi-sert-oldu-42030258

12. Pierre Hecker, "Satan, Sex and an Islamist Zombie Apocalypse: Religion-Sceptical Publicity and Blasphemy in Turkish Cartoons and Comic Books," in *Global Sceptical Publics: From Non-Religious Print Media to Digital Atheism*, ed. Jacob Copeman and Mascha Schulz (London: UCL Press, 2022), 196.

13. Tanıl Bora, *Türkiye'nin Linç Rejimi* (Birikim Yayınları, 2008), 34.

14. Quoted in Jonah E. Bromwich, "Everyone Is Canceled," *New York Times* (June 28, 2018): https://www.nytimes.com/2018/06/28/style/is-it-canceled.html

15. "Linç edilen ünlüler paylaşım yapmaktan çekinmedi," *Yeni Şafak* (June 13, 2017): https://www.yenisafak.com/hayat/linc-edilen-unluler-paylasim-yapmaktan -cekinmedi-2719412

16. Nedim Şener, "Akşener ve İnce'ye 'Cancel Culture' yöntemi: Öve öve olmazsa söve söve-döve dove," *Hürriyet* (March 20, 2023): https://www.hurriyet.com.tr/yazarlar/

nedim-sener/aksener-ve-inceye-cancel-culture-yontemi-ove-ove-olmazsa-sove
-sove-dove-dove-42237021

17. Bruno Molinero, "Boicotes virtuais se descolam de atos concretos e alimentam a intolerância," *Folha de Sao Paulo* (December 30, 2019): https://advance.lexis.com/api/document?collection=news&id=urn:contentItem:5Y61-8WD1-JBJN-M121-00000-00&context=1516831

18. Carlos Manfroni, "La izquierda, la derecha y la cultura de la cancelación," *La Nación* (Argentina) (November 17, 2021): https://advance.lexis.com/api/document?collection=news&id=urn:contentItem:644F-3NY1-DY1R-B0F0-00000-00&context=1516831

19. "Cumhurbaşkanı Erdoğan, linç kültürü CHP'nin ruhuna işlemiş," *Medyasamsun* (May 23, 2023): https://www.medyasamsun.com/cumhurbaskani-erdogan-linc-kulturu-chp-nin-ruhuna-islemis/44444/

20. Ahmet Hakan, "Onlarda iptal kültürü . . . Bizde linç kültürü . . .," *Hürriyet* (November 8, 2021): https://www.hurriyet.com.tr/yazarlar/ahmet-hakan/onlarda-iptal-kulturu-bizde-linc-kulturu-41934429

21. Şener, "Akşener ve İnce'ye 'Cancel Culture' yöntemi."

Conclusion

1. Post on X (Twitter) by Bill Ackman (January 2, 2024): https://twitter.com/BillAckman/status/1742441534627184760

2. DeSantis's speech text can be found at https://www.democracyinaction.us/2022/cpac/desantis022422spt.html

3. Tressie McMillan Cottom, "Who Would Want to Go to a College Like This?," *New York Times* (March 28, 2024): https://www.nytimes.com/2024/03/28/opinion/dei-ban-college-students.html?smid=nytcore-ios-share&referringSource=articleShare

4. See e.g. Greg Lukianoff and Rikki Schlott, *The Canceling of the American Mind* (New York: Simon & Schuster, 2023), 157; René Pfister, *Ein Falsches Wort: Wie eine neue linke Ideologie aus Amerika unsere Meinungsfreiheit bedroht* (München: DVA, 2022), 197ff.

5. Angelo Amante, "Italian First! Meloni's Nationalists Defend Cultural Identity at Risk of Irking EU," *Reuters* (April 12, 2023): https://www.reuters.com/world/europe/italian-first-melonis-nationalists-defend-cultural-identity-risk-irking-eu-2023-04-12/

6. Her speech can be found here: https://www.culture.gouv.fr/Presse/Discours/Transcription-du-discours-de-la-ministre-de-la-Culture-Rima-Abdul-Malak-de-presentation-des-vaeux-aux-acteurs-culturels-le-16-janvier-2023-a-la

7. Heather Stewart and Aubrey Allegretti, "Rishi Sunak Seeks to Revive Faltering No 10 Bid by Attacking 'Woke Nonsense,'" *Guardian* (July 29, 2022): https://www.theguardian.com/politics/2022/jul/29/rishi-sunak-liz-truss-culture-war-woke-nonsense

8. Post by Bill Ackman.

9. Jim Carl, *Freedom of Choice: Vouchers in American Education* (Santa Barbara: Praeger, 2011), 70.

10. Elif Özmen, *Was ist Liberalismus?* (Frankfurt: Suhrkamp, 2023).

11. Jason Stanley, *How Fascism Works: The Politics of Us and Them* (New York: Random House, 2020), 179.

12. Bruno Perreau, *Queer Theory: The French Response* (Stanford: Stanford University Press, 2016).

13. Joshua Paul, "'Not Black and White, but Black and Red': Anti-Identity Identity Politics and #AllLivesMatter," *Ethnicities* 19, no. 1 (2019): 3–19, quote at 10.

14. Moira Weigel, "How Elite US Liberals Have Turned Rightwards," *Guardian* (September 20, 2018): https://www.theguardian.com/books/2018/sep/20/the-coddling-of-the-american-mind-review

15. Jordan B. Peterson, "Professor Against Political Correctness: Part I" (September 27, 2016): https://literallyanscombe.medium.com/jordan-petersons-professor-against-political-correctness-70626ea78c20

16. Ulf Poschardt, "Die Heimlich Verschwundenen," *Die Welt* (January 5, 2019): https://www.welt.de/debatte/kommentare/plus186548868/FDP-vor-Dreikoenigstreffen-Die-heimlich-Verschwundenen.html

17. Ulf Poschardt, "Diese Frau bricht den FDP-Boysclub auf," *Die Welt* (April 17, 2019): https://www.welt.de/debatte/kommentare/plus192097475/Linda-Teuteberg-Diese-Frau-bricht-den-FDP-Boysclub-auf.html

18. Ulf Poschardt, "Wo bleiben die Öko-Avengers?" *Die Welt* (June 21, 2019): https://www.welt.de/debatte/kommentare/plus195695319/Vermeintliche-Umweltschuetzer-Wo-bleiben-die-Oeko-Avengers.html

19. Ulf Poschardt, "Der einzig richtige Vorname des Liberalismus lautet Neo," *Die Welt* (October 9, 2019): https://www.welt.de/debatte/kommentare/plus201419350/FDP-Der-einzig-richtige-Vorname-des-Liberalismus-lautet-Neo.html

20. Ulf Poschardt, "Mannschaftsspieler und Abenteurer—Wir brauchen beide," *Die Welt* (August 17, 2019): https://www.welt.de/debatte/kommentare/plus198676445/Zukunftsfaehige-Republik-Mannschaftsspieler-und-Abenteurer-Wir-brauchen-beide.html

21. This language appeared for months at https://about.gettr.com/ and can be retrieved via the Internet Archive's Wayback Machine. It is not part of Gettr's current "about" page.

22. Giorgia Meloni, *Io sono Giorgia: Le Mie radici le mie idee* (Milan: Rizzoli, 2021), 204.

23. Thomas Biebricher, *Mitte/Rechts: Die Internationale Krise der Konservatismus* (Berlin: Suhrkamp, 2023).

24. Corey Robin, *The Reactionary Mind: Conservatism from Edmund Burke to Donald Trump* (New York: Oxford University Press, 2017).